Bill Jack

LITTLE BOY BLUE

To Vanessa – Enjoy
Bill

Austin Macauley Publishers™
LONDON • CAMBRIDGE • NEW YORK • SHARJAH

Copyright © Bill Jack (2018)

The right of Bill Jack to be identified as author of this work has been asserted by him in accordance with section 77 and 78 of the Copyright, Designs and Patents Act 1988.

All rights reserved. No part of this publication may be reproduced, stored in a retrieval system, or transmitted in any form or by any means, electronic, mechanical, photocopying, recording, or otherwise, without the prior permission of the publishers.

Any person who commits any unauthorized act in relation to this publication may be liable to criminal prosecution and civil claims for damages.

A CIP catalogue record for this title is available from the British Library.

ISBN 9781787104525 (Paperback)
ISBN 9781787104532 (E-Book)
www.austinmacauley.com

First Published (2018)
Austin Macauley Publishers Ltd.
25 Canada Square
Canary Wharf
London
E14 5LQ

Introduction

The following is based on my involvement from 1969 to 1972 as a police cadet with Lanarkshire Constabulary, a now defunct and largely forgotten organization which was archaic even before its abolition. A few years later, Lanarkshire was amalgamated with several other forces to form Strathclyde Police, where I remained until 1999, retiring as a sergeant from the infamous Gorbals district of Glasgow.

The period in question pre-dates the huge upheaval of the mid-Seventies when the Scottish Police Service was belatedly dragged into the twentieth century and introduced to novelties like modern technology, equal rights, health and safety, political correctness and large regional police forces. It also saw the abolition of attitudes and practices, officially sanctioned and otherwise, which nowadays tend to be met with scepticism by those who weren't there, although TV has since resurrected it all, complete with camel coats and Ford Cortinas. It's a bit depressing to wake up and realise you've lasted long enough to have become period drama.

Some former colleagues with longer memories may wonder why I, a comparative youth in his sixties, should be writing about an era I only saw the end of, but the fact is that nobody else has done it yet and, besides, nothing much had changed for years before I turned up.

The locations are real but, like the equally real episodes in the story, have been moved about a bit to help the story along, and while some of the characters are purely fictional, although firmly based in reality, some are amalgams based on real people. Having said all that, the essence and the background are as authentic as I can make them. I have avoided any forlorn attempt to reproduce the West of Scotland dialect which can be either phonetically accurate or comprehensible, but seldom both.

Lastly, if you think you see yourself or someone you know you must be mistaken because, of course, this is only a story.

Chapter 1

Late 1969 is the period when my chequered career as a police officer unfolds. To put it in perspective, wages were still paid in pounds, shillings and pence and £2000 could buy you a Jaguar XJ6, then newly arrived on the market. £3000 could buy you a decent semi-detached house, in Lanarkshire at any rate. Harold Wilson was Prime Minister, Richard Nixon was President of the United States, John Wayne starred in *True Grit* and Neil Armstrong walked on the Moon. The Hippies cavorted at Woodstock believing themselves to be walking on the Moon too, and I applied to join Lanarkshire Constabulary as a police cadet.

If you know what police cadets were – I don't know if they have them now, but if so it will certainly be on a very different footing – skip the next bit. If you don't, they were basically underage police officers who'd been taken on the strength but weren't legally of age to be sworn in as holding the office of constable. They wore blue hatbands instead of black and white chequered ones, didn't have any official police powers and didn't actually go out on patrol unless they were tagging along with someone else. They also didn't get paid much.

Maybe they got decent crust in later years, though I doubt it.

I'm sure that, given 21st century management ethos, today's cadets, if such beings now exist, have a well-planned and rewarding career laid out for them, and are no doubt nurtured, supervised and mentored by carefully chosen tutors at every turn. Good for them if they are. I can't comment at first hand, you see, being happily retired from the wonderful world of policing these last seventeen years, at time of writing, but not to put too fine a point on it, it wasn't always quite like that.

I didn't really want to be a police cadet, if I'm to be entirely honest about things. What I wanted was to be a real police officer and share smoky pubs and clubs with distinguished company like the Kray Twins, then recently put away and still fresh news, but at the age of sixteen I was some way short of the statutory entry age of nineteen. Having no particular urge to kill time elsewhere while I waited for 1972 to come round I duly applied.

It wasn't killing time as such that I objected to, of course, it was having to do it while working for a living. Being, like most teenagers, a bone idle layabout at heart and not given to undue exertion, I put forward a beautifully argued case that I didn't want to take advantage of any potential employers by accepting a job then leaving them distraught by moving on a couple of years later. Assuming rather optimistically that my story would be swallowed, I settled down to enjoy a nice long rest while waiting to attain the required age. I understand the expression among the idle of the world is Finding Yourself, but sadly the nice long rest was depressingly short-lived. My parents, unaccountably, didn't share my vision and indicated that retirement was a privilege reserved for those who had already worked for a living, ideally for about fifty years. I was therefore instructed to Find Myself without further delay, vacate my bed and attend to the vexed question of employment.

Like most prospective school leavers, I had considered various careers, all ridiculous, some particularly so and all sharing the common attraction of minimal work. Having read with intense interest of Brigadier the Lord Lovat, the wartime commando leader, and having discussed the whole matter at some length at school with other potential adventurers, I settled on becoming a commando and ideally one in Lovat's own unit. This idea stayed firmly fixed in my head for some time and excluded other career paths which might have been more sensible and founded in the real world.

There were serious problems with my ambitions, though. Firstly, Lovat himself had been badly wounded in Normandy in 1944 and medically discharged. By 1969 he would also have been pushing sixty, an age when most action heroes have decided to call it a day and take up golf, so what with one thing and another it didn't look like he would be doing much in the way of commando raids, even if I promised to come with him. Secondly, the army commando units were disbanded shortly after the war, an event then unknown to me, and when I later learned of it one which caused me deep disillusionment with the post-war Labour Government. I haven't been too enamoured of any Labour Governments since and now they know why. Thirdly, having surrendered in 1945 and taken no further part in hostilities since then, Germans had ceased to be fair game during raids on moonless nights, which rather took the fun out of being a commando. After all, if you can't creep up behind German sentries with your genuine Fairbairn-Sykes Commando Knife and have at them prior to blowing up a radar installation or carrying out some other dashing exploit of the sort, what's the point of it all? Finally, I had to accept that by the tail end of the Swinging Sixties there was little or no demand for night landing in occupied Europe and generally doing down the Fatherland. As for current military adventures, the Americans were still going hard at it in Vietnam, of course, but Britain was going through an unusually quiet spell as far as overseas wars were concerned. We had pacified Aden, albeit with some controversy involving the tactics employed by the Argyll and Sutherland Highlanders, and Northern Ireland was beginning to show signs of restlessness again, but it wasn't the same somehow.

My career ambitions, though no doubt patriotic and just the thing for a keen young man to set his sights on had it been circa 1940, were looking a bit lame nearly thirty years down the line. In fact, I might as well have set my heart on being a lamplighter or a tramcar conductor. There were still commandos in the Royal Marines, of course, and damned fine fellows they were by all accounts, but a quick dive into school career books suggested a lot of extremely arduous training with minimal chances of being turned loose on the Hun.

So far as bloodthirsty teenage war enthusiasts, and indeed the producers of comic-book fiction, were concerned Nazi Germany was still the enemy in 1969 and it never really occurred to clots like me to query it. Even the Action Man toy was still squaring up to opponents clad in full Wehrmacht equipment in those days, though for some reason it never seemed to take on the Japanese. Years of reading war comics and watching British films starring such heroic figures as John Mills and Jack Hawkins had rather stereotyped Germans as goose-stepping krauts whose sole function in life seemed to be providing legitimate target practice for our plucky British Tommies and it was hard to adapt to them as friendly civilians. I have since heard holidaymakers coming home from Spain express similar sentiments, although I understand their territorial conquests these days tend to involve sun beds rather than the invasion of Poland.

When it became obvious that I had been born a generation late for saving the nation from the Third Reich, I cast about elsewhere. I briefly considered the Church, largely focusing on the attractive prospect of working one day a week, and was for a time enamoured with school teaching on the strength of the long holidays. Both, however, entailed a lengthy period of university-level study which didn't fit in with my overall strategy at all.

I considered a life of crime, the revelations of the Kray and Richardson trials having inspired a generation of impressionable youth like myself to consider moving to the Smoke to fill the vacancies which cropped up after the trials. The thirty-year stretches which led to the openings didn't in any way dampen my boyish enthusiasm. Similarly, the 1967 cinema portrayal of Bonnie and Clyde by Faye Dunaway and Warren Beattie had helped in its way to boost the image of the professional criminal, although robbing banks in the American Midwest was considered impractical. London was but a bus trip away while America wasn't, and while it's one thing to have a bash at controlling the London underworld knowing you can always phone home for your bus fare if it doesn't work out, America is an awfully long way off. I suppose in finally electing to grace the police service with my presence, a life of crime wasn't too far from what I finished up doing.

I made one uncharacteristically wise decision by choosing a career in the branch of crime which carries a pension scheme and sickness benefits, a shrewd move which showed more foresight than displayed by some of my former schoolmates who found themselves in the mailbag-sewing side of the business. The work was steady and the chances of being shot or locked away for thirty years, while still entirely possible, was less likely.

What I definitely didn't want was a routine, respectable, boring job at a desk as recommended by parents, teachers and other bad influences on a developing teenager. Looking back, I must have needed my head examining. You don't get cold or wet at a desk job in a bank or the Civil Service, your chances of dying a hero's death with your boots on are minimal and nobody expects you work nightshifts, but eleven years of school had put me off desks of any description and I craved a life of action and adventure. On many a wintry nightshift in later years, semi-conscious from a combination of sleep deprivation and hypothermia, terminally bored and huddled against the elements in a shop doorway, I had ample leisure to ponder the wisdom of my youthful zeal and spent many a night dreaming wistfully of a safe, warm, little office to call my own. Even the bad guys in Barlinnie Prison were cosily tucked up in their little beds while I slowly froze to death on a street corner, protecting the public weal and Her Majesty's lieges. At the time though, and barring a sudden resumption of hostilities against Germany and her allies when I would become the man of the hour, policing was the life for me.

I don't know what I thought I was getting into. I had some police tradition in the family, notably an uncle who had done rather well out of it, and one of my Grannies had taken in police lodgers when such arrangements were commonplace, but for all I knew about the actual day to day activities of police officers I might as well have been related to Eskimo seal hunters. Television wasn't a great help either as Dixon of Dock Green and Z-Cars were about as earthy as it got at the time, TV being still in the pre-Sweeney era, and even as a sixteen-year-old I had doubts about the authenticity of good old PC George Dixon with his wise sayings and avuncular image. Being far from streetwise, my limited contacts with the local gendarmes suggested large, intimidating characters who occasionally smelled of drink and went about putting the fear of God into people I personally felt happier avoiding.

Tales of the Bellshill police, that is to say the branch of the constabulary based in my home town in Lanarkshire, were many and varied. There were so many in circulation that surely some of them must have been true and one in particular caught my imagination. A classmate at school had several older brothers, some of whom frequented an establishment called the Berkeley Club. This was not as grand as it sounded, being nothing more than an open area behind the old Co-op Butchers near Bellshill Cross, albeit one adorned by a professionally painted sign on the wall advertising its presence and giving the misleading impression that something like White's or the Athenaeum lay beyond. Caesar's Palace at the very least.

That aside, the open area was used as a venue for Sunday morning games of pitch and toss where serious money was gambled on the heads or tails result of pitching coins from a stick against a wall. These tossing schools, as they were known, were nothing more than illegal gambling dens and the haunt of most of the local bad characters. They were well organised, generally under the watchful eye of some prominent local ned who, for a share of the proceeds, ensured that the lucky gamblers and their winnings made it safely home under his wing. If he didn't get his cut, of course, the lucky winner would be even luckier if he got fifty yards down the road in one piece. Given the size of these events, which were to be found in shadowy corners all over Lanarkshire at that time, periodic police raids took advance planning and involved rounding up substantial numbers of men and several large vans to transport the day's catch.

There was, naturally, a degree of friction to be expected when two rival factions such as the Bellshill police and the Bellshill neds, each bringing supporters from out of town to make up numbers, met in force. The situation wasn't improved by both sides containing a substantial element famous for their ability to start a fight in an empty house. On this occasion the friction was expressed in a difference of opinion over the moral rights and wrongs of police intervention in a harmless game of chance among friends. The ned in charge apparently asked the Inspector, in fairly unguarded language, who he thought he was and the Inspector told him in equally unguarded language exactly who he thought he was. A brisk exchange of views took place which in turn touched off a running battle which spilled out of the Berkeley Club, spread up the Main Street and enlivened the Cross area just as worshipers from morning service were dispersing from the adjacent church. After the dust had cleared and several old ladies had been revived from fainting fits the final result was that half the rogues in Lanarkshire were locked up for the night, the other half doing the locking up, and the police casualty surgeon on call that day made more money than the patrons of the Berkeley Club combined.

The relevant part of the story, which distinguished it from the normal weekend entertainment around Bellshill town centre, was that when the Berkeley Club patrons were liberated in the small hours of Monday morning and compared notes, it transpired that much of the pitch and toss winnings had unaccountably disappeared. Intense speculation revolved around the loss which remains a mystery to this day.

Maybe it happened like that and maybe it didn't, but either way it was the talk of the place for weeks and gives some flavour of how things have changed. For my money, the most likely explanation is that a raid undoubtedly took place, that there was some predictable unpleasantness involving arrests and minor injuries and that the story took on arms and legs as it was told and retold. On the other hand, the difference between the image of the Scottish Police Service then and now is that the story was believed without question in the lower strata of Bellshill society, which may tell you something.

There was another episode, this time one I witnessed personally, which impressed me hugely and contributed in no small way to my later ambitions to become a policeman. While quite young I had been taken to Glasgow to watch Rangers, then more or less unbeatable on the football field, thrashing their old enemy Celtic in fine style. As was often the case at these events, an unsportsmanlike reaction to the result among certain factions of the paying customers led to an eruption of after-match violence outside the stadium entailing a large mob of Rangers supporters and a large mob of Celtic supporters meeting up with mutual genocide in mind.

Two of the Glasgow Police Mounted Branch, hitherto half asleep in the saddle, spurred their mounts into a spirited gallop and engaged the enemy, both officers drawing three-foot horse batons from their saddles as they entered the fray and laying about them left and right with commendable vigour and a total disregard for which side was on the receiving end. Bigotry and intolerance may have existed within the ranks of the supporters, but Glasgow's guardians of law and order were scrupulously fair when it came to smiting the wicked. Within moments the sectarian warriors, seeing themselves outgunned, were dispersing rapidly, licking their wounds and leaving the City of Glasgow's very own horse cavalry the masters of the field. I understand that these robust though effective tactics have been officially frowned upon for some years, which seems a pity, and as I recall it the comments from respectable, non-violent football supporters who were present were extremely favourable, and not entirely because of the good, wholesome entertainment value. The "polis" were quite good at laying on entertainment for the public in those days when you think of it.

Apart from watching from a safe distance as Glasgow's horse dragoons scattered the unwashed rabble, I had only one personal experience of policing to fall back on and it happened in the early part of 1969 when I was fifteen and still at school. One day, leaving Bellshill Academy at throwing-out time, I was grabbed from behind by the collar and shoved against the school wall. Fearing the worst, our dear old school being a noted venue for serious and completely random assaults, I ducked and turned to find two sour-faced uniformed cops exchanging glances and nodding. Without a word of explanation I was directed to cross the main road and wait for them inside the police station door, that building being conveniently situated fifty yards from the school gates, and advised that I had better be there when they arrived. Public relations, you may gather, was a concept in its infancy at the time.

As I moved away, grateful to be alive and in one piece, I saw a few others, all roughly of my height and build, being similarly accosted and directed to follow me. To cut a long story short, I had apparently volunteered to be a stand-in for an identification parade, the sole qualification for selection being an approximate resemblance to the accused, thus complying with the law by giving him a sporting chance of being missed by the witnesses.

That settled, I joined the other volunteers to be shuffled around in a line, told not to scowl, smile, laugh, cough, stare at the witnesses, point at the suspect or in any way whatsoever contribute to the witness identification process beyond standing rigidly to attention and looking dead ahead. The accused, it seemed, was allowed to do anything he liked and I wondered if it was because the officers conducting the parade didn't want to be seen to interfere while under the eagle eye of the suspect's lawyer. It might also have been because they didn't mind in the least if he drew attention to himself, an uncharitable thought on my part.

One day some years later, when I had become more familiar with ID parades, it struck me that I should have been paid a modest sum of money for appearing, but somehow the reward failed to materialise. Instead, having stood in line trying to look like Humphrey Bogart and hoping with all my heart to be picked out as a desperado, which of course didn't happen, I was ejected from the building in the company of the other volunteers as soon as the parade was over.

I thought some word of appreciation might have been in order, some small token of official recognition perhaps, but had to settle for a growled warning to get straight home and not hang about the streets. I could have pointed out that I had no intention of hanging about the streets and but for being shanghaied as a stand-in would have been safely home with the nosebag on by then. I could have said that and much more, but sensibly didn't. For the record, not only did the officers not seem to know much about the financial aspect of things, they were downright careless when they chose their stand-ins at the school gates. The accused, picked out unerringly by the honest and upright witnesses, was at least fifty years old and stood about a foot shorter than any of us did. He was also the only one with no shoes.

The reception I'd had and the stories I had already heard disinclined me to stay about the place and pass comment, and I was actually quite happy to get out, having come to no harm. Not everyone who passed through these hallowed portals could say the same. I'm not saying that there weren't any Dixon of Dock Green types about Bellshill, widely regarded then as now as one of Scotland's premier rat-holes, just that they weren't immediately apparent to the casual passer-by. More likely they had been posted to more genteel areas where their qualities would be appreciated.

Having given up my ideas about defeating Hitler by joining the commandos or the Devil by joining the church, I had submitted my job application to Lanarkshire Constabulary some time before I was due to leave school and, having done my duty by making a stab at finding a job, slipped craftily back into idleness. I had therefore forgotten about the whole thing until one evening in early 1970 when I wandered into the family seat to find a sizeable part of the living room occupied by one of the local police sergeants. It seems he had arranged the home visit a day or two earlier as part of the standard recruiting process and my mother, who had immediately knocked out enough home baking to have fed not only Lanarkshire Constabulary but visiting delegates from other forces, had omitted to tell anyone else about it. Fortunately, I was in a presentable state and fit for inspection. Having attained sixteen, which passed for legal drinking age in most Bellshill pubs at the time, it wasn't unknown for your correspondent to be sneaking quietly in the back door with a mouthful of Polo mints and heading straight upstairs.

As an aside, while I was fit for a police visit not everyone else in the house was. At that time substandard car exhausts were sent from the Hillman Imp factory at Linwood to the Ravenscraig steelworks in Motherwell for melting down as scrap. Naturally, the employees at Ravenscraig were able to think of a far better use for them and sold them on to grateful Hillman Imp owners, usually for about forty Embassy Tipped a unit. One of the grateful Hillman Imp owners, my father, was under the car fitting one of the liberated exhausts at the time and I'm sure you can imagine his reaction when my mother called out to announce the arrival of the police at the door.

An hour or so passed during which my family, my house and presumably myself were subjected to a searching examination for suitability. How this was achieved I am unsure, as our visitor spent the entire period working his way through the buffet like a mechanical digger, pausing only to accept refills for his teacup, while we watched, fascinated. I thought I could eat but this character was in another league. When the tea was done and a quick scan of the room revealed that the cakes were too, he took his leave with a brief word of thanks and disappeared into the night. We must have made some sort of impression on him, though, because a short time later a letter arrived inviting me to drop in to the Recruiting and Training Department at Police Headquarters, Beckford Street, Hamilton for a written examination.

When I say written examination, I don't wish to give a misleading impression or make more of it than it was. I was given something like an hour to complete a paper on elementary English which could have been managed by a reasonably well-read baboon – some might say that's exactly what happened – then invited to write a short essay, no more than a page long, on why I wanted to join Lanarkshire Constabulary. Not exactly taxing stuff, you'll admit.

Later, I sometimes wondered whether it was a test on my grasp of the English language or whether they genuinely couldn't understand why anyone wanted to join. At that time, you see, police wages were low and employment was healthy in the area, the steelworks and heavy engineering firms being still very much to the fore. I'm still not sure. I was also pleasantly surprised when one of the police training sergeants, a cheery soul, popped in at regular intervals to make sure I was managing without assistance and looked slightly taken aback when he saw that I was. With hindsight, it's obvious that I was meant to pass. If I hadn't been considered suitable and already accepted in all but name, I would never have seen the inside of the building, equal opportunity employers being very much the stuff of dreams at the dawn of the Seventies.

I did some quick mental calculation and indicated to the cheery soul that if fortunate enough to be accepted I would be able to take up my appointment on June 1st, the first working day after my last scheduled exam at school. That went down well as it showed enthusiasm and a certain degree of confidence in my own scholastic ability. What I didn't bother to mention was that I had already decided that if the exams were unsuccessful I wasn't going back to school anyway, having seen more than enough of the place. It's a sobering thought that I was so carried away by the whole thing, not least the prospect of getting out of school forever, that it never occurred to me to make myself available from about September, rather than June, thus awarding myself the summer off to loaf around in the sun with a clear conscience, preparing myself mentally for the challenge ahead.

About a year earlier there had been a degree of coolness in the family home when I announced that having achieved the age of fifteen, I was leaving school to join the Royal Navy, become a police cadet, a commando, an astronaut, a vampire hunter or the main character from whatever other dream world I was living in at the time. I think running away to be a mercenary in Angola came into it somewhere too, as did the French Foreign Legion which may give you some idea of my level of mature deliberation at the time. It was still legal to leave school at fifteen and Lanarkshire Constabulary was taking on cadets at that age, though God alone knows why. I can't comment on the minimum entry age for being an astronaut with NASA or one of Lovat's commandos, not having pursued those lines of enquiry to any extent. Vampire hunters seemed to be self-employed, if the movies were anything to go by, so that didn't matter.

I was duly advised that I would, like it or not, be staying on to at least make an attempt at sitting Highers, the exams encountered in fifth year of Scottish secondary schools. Stay on I did with the result that I somehow acquired a couple of these much-vaunted Highers and Lanarkshire Constabulary had to soldier on without me until 1970 when I turned up for the entrance test, made a fair stab at it and in the fullness of time was advised to report to the same place for induction as a police cadet.

Chapter 2

On June 1st in the Year of Our Lord 1970 I arrived suitably scrubbed and polished to find that I was one of a small group of initiates. Not yet having signed the dotted line and as such still entitled to a measure of civility as members of the public, we were warmly greeted by one of the training staff whose life was now clearly complete by having lived to see this day. Having had our hands enthusiastically wrung, assured that we were making a wise career choice, and advised that the future of the police service was now in good hands, we were lined up to be marched around the building and shown the wonders of Force Headquarters. This was an edifice of vaguely Georgian appearance forming one half of a building which also housed the Sheriff Court. In addition it sported some pretentiously Roman or Greek-looking pillars which suggested that the architects and town fathers of Victorian Hamilton had suffered from a serious identity crisis. Since the demise of Lanarkshire Constabulary it's been used by court officials from next door.

I hadn't given much thought to what a police HQ should look like. I suppose I vaguely expected incident rooms full of chain-smoking detectives, uniformed officers racing to the door to attend emergencies and large, fast cars screaming in and out of the yard with blue lights ablaze. I certainly hadn't realised that a police headquarters isn't really a police station at all and is basically nothing more than an office block, albeit one where some of the staff wear uniforms. They don't do police work as such, of course, just wear uniforms.

A member of the public calling at the door in the fond hope of reporting a crime would have been disappointed, which is why, years later and after countless embarrassing episodes, the Strathclyde HQ was upgraded to include a small police station on the corner where Joe Public could walk in and speak to an operational police officer about something we were supposed to show an interest in. Until that happened, a caller appearing in all innocence at the main entrance would be stopped by an officious uniformed doorman and asked to hang around, in any and all weather, until the nearest beat cop could be dug out and sent along to interview him in the street, always assuming you were presentable enough to be seen hanging about the main door. If the Chief Constable was expected you'd be shooed down the street to wait. This of course could take some time if the officer unlucky enough to be on the Headquarters beat was busy and the caller might, with some justification, wonder why nobody else in the building could help. While wondering, he would be treated to the curious spectacle of passing senior officers turning themselves inside out to avoid eye contact and consequent involvement in the sort of sordid affairs best left to junior ranks. This, however, was in the future and so admin office block or not, a tour we were going to have.

Our first stop was something between a small room and a large cupboard where we were privileged to witness – believe it or not – a demonstration of the Gestetner Spirit Copier, a prehistoric printing device long since made redundant by the advent of the electronic photocopier. Our guide introduced it with a theatrical flourish like a magician producing a rabbit which suggested that, firstly, we were seeing the cutting edge of policing technology and, secondly, they had probably just bought it and were still excited by the whole business. Wondering what on earth this had to do with me or why I should be remotely interested in it, I watched a batch of Force Orders – something about frivolous over-use of torch batteries on nightshift as I recall – being run off by an elderly policeman turning a handle on the side of the machine while our guide pointed and nodded enthusiastically. The operator reminded me of my Grannie turning the mangle on washing day, a thought I decided to keep to myself, although I also remember wondering why the job needed an obviously senior and experienced constable to do it. Even I could have done it.

At that early point in my career I wasn't aware that conniving light duties was something of a cottage industry among older cops of the time. The trick was to go off with a bad back, dizzy spells, angelic visions, trench foot or whatever other exotic ailment could be dreamed up then enjoy a long absence until your GP got fed up writing certificates. At this point, when you were about to be de-certified anyway, you limped bravely back to work, a selfless martyr offering to take on light duties instead of lying about the house which, of course, was anathema to your industrious nature. Ideally, the light duties should be located where you were unknown and nobody would pass sarcastic remarks on how well you were looking for an invalid supposedly at death's door.

If you kept your head down and melted into the background there was a fair chance that everyone would forget why you were there in the first place and, as your own bosses back at the station retired, were promoted or otherwise lost interest in you, people stopped phoning up to see when you were coming back. To make doubly sure, your next step in the campaign was to gradually take on jobs which lightened your new bosses' load until they realised that they would be lost without you. At that stage of the campaign, with luck and a fair wind, the indoor dayshift job became more or less permanent.

When the excitement died down and the Gestetner operator drifted off, no doubt to lie down for a bit on doctor's orders, nothing would do but we had to visit the Force Museum, a treat heralded by arch looks and meaningfully raised eyebrows which suggested that something along the lines of the Glasgow Hunterian or the Tutankhamen Exhibition was about to be revealed to us.

We moved through the building en route to the museum, while our guide waved vaguely at a series of nondescript offices containing a series of nondescript people who peered over teacups at us. Nothing further was forthcoming about who they were or what they did, or indeed if they did anything. I also remember seeing for the first time examples of the species known as Bright Young Men who inhabit headquarters buildings the world over. I don't know what the requirements were for being a Bright Young Man in the Lanarkshire Constabulary of 1970, although I suspect that sobriety and the ability to converse without the use of foul language got you past the first hurdle, but some of them went on to great things in later years while others gradually slipped into obscurity as the shine wore off, an occupational hazard. Like pop idols, it's all right for rising stars of the police service to get old and grey and paunchy if they've already made it to the big time but it's the kiss of death if you're still waiting your turn.

There was also one unfortunate effect of Regionalisation a few years later which saw a few of them off. When Lanarkshire amalgamated with the much larger City of Glasgow and other surrounding county forces the first Chief Constable of the new Strathclyde Police was also, predictably, the former Glasgow Chief. He remained in Glasgow HQ which became Strathclyde HQ and came fully equipped with its own army of Bright Young Men already dug in and well placed to repel boarders. Our rising stars had to compete with them and while some of them thrived on it others never recovered from the blow, being reduced to doing police work for a living in their declining years.

We continued to pass through what I remember as a sort of rabbit warren of small offices and staircases until we reached the main foyer. I would have called it the reception area had there been anyone there to receive visitors, but it was deserted. Anyone could have walked in. Our guide stopped and we all stood behind him, waiting for something to happen. A few moments passed before a meaningful cough and a sideways glance indicated that we had in fact come to journey's end and were looking at the museum itself which turned out to be a grimy glass case about the size of a double wardrobe standing just inside the main door. It contained a collection of leg-irons, ornamental batons commemorating long-forgotten confrontations with the civil populace and ancient, disintegrating uniforms which appeared to have things living in them and should have been burned as a public health hazard. There was also a collection of sepia photos depicting long-dead Inspectors and Superintendents of Police in mutton-chop whiskers whose facial expressions suggested that painful haemorrhoids were an occupational hazard of policing in times gone by. They all seemed to be looking forward to death as a welcome release and one or two might even have been dead when the pictures were taken by the look of them.

Our guide was obviously proud of it, though, and as nobody wanted to offend him we examined the collection of ancient relics keenly until it became apparent that the artefacts didn't actually do anything, and weren't going to do anything, except gather dust.

I wondered if some sort of moving exhibit like the laughing clown at Blackpool would have been a useful addition. I don't know if you've seen it, but it's a huge mechanical clown in a glass case which sits at the entrance to the Pleasure Beach. It's got an irresistibly infectious, manic laugh which never fails to cause hilarity among the crowds of holidaymakers who stop to watch it as they arrive for a day's fun. Try as you will, you can't help laughing back. I decided that an eight-foot moving clown in a Victorian Chief Constable's uniform rolling about on a stool and howling at passers-by would have been just the thing to impress visitors to Headquarters. A touch of class, really. I couldn't imagine why nobody else had thought of it and the idea stayed with me, so one day, a few months later, I put the idea to an old cop I was out on patrol with. He considered the idea quite seriously for a few minutes before rejecting it. He reckoned Headquarters had enough clowns in it already.

Perhaps realising that the tour wasn't really gripping the audience as much as it might have, our guide peered outside and managed to locate a marked police traffic car in the yard for us to marvel at, a Ford Zephyr if I remember correctly. Although the HQ building wasn't a police office as such, operational cops and vehicles did pop in and out from time to time and the yard was also shared with the Force Vehicle Workshop so there was a certain police atmosphere about it. As we were being led outside, the driver of the Zephyr, stubbing out a cigarette as he realised that he was being watched, scowled at us and drove off, leaving us to admire an empty yard and a petrol pump. The garage itself appeared shut, or maybe they didn't feel like visitors that day.

Our guide, rapidly running out of commentary but game to the end, pointed at an unmarked Rover which he told us, in hushed tones, was the Chief Constable's car. The rain came on and things more or less petered out after that as the Force Control Room, normally the big finale to the tour, was also closed to visitors that day for reasons unspecified. Our guide turned away, nodding despondently at us to follow, and I gathered that the full range of attractions had been covered. Nonetheless, we were sensible enough to look impressed and eager.

We were then shown into the presence of the Recruiting and Training Chief Inspector, who laughed and slapped his thigh before rising from behind his desk to shake hands all round, the last official courtesy I was to experience for some time. He was probably the biggest man I had ever seen. Even at sixteen I was tall, albeit painfully thin – a problem which I unfortunately don't have today – but he was, if anything, taller than me and looked like Desperate Dan. Maybe it was Desperate Dan. His chest and waist measurements must have been close on sixty inches each. He blocked the sunlight from the window and it was only after he resumed his seat that we could see him again.

He beamed in delight as he surveyed us, again giving the impression that having met us life could hold no more. Once in control of his emotions, he advised us of our first postings, assuring each of us that we were indeed fortunate in getting the plum position in the entire force. The force seemed full of plum positions. I was suitably impressed and not a little envious when the recruit in front of me was told that he would be working in the Force Control Room there in that very building, the hub of Lanarkshire and therefore, by implication, of the British Empire. I was slightly less overawed when I was informed that I was to report to the Police Office, Muiryhall Street, Coatbridge on the following morning where I would undertake certain duties which he neglected to clarify. I soon learned that things would seldom be clarified, and that orders to cadets from on high tended to leave a lot to the imagination. Coatbridge, although only a few miles from my home, was a town I had never had cause to visit, and from the little I knew of the place the arrangement had suited me just fine until now.

The Chief Inspector, still visibly moved by the occasion, wrung our hands again and finally tore himself away, handing us over to his staff who smiled indulgently until he had gone then got down to business. I noticed that the cheery soul I'd met earlier, obviously the acceptable face of the Training Department and the one used to lure recruits inside, was missing and been replaced by a different breed.

This lot didn't laugh much and it was obvious that the honeymoon period was over. Before leaving the outer office, we were obliged to sign various papers, none of which was explained to us and whose contents were obscured by a large hand. I later found out that one was the Official Secrets Act which started off all sorts of ideas in my fertile imagination, one of which was that I might become involved with foreign spies and such. The others I am told authorised deductions for welfare, life insurance premiums and the like but I'm still not entirely sure what I had signed. Nobody else I ever met was sure either and I gather the official view was that the young recruits had enough on their minds without bothering them with tiresome details like where their wages were being siphoned off to.

I was also sold a Scottish Police Federation tie which I didn't want, and to the best of my recollection never wore, and told that although I could and should wear it proudly I should keep in mind that as a cadet I didn't actually have employment rights and could expect absolutely no help from that quarter if I someone decided to sack me. I was given to understand that virtually anybody from the office cat upwards could arrange my dismissal, and that the Federation, the police equivalent of a trade union, would actually be selling me a tie without any intention of representing me.

Having been appraised of our new status in life, which tended to contradict the emotional scenes encountered earlier, we were taken to the supplies store where we could look forward to being kitted out in the full uniformed splendour of the police service.

The supplies department turned out to be in the basement of the building, a dusty, ill-lit dungeon of a place with severely limited headroom where great piles of dusty clothing covered the floor to a depth of several feet. You got the impression that it was seldom moved and if you dug down far enough you'd find suits of armour. The place smelled of mildew and cigarette smoke, like most police establishments I would visit over the next few years.

We were met by the stores man, another elderly cop with some ailment or other which had prevented him from doing outdoor duty for the past twenty years. Rumour had it that many moons ago, while attending the derailment of a steam engine somewhere up-country and standing closer than was perhaps wise, the said engine had toppled over and caught him a crack across the skull, necessitating the insertion of a metal plate in his head, but all sorts of stories circulated in the police, many specially concocted specially for impressionable youth like me. That said, however, the ones which turned out to be true were usually the least plausible and I was soon to appreciate the old adage that truth is stranger than fiction. In Lanarkshire Constabulary it certainly was. Being a member of the force Pipe Band, in addition to his function as Gents Outfitter by Appointment to the Chief Constable, this worthy whiled away the hours by practising drum rolls on his desktop unless duty in the form of new recruits called. I remember wondering when his job would fall vacant and whether the ability to play the snare drum was a necessary qualification.

If we thought that we were going to leave the building dressed as police officers in brand new uniforms, ready to strike terror into the hearts of wrongdoers, we were to be disappointed on two counts. Firstly, the uniforms wouldn't be ready for some weeks, and secondly they wouldn't actually be new. This was my first brush with what would become a familiar pattern in Lanarkshire Constabulary – they invariably did things on the cheap. Whether it was unavoidable due to tight budgets or whether they were just naturally tight-fisted I still don't know. What I do know is that every penny was a prisoner and that if we, as new cadets, thought that we were going to have money spent recklessly on us, we were mistaken. You will gather that having signed the forms relinquishing our human rights, the rather strained bonhomie from authority hitherto experienced had been withdrawn.

I presented a slight difficulty due to my height as only a few of the second-hand or maybe third-hand items of uniform in the upper layers of the clothing pile were even close to my fitting. The hat was no problem and that was about as far as it went, although the black and white chequered band had to be removed and replaced by a blue one, as worn by cadets. With much muttering, the storeman dug around until he had identified a suitable tunic for alteration, an ancient, musty garment which must have been about the same age as the building, dusting it down and helping me into it before taking in several handfuls of cloth in the time-honoured manner and scribbling down some notes on a scrap of paper.

A raincoat was located which had possibly been first worn by Herman Munster, and which I was assured I would grow into. Standing like a pole supporting a collapsed circus tent I had my doubts but decided not to press the issue. No doubt he knew best. Trousers were similarly issued on the principle that they would fit where they touched, despite being a couple of inches short. I enquired if I was expected to shrink into the trousers while I grew into the coat but the storeman obviously didn't hear me.

The shirts were the star of the show. The standard issue was four shirts, blue cotton, with a dozen collars, police officers for the use of. I recall staring at the collars for some time, wondering if someone was having me on, before enquiring what I was supposed to do with them. Was I – or more realistically my mother – meant to sew the collars on or did they just sort of sit loosely, held in place by a tie? Collar studs were the answer, I was informed, with a sideways look suggesting I wasn't firing on all cylinders. This in 1970, mind. Man was conquering space and Lanarkshire Constabulary was issuing stud-collar shirts. I doubt if any other force had issued them since the General Strike.

Anyway, I left the store carrying a brown paper bag containing my shirts, collars, hat, ties and raincoat with an assurance that the remainder of the uniform, once tailored to my complete satisfaction by master craftsmen, would be forwarded to Coatbridge. I was disappointed to learn that the police issue baton, the one item of equipment I was looking forward to getting my hands on, was not for issue to cadets. Only duly sworn constables carried batons or handcuffs, I was informed by one of the training sergeants, his narrowed eyes suggesting my reputation was already suspect by having indicated I wanted them.

Before leaving we were shown a tantalising glimpse of the snooker room, also in the bowels of the earth next door to the stores, which could be used by anyone in the building during breaks or by cops attending the court next door. Like much else in the place, it was an improvisation, the table being barely smaller than the room it had been fitted into. The actual installation would have been like building a ship in a bottle. The players, who must have been fanatics, edged along the gaps between the sides of the table and the locker-lined walls, drawing stomachs in as they squeezed past each other, and used specially cut-down cues about two feet long to play most shots. I also seem to remember a dartboard at one side and lethal missiles flying over the heads of crouching snooker enthusiasts as both games continued simultaneously. The far end of the low, windowless room was invisible through a wall of cigarette smoke so anything could have been happening over there.

Clutching my brown paper parcel like some old lag newly ejected from prison, I made my way home, taking good care to conceal the contents as the bus crawled through the less touristy bits of Lanarkshire where the inhabitants store their cars on piles of bricks and don't always get on well with the police. It was about then that I stopped thinking about it all as some sort of school outing and realised that the owners of the old bangers on the bricks would shortly be playing a major part in my life.

Chapter 3

8.30am the next morning found me in my Sunday best, walking towards my new police station with some fluttering in the tum. For all that Coatbridge was only a few miles from home, it wasn't very convenient to reach by public transport. Buses did travel between the two, but apparently didn't do so very often and fetched up in a desolate, uninhabited area among old buildings, optimistically named a bus terminus, which looked more like the end of the world. It seemed at first glance like some Western ghost town, all that was missing being tumbleweed and a bearded prospector with a mule. I had left home at an early hour, not having the faintest idea where the police station was, and it was just as well that I'd allowed myself plenty of time by the look of things. I carefully ventured out of the terminus area and by pure chance went in the right direction, arriving in what I presumed was the town centre as it had lots of shops, albeit still shut. I asked directions from a passing native, there being no sign of any police officers I might have approached, and eventually found my new workplace.

The first impression was anything but reassuring, the office being one end of a high, gloomy municipal building which also housed the town hall and the Burgh

Court and was perched at the top of a hill like a haunted castle. It's still sitting there although it's no longer the police station, having been replaced years ago by a newer one, but at that time was typical of most large police offices, being Victorian, neglected and depressing in appearance.

I approached the door like Peter Cushing approaching Castle Dracula, paused, took a deep breath and jumped about a foot in the air when it opened just as I reached for the handle. An oldish uniformed cop looked me up and down for a moment then walked past me without comment, from which I cleverly deduced I had arrived at the right place. I entered a small ill-lit hallway with swing doors directly ahead and a counter to the left where I stood for a few minutes being ignored by passing police officers until another oldish cop appeared, this time behind the counter, and eyed me silently. Apparently a cheery welcome or even just asking callers what they wanted wasn't the done thing and it was up to the visitor to open negotiations. I wondered if all the occupants of the building were elderly and mute.

I cleared my throat and began a small prepared speech, intended to identify myself and gain access to the Superintendent, whom I had been instructed to ask for – him and no other, mind. I had no sooner given my name than the old PC, who I discovered to be a functionary known as the bar officer, raised a hand to silence me and indicated that I should come inside. From this I gathered that he was expecting me.

He opened a side door from within and I was admitted to the business side of the counter, apparently known as the uniform bar or just the bar. I suddenly felt important. Me, only a few days earlier a schoolboy, now allowed into the private area of a police station, the sanctum sanctorum itself, as one of the crew. I remember wondering if I'd be allowed to touch anything or sit down. I had visited Headquarters already but that had seemed more like a day out and I'd been inside the one in Bellshill, albeit under sufferance and quickly ejected when I'd done my bit for the war against crime. This was the real thing. I enjoyed a moment of euphoria before it hit me rather forcefully that I really was finished with school completely and, much as I'd never had any great regard for the place, it had at least been familiar. I was now entering the big, cold world and whether I found it to my liking or not, I couldn't go back. Not ever.

The bar officer, less impressed by the occasion, cleared his throat with a hint of impatience and broke the spell by suggesting that if I had nothing better to do than stand with my mouth hanging open, he had. He ushered me through another door into the area where I was told I would be spending my day. My moment of uncertainty forgotten, I asked hopefully if this was the control room to which he replied that he supposed it was, but not to get too far ahead of things too soon. I discovered that the little room contained several items of police equipment, one of which being the kettle was apparently to be the focus of my first training session.

I realised that he had been anxiously waiting for me, not because my arrival was the high spot of his week, but because he was on his own in the bar and I was required to make his tea. We got that attended to after which he introduced me to my new world, grumbling about having to run the whole office and break in new boys at the same time. In case you're wondering, this was the nearest I got to be officially welcomed to my new station. Somebody obviously forgot to organise the brass band.

I suppose the Superintendent was notified I'd turned up, but if so it didn't make much of a ripple in his life either. Perhaps I overestimated the impact of my arrival which I dare say was more of an occasion to me than to anyone else, and while I certainly didn't expect him to run downstairs and clutch me to his bosom with tears of joy, I think he might at least have stuck his head in to say hello, or more likely sent for me, senior officers being acutely conscious of their status in those days. In fact I didn't set eyes on him for about another three weeks and that was only to be sent out for his fags.

In fairness, our Super at Coatbridge, when I eventually had the chance to speak with him for a few minutes, turned out to be a decent old spud who kept sweets in his drawer and offered me one every time I came into his room. After a while I was told to come in and help myself if he wasn't there. Forget the obvious conclusion which no doubt springs to your sordid little mind as it did to my sordid little mind initially, it's not true. He was an old gentleman, most of the time anyway and providing nobody annoyed him or disagreed with him, but they weren't all like that. Some of the old bosses had a tremendous conceit of themselves and cultivated a ponderous dignity more suited to someone like a Roman emperor or one of the ancient Pharaohs than moderately senior cops in Lanarkshire.

The one who dropped in from Airdrie now and then and was apparently our Super's immediate boss was one such, and I saw him on my first day. He was a grave, self-important character who gave the impression that he'd been a police Superintendent for about a hundred years, like a lot of them did at that time, but the fact is that when he went to his reward many years later at a ripe old age and I read his obituary, a quick bit of mental arithmetic revealed that he couldn't have been fifty at the time. Thinking back, the job seemed full of men in early middle age who could have passed for Methuselah the Son of Enoch and that's not entirely because I was very young at the time either. As I became more familiar with them it seemed that they had omitted childhood completely and drawn their first breaths as National Servicemen.

As the great man strode majestically through the building, looking as if he'd have found it more appropriate to be carried on a litter by sweating slaves to the *Grand March* from *Aida*, he expected to find the corridors and stairways cleared in advance of his arrival. How anyone was supposed to know he was coming and vacate the premises was a trick never made clear to me and remains a mystery, as does the reason why anyone had to try in the first place. When he did encounter one of the lower orders he would draw a sharp breath with barely concealed anger. I was safe enough, being utterly beneath his notice as mere cadet, and one without a uniform at that, which is just as well really as I exercised my well-known common sense by tugging my forelock as he passed. The bar officer, bustling about with a handful of paper in case the big boss offered to find him something to do, the usual response to seeing a subordinate standing idle, nearly had an apoplexy and hauled me out of sight immediately.

The control room I was shown into was a small, narrow, cave-like area which, in the days before such wonders as police radios, had been a sort of kitchen, a theory borne out by the serving hatch on the wall which allowed heads to appear every so often, shout at the office staff, then disappear again. Why they had ever needed a kitchen there was another mystery. The room contained a large, dark device, not unlike a Wurlitzer cinema organ in proportion, with little numbered flaps, spring loaded cables and sockets which I discovered to be a telephone switchboard. It was all dingy brown Bakelite and the thing's probably worth a fortune today if anyone had the foresight to hang on to it, but it probably went into a builder's skip in case anyone should be seen to be benefiting in any way from its disposal. On the window sill sat a green metal box with a wickerwork speaker which turned out to be a radio. It looked like something retrieved from a German bomber and, knowing Lanarkshire Constabulary as I now do, possibly was. I could imagine my friend from the stores in 1945, scavenging in the wreckage of a crashed Dornier for discarded equipment.

A bank of personal radios and a terminal sat on a small table, and a sinister looking contraption in the corner, known apparently as a teleprinter, completed the inventory. Anyone could take messages from it by the simple expedient of tearing the paper off after it stopped rolling out, but I was warned that I should under no circumstances attempt to send anything. Only the office typists could do that as they and they alone in the building had mastered the mystic art of typing. My suggestion that it couldn't be as difficult as all that was met by a horrified silence and I realised that I had spoken out of turn. In a nutshell, typing was regarded as women's work and the bar staff, all male of course, were as likely to be seen knitting baby clothes as typing messages. And yes, this was the latter half of the 20th century, not the 19th.

Training in the police being the advanced science it was then, it was assumed that I would know how to operate switchboards and radios and if I didn't it was no concern of the bar officer who was employed as a police constable, not a college lecturer in advanced electronics. As time progressed I came to realise that he had only a scanty knowledge of the office himself, being a temporary replacement for the regular incumbent who was off on holiday or sick or something, and had hitherto managed by luck rather than judgement. I also learned that his surly manner wasn't his normal attitude but rather one brought on by his being removed from his normal haunts and forced to man the office. The attractions of his regular beat also became more apparent at a subsequent date, but more of that later.

It turned out that the office cadet was to be a man of many parts. I was to operate the antique switchboard, a full time task in itself, and listen to the two radio frequencies, the large green affair which was apparently connected to the county cars and Force Headquarters, and the small one which governed the personal sets for the local area only. I was, of course, to monitor the teleprinter, a fearsome device which periodically exploded into life like an anti-aircraft battery and made a noise which, in the confines of a small room, defied description. It seems that it should have had a sound-deadening hood, but for some reason didn't. Possibly it was cheaper if you deleted the soundproofing option.

I was to listen for members of the public calling at the bar – you couldn't actually see them from most of the office area – and render such services to them as I could, not forgetting to keep the bar officer supplied with regular cups of tea while he sat at his desk in lordly splendour like the King of Siam. The radio duties, in those pre-computer days, included catching a numbered and never-ending series of messages and notifications of stolen cars from all over Britain, and transcribing them into a huge ledger. Failure to catch one led to phone calls to other offices to get the details, a practice which entailed suffering verbal abuse from the bar staff at the other end. I was also amazed to discover that my duties also included washing vans when the janitor was conveniently absent, or in hiding, and destroying stray cats.

Feeding and eventual destruction of unclaimed stray dogs in the main offices was the remit of the bar officer, who would stir himself into activity with uncommon diligence when an animal appeared, not because he wanted to relieve me of the task, but because he was paid an allowance for each animal he fed and / or shot. If I'd helped him in any way, I might have been entitled to a cut of the profits. Nowadays the cat and dog homes collect them and try to unite them with loving owners, but that was some way off then. Cats, I have to say, were a rare visitor as the police have no statutory duty to accept them as strays. Don't ask me why, I don't know. When presented with one by a well-meaning animal lover who wouldn't take no for an answer and couldn't bear to see the poor creature wandering the streets, the bar officers had a tendency to toe them outside once the finder had gone. Nevertheless, the odd one would find its way in and, there being no money in cats, the job would make its way down to me. The method of disposal was by inserting puss into a lidded box with a small glass window then pouring in enough chloroform to see it off. Later, the cat went in the bins outside. I didn't care much for the job at all but I wasn't asked my opinion, just told to get on with it, and I also reckoned the bar officer was welcome to his income from the dogs.

I later found that the ready acceptance of dogs was more prevalent in the larger offices like Coatbridge, where kennel facilities were available and the bar officer could make some pocket money on the deal, than in the small, unmanned "County" stations. In these remoter outposts, a dog handed in meant that the local cops had to transport the thing in a small van, with no cage between snarling mutt and crew, to the nearest large office, a trip which could be both hazardous and a serious waste of valuable policing time. As with cats, a sharp tap to the rear end frequently got rid of it via the back door, the Found Dog Register being endorsed as "Dog turned savage and escaped." As one worthy remarked to me while the topic was under discussion, a size ten boot buried halfway up my arse would make me turn savage and escape too. Had I rumbled this admirable scheme earlier, a few Lanarkshire cats and dogs might have lived to fight another day.

Nobody bothered to tell me, but I soon realised that I was expected to down tools about midday and lose myself for an hour. Also, nobody told me that while I was working a nine to five, the regular shifts changed at two, or 1400 hours in the official lingo. I was on the point of joining the earlyshift in leaving at two, thinking what a nice short working day the police had, when the backshift bar officer, who on his arrival had given me no more than a disdainful grunt while eyeing me over his spectacles, advised me that I was here until five and to get the kettle on. He, if anything, was even less sociable than the earlyshift man. He was of advanced years, being old even in an office which seemed at first sight to a sixteen year old to contain nobody under the age of fifty, an impression helped along by his habit of wearing braces over his uniform shirt and smoking a greasy old pipe constantly. I believe he removed it while drinking tea but I can't remember for certain and rumour had it, among the younger men on the shift, that his children had been conceived with it firmly in place.

Shortly thereafter a cloud of cigarette smoke containing a mass of large, noisy, uniformed cops appeared at the counter, shouting and swearing at each other and demanding radios. As the bar officer remained rooted to his chair and looked over his specs at me in a marked manner, I gathered that this was another of my duties and issued each outgoing officer with a radio and battery for which they showed their appreciation by shouting and swearing at me instead. Shouting and swearing back at them, as I found early on in the game, was optional and not resented in the least. They milled about, installing the radios, heavy metal devices in leather harnesses, under their raincoats and drawing hard on their cigarettes, and appeared to be settling in for the day until the arrival of one of the shift Sergeants put them to flight and cleared the office. Peace settled as their profane cries faded into the distance.

The shift Sergeant was joined by another Sergeant and the shift Inspector who all marched into the control room and squeezed themselves into the limited space, moving over to allow the bar officer to join them. They looked expectantly at me, and for a moment I wondered if I was expected to sing or perform some sort of trick. The penny soon dropped, however, when the bar officer enquired if the dayshift man had shown me around the building and if so did I remember where the cups were kept, an amusing sally which raised a ripple of wheezy laughter all round. Refreshments were duly produced while the guests lit up and began slurping tea and shouting at each other.

During this daily soiree, I was expected to answer radios and operate the switchboard, which might have been feasible if the room had been bigger than a broom cupboard and the tea drinkers, all of whom weighed sixteen stone and upwards, disposed to squeeze over to let me move about. As it was, the next half hour was bedlam as I hopped nimbly over extended legs and answered telephone calls with one hand covering my ear, trying to make myself heard above the din while I enquired at which extension the CID were to be found and what did one do when a road accident was reported.

Apparently I was expected to come pre-programmed with this information, together with an encyclopaedic knowledge of the town of Coatbridge and the identity of everyone who worked in its police office. For this, I found, I was to be paid the princely sum of eleven pounds-odd per fortnight once some ongoing pay deal was ratified.

Eventually the social club left to annoy someone else and presumably involve themselves in some form of police duties, and the bar officer edged over to begin enquiries. What school did I go to? Which team did I support? What was my status and views regarding girlfriends? How did I get on at school? What was the name of the school again? Within a few minutes of these and other searching questions, he had established to his satisfaction that I had not attended a Roman Catholic school – a key issue apparently – heterosexual, a non-smoker – also important as I was thus unable to be tapped for smokes – and a smart-arse who obviously intended to be the next Chief Constable on the strength of possessing a handful of O-Levels and awaiting the results of Highers.

The last, as a matter of interest, wasn't as ridiculous as it sounds. In Lanarkshire Constabulary, as opposed to the well-educated force of today, Highers were considered to be pretty advanced education. Degrees were something you got in the Masonic Lodge. They weren't joking about the religious aspect either. In those days, not too far gone and before discrimination became a political issue, Roman Catholics were as near to an ethnic minority as Lanarkshire Constabulary got, although even then it was beginning to change for the better despite the inbred bigotry of some of the old guard. Had anyone suggested that recruits of, say, Asian origin might turn up one day at Coatbridge, he would probably have been told to go home and lie down in a dark room till he felt better. Quite incredible, but that was the thinking of the times.

One thing was passed on to me – I was advised that another cadet existed in the station. He was then on holiday, or on a course or something – I don't think anyone actually knew – but on his return the following week he and I would begin working alternate shifts. That meant that on one week I would work a seven-to-two earlyshift, and on the other a two-to-eleven late shift, or backshift. I also discovered that when my uniform eventually arrived I might even be sent out of the office on patrol from time to time, albeit under the wing of some carefully selected mentor. I would, on that subject, soon discover that their definition of a suitable mentor for a cadet of sixteen was quite a flexible one as we will see. At five o'clock that day I went home full of my forthcoming career on the mean streets.

Chapter 4

I didn't realise that the world came to life so early. To be at Coatbridge Police Office by seven in the morning necessitated catching a bus in Bellshill at five forty-five. This dropped me off at the terminus, which in turn lay about a mile from the office. Needless to say the bus which came nearest to the ideal left me arriving about five minutes late, even if I ran, and I was advised that such an arrangement was not on. I had duties to perform at the start of the shift, not at five minutes past. I therefore presented myself, half asleep, at six thirty which was about the time the bar officers changed over and the events of the preceding night were passed on. The bar officer, of course, had enjoyed a longer sleep than me.

At that time almost all the cops lived in police owned housing, invariably close to their station and certainly in the same town. Most of them fell out of bed and were in work ten minutes later. They were parochial in the extreme in those days, and to suggest to any of them that they might live in another town and commute was to invite ridicule and general hilarity. The Coatbridge men would grudgingly admit that the adjacent town of Airdrie was acceptable, it being so close that only a local could tell where one town finished and the other started, but anything further was simply unheard of. The north of Lanarkshire is and was fairly densely populated with most of the larger towns being in close proximity, but the idea of living in any one of half a dozen other places, none more than a few miles distant, was as likely as daily commuting from Tibet.

This had its roots in the history of policing and local government in the Lanarkshire area which, with hindsight, has an unmistakeable air of the farcical about it. Until about 1968, a very short time before the period in question, there had been several police forces within the geographical area of Lanarkshire. There were small Burgh Councils in Hamilton, Airdrie, Coatbridge, and the twinned towns of Motherwell and Wishaw. Each of these, until two sets of amalgamations 1967-1968, had its own police force, usually numbering less than one hundred officers, and was completely self-contained and ruled over by its own Chief Constable who, in theory at least, enjoyed the same power and status as the Commissioner of the Metropolitan Police in London or the Chief Constable of Glasgow. The remaining landward or non-burgh area of Lanarkshire also had its own force. Just to top it all, the county force had its headquarters within Hamilton Burgh. That meant that unless there was some arrangement I don't know about, a hypothetical crime or a sudden death within Lanarkshire County Police Headquarters would have fallen to another force, Hamilton Burgh, to investigate.

More specifically, I heard a tale of a dead body which briefly became something of a celebrity and came very close to assuming the status of a diplomatic incident. The River Clyde joined the River Avon and then, as rivers do, meandered a bit through an area where three local authorities, namely the Burgh of Motherwell and Wishaw, the Burgh of Hamilton and the County of Lanark, met in a sort of vaguely defined Bermuda Triangle with little in the way of landmarks to pinpoint boundaries. Also, as there was nothing there of any value, everyone chose to assume it belonged to someone else, particularly if some incident entailing paperwork occurred within it. One day, a keen-eyed member of the public spotted the aforesaid body bobbing about near the Motherwell shore and duly reported it. By the time the Motherwell cops arrived, assessed the situation and reported back to their HQ, it had somehow drifted over to the Hamilton side and thus become a Hamilton Burgh matter, despite their avowed efforts to recover it using the long branches they were seen splashing about in the water. Hamilton was duly notified but strangely, when the Hamilton men arrived, assessed the situation and reported in, it was to say with cries of dismay that the body appeared to have been moved by the treacherous currents and would the bar officer kindly alert the County. Even stranger, when the County men reported in it was to say that they feared the currents or some other malignant force of nature had again been at work and the deceased was once more resident in Motherwell.

By now you may be catching the drift of the story, if you'll excuse the term. The deceased, having posthumously discovered the secret of perpetual motion, seemed destined to spend eternity cruising the environs of the River Clyde like some dead Viking chief searching for Valhalla and, to cut a long story short, it took the eventual arrival of an Inspector to ensure that the forces of nature desisted from their mischief and allowed the departed to find a place of rest. The whole situation was a bit like a comedy script and remained so until the various forces in question eventually amalgamated to become Lanarkshire Constabulary. Even then the resulting force wasn't all that big although it seemed vast compared to some of the one-horse outfits which survived in the more rural parts of Scotland.

Thus in 1970 when I started work, the old Burgh Forces were still very much alive in spirit. Although theoretically part of Lanarkshire, Coatbridge was largely manned by the same officers who had served in the Burgh and who retained their disdain for the other constituent forces. To them, the world still began and ended at the Burgh boundary, a matter not helped by the fact that the Burgh authorities, complete with Provosts and Councillors and all the incestuous practices of small local governments which went with them, survived until the creation of the Regional and District Councils in 1975. All the old allegiances and loyalties and mutual back-scratching remained, as did the prejudices against anything not of their Burghs which seemed like little, self-contained kingdoms. An old Glasgow City officer of my acquaintance who was one of the first promotions from Glasgow to Lanarkshire in 1975 referred to one former burgh as a banana republic and he may not have been too far from the truth.

The old timers would roundly condemn, at every opportunity, the former burgh forces of Motherwell or Hamilton or indeed anywhere else they hadn't personally served, and all regarded the former Lanark County force as Dickensian, even by the burgh standards which were anything but progressive. Only one thing was granted in the former Lanarkshire County's favour and that was its hat badge. When all forces were permitted to display their own distinctive hat badge, Lanark County's was a thing of beauty, a double-headed eagle which was the secret envy of many another force although, according to the burgh men, the only thing Lanark County had going for it. Naturally, Lanark County men had an equally low opinion of the burghs, and so it went on.

The City of Glasgow, itself just a few miles to the West, wasn't even considered worthy of discussion. Glasgow City cops might as well have hailed from the Andaman Islands for all the relevance they were held to have to Lanarkshire, and were widely – though I hasten to add wrongly – believed to be drawn mainly from the criminal classes themselves. In fact, had you travelled into Glasgow at that time and visited one of their large, dark, Gothic police stations you might well have wondered if you really were in a foreign land as many of them didn't seem to speak English. You think I'm joking?

For years Glasgow had maintained a policy of actively recruiting from the Highlands and Islands and even sent teams of officers up North to set up shop in a series of rural Hebridean hotels, encouraging big, brawny farm boys to sign up for a career with Glasgow's Finest. The farm boys probably had to prop up the Glasgow visitors to stop them sliding off the chairs after a day's recruiting – on expenses – in the bar of a Portree hotel, but I digress. Employment for young men was a perennial problem on the islands where the oldest son was expected to inherit the croft, and the others expected to sling their hook when they reached adulthood. There just wasn't enough work on a small farm to support them. Many of them went to sea, and in later years the North Sea oil rigs, but just as many were scooped up to work in the big city, Glasgow having a strong Highland tradition, and City of Glasgow Police was a major employer. Just as the New York Police Department was famously full of the Irish, City of Glasgow Police was full of expatriates from the Western Isles.

Experience in the Twenties and Thirties had shown the police management of the time that the most effective answer to violent, razor-wielding hooligans from places like the Gorbals was the importation of violent, baton-wielding hooligans from places like Skye. An enlightened policy by early Chief Constables, notably one Sir Percy Sillitoe, of terrorising the terrorists had set the pattern for later decades and the force continued to draw recruits from the islands where the natives had always shown a splendid aptitude for the work.

Because of this, many of the older men spoke fluent Gaelic, having been, in some cases, brought up with it as their first language. Some of them, even after twenty or thirty years in Glasgow, still spoke English more or less as a second language and would drop into the old tongue at every opportunity – certainly if they didn't want to be overheard by non-Gaelic speaking bosses. It was almost like the Mafia except that membership was conferred by hailing from the Hebrides rather than by bumping off a rival gangster, but then again given the fearsome reputation of the Glasgow polis in those days I wouldn't like to be too firm on the point.

In any case, huddled groups of old Glasgow cops plotting together in what to lowlanders like me might have been Ancient Chinese, was a common sight well into the Eighties when the supply of bilingual islanders started to run out. I don't know why, it just did.

I personally met one of the old brigade in the early Eighties who had been living and working in Glasgow for thirty years and still had trouble making himself understood in English. The neds thought he was a Pole and he was so unbelievable as a British police officer that he was used to infiltrate illegal gambling dens in disguise. Being on the small side for a Glasgow cop of the time, he borrowed a jacket from one of his much larger colleagues which made him look like a Glasgow ned wearing a teddy-boy drapecoat – the story sets a definite historical period of sometime in the nineteen-fifties – and kept his head down until the gambling was under way, at which point he threw open the fire door then threw himself on top of the cards and money to preserve the evidence as the rest of the plainclothes cavalry charged through the open door.

A county or burgh man transferring voluntarily to the city, had such a thing ever happened, would have been discussed in hushed tones as if the subject of the scandal had deserted from the army or defected to Russia. Renounced drink, even. On that subject, the Glasgow cops' well known love of strong drink was tactfully avoided as the practice was just as rife in Lanarkshire as in the city, and especially so in the former Burgh areas where everybody knew everybody else. In fairness, the other constituent parts of Lanarkshire held my new station in the same degree of esteem and the City men regarded all County or Burgh forces as rest homes for sheep-molesting bumpkins. I am pleased to say that although this widespread nonsense prevailed until well after the 1975 inception of Strathclyde Police and kept going by younger officers who had joined a regional force and never served in a county, burgh or city force of any description, it has now all but vanished. Two episodes, however, illustrates the ridiculous level of rivalry which prevailed.

Due to a dispute between the local Lanarkshire bus company, the now defunct Central SMT, and one of the burghs, which shall remain nameless, the conductresses were instructed that the police officers from that particular force would be required to pay their fares, a practice unheard of when policemen in uniform travelled free on the buses as an accepted perk. For a time, the conductresses were seen to go around the buses examining shoulder numerals to identify which force the officer belonged to. This, mark you, on a bus containing possibly half a dozen cops travelling back and forth between courts or heading to and from work. When one was identified from the offending force, the conductress would loudly demand his fare to even louder catcalls and whistling from the others. Childish it may be, but it illustrates the small-town mentality of these old forces.

The second episode shows it up even more clearly, although in this case individual officers are perhaps guiltier than the institutions. Young officer X lived in Burgh A and worked in Burgh B, both separated by a few miles of County. Having no car of his own, this being in the early Sixties, young officer X, if working overtime past the hour when the bus services closed down, was officially allowed a lift in the burgh traffic car to the edge of town, after which he was considered to be behind enemy lines and on his own, no doubt liable to attack by cannibals and other dangerous county wildlife. He would be ceremoniously collected in the Traffic Jaguar, dropped off exactly midway over the bridge which represented the frontier, then watch as the car carried on another half mile into the county to turn at a roundabout and head back. The notion that it could have dropped him off at the turning point and saved him ten minutes on his journey didn't seem to occur to anyone except him and as a probationer his opinion didn't count for anything.

Returning to my new routine, it's needless to say I received precious little sympathy for my excessively early rises. If I was so ill-advised as to have been born in the remote wastelands of Bellshill – which started about half a mile beyond the southern tip of the Coatbridge boundary – a place lacking even the status of being a burgh, that was my problem. Nonetheless, it began my real education in the police.

I soon realised that in the police world, despite what the nine-to-five senior officers maintain, office hours are a nuisance, a sort of limbo time when, as a rule, nothing very much happens and the cops kill time until the bosses have gone home and they can get on with things, free from unwanted senior management supervision. This much has never changed, and senior officers strode through offices, castigating cops, sergeants and inspectors for being indoors report writing or catching up with admin when they should have been outdoors on patrol. They refused to accept that daylight hours, particularly between nine and five, are the times when the police are least needed on the streets and can safely settle down to the much-dreaded and despised paperwork so long as somebody's out and about. It had to be dealt with sometime although some of our leaders seemed to think the pixies did it when everyone else was asleep.

The fact remains that come five or six in the evening when the great and the good disappear, or before about eight in the morning when they begin to re-emerge, a police station is a completely different place. It also explains why so many cops, given the choice, want to work in the smaller outlying offices where there aren't any bosses at all apart from the occasional unwelcome visitor. In the offices where bosses live, the street cops become cunningly adept at keeping a low profile.

My first earlyshift also introduced me to the nightshift, hanging about the bar area until heads had been counted and showing little patience or good humour while they waited. Nobody goes home at the end of a shift, particularly a nightshift, until everybody has been safely accounted for, given the nature of the job, and should someone be missing and unable to be raised on the radio to confirm he was still busy and held up, the rest of the shift would have to forego their beds and go out looking for him. In almost every case, of course, the culprit would be found lying sound asleep somewhere rather than in any desperate peril but he still had to be accounted for. In such events the comments directed by the good shepherds to the lost lamb once located were choice.

Like their daytime equivalents they shouted and swore a lot. I also noticed for the first time a distinctly alcoholic aroma from certain parties filtering through the haze of tobacco smoke. Most were red-eyed and one or two seemed to be having trouble keeping awake, or at least I assumed that was the problem as they seemed unsteady on their feet and had difficulty in speaking clearly. I wondered, in my innocence, what they got up to during the night to exhaust them like this and was likely to remain in ignorance as I, being a mere cadet, was not permitted to work nights at all.

Listening eagerly, I heard some talk of having found an insecure pub earlier, and calling out the manager, so no doubt they were tired from having been so busy. At the time it didn't occur to me that perhaps the manager had also been busy making free with the hospitality of the house on his arrival, but perhaps that would have been doing them an injustice. Or perhaps not. One way or another, they certainly all mucked in when a job needed doing – I gathered that most of the shift had turned up to help search the insecure pub and had to be forcibly removed and sent about their business by the shift Inspector.

Anyway, come the hour of seven and all declared alive and well they didn't hang about much. Neither did the earlyshift. It being a wet morning I assumed they would be slow in rousing themselves into activity, some of the specimens I had watched dragging themselves past the bar en route to the muster room looking like survivors from a shipwreck, but I was mistaken. Radios were called for and quickly supplied as I was now up to speed and had them sitting out in readiness. Only one of the cops, the oldest man on the shift and the one who did bar relief at mealtime, hung about and settled in the control room with the shift supervisors who, I found, arrived at the start of every shift seeking refreshment. The remainder shot from the office with commendable ardour, no doubt to examine their beats for signs of lawlessness. The truth as ever was more mundane.

Each and every one of them had a "doss" or "howf" where a free breakfast was to be had, or at the very least a chair and a cup of tea. The old cop who didn't was unfortunate in having nothing suitable on the beat he was temporarily occupying and, as it transpired, couldn't be troubled to latch onto someone else and breakfast with him. Even a man of his advanced years and service couldn't just walk in somewhere without breaching protocol and would have to have been invited by the incumbent beat man, however junior. That was when I learned the First Commandment of beat work; Thou Shalt Not Scrounge On Somebody Else's Beat. Fights had broken out and blood had been spilled over less, and unless you wanted to find yourself in serious trouble you would no more have used a doss on another cop's beat than you would have walked into his house and helped yourself from the fridge. Some did, of course, which makes you wonder what kind of next-door neighbours they would have made, but mostly a good doss was a treasure to be cultivated carefully and protected from raiders.

A good doss, it was carefully explained to me, has to be used sparingly. Spread out your visits and don't bleed it dry, see? It follows, then, that if you carefully ration your own visits so as not to wear out the welcome mat, the last thing you want is some parasite sneaking in when your back's turned. Further, unless a doss was a known open house, which some were, you never told anyone else about it. The ideal doss was somewhere that you and you alone had found and cultivated, which was why cops who were forced to neighbour up with a new face like me got very cagey about where they were going. In the City of Glasgow, the senior men used to leave newcomers in the Doctor Who police boxes while they did their round of visits. If a new face was taken into one of these hallowed places, it was after being sworn to secrecy with dire threats of retribution if its location was revealed.

Naturally, old compatriots who had fought and died together for years would share their secrets with each other and perform the necessary introductions, but even there a strong element of trust was involved and not undertaken lightly. If two old cronies fell out, dividing up the good dosses fairly and equitably must have been like a Hollywood divorce.

A doss could take many forms and, if a good one, could allow the beat man to disappear without trace despite the best efforts of his sergeant or inspector to track him down. Some were universally known, and were local institutions. Go into one of those and it wasn't even considered dossing by the bosses as they knew exactly where to find you. Some were known to a carefully chosen few, and the occupier of the doss was instructed to discourage interlopers. The real prize, however, was a doss which nobody in the world but you knew. Strangely enough, when my uniform arrived and I started being sent out on the street with the cops, I became privy to the location of the most treasured boltholes in town. They had no option, you see. Being responsible for a sixteen year old cadet even the most disreputable old cop, and there were more than a few who fitted that description, wouldn't leave me on my own and had to take me along. It wasn't necessarily the case that they were concerned about my wellbeing, although some possibly were, but had the cadet come to grief the repercussions would have been unthinkable.

I suspect the sergeants did it for devilment. They would send me out with the office reprobates, assuming that having me along would spoil their plans for the day. Little did they know that I went everywhere the boys did, having been sworn to secrecy in lurid terms which wouldn't have been out of place in a Triad initiation ceremony. After a few mutually uncomfortable days, it became obvious that I could be relied on to keep quiet and the word went out. From then on I was readily accepted as a "neighbour".

The sergeants never quite grasped this, strangely, and the old cops went through the motions of mumping and moaning about being saddled with a cadet, crying to the heavens in despair before grabbing my sleeve and heading smartly for their favourite watering hole. Nor was there any question of it being done for my benefit. The sergeants felt that my presence would be a deterrent to mischief, and the old cops knew that with me along the sergeants would stop following them about and trying to catch them up to no good. As it got me out of the office, which suited me very well, everyone concerned was happy with the arrangement.

If the earlyshift gave a glimpse of reality, the backshift was an eye-opener. By five thirty or six the senior management had gone home to the bosoms of their families, and a whole new atmosphere descended on the building. Instead of a busy office full of Superintendents, senior detectives, traffic wardens, cleaners, typists and sundry other dayshift wallahs, the large building became quiet and private. Just me, the bar officer and any passing visitor. A quiet cough or an escape of wind might indicate that someone was sitting in a side room report writing, or the odd raucous outburst from one of the cells remind us that we were entertaining company, but that was all. Nobody felt they had to jump about and the decoy crime report forms, which the boys carried to look busy, were dumped. Cops would periodically stroll into the bar and others like passing Traffic crews or dog handlers could hang about without looking furtive. That's when I started to hear things about my new job. Strange things too, some of them, and generally in the early evening the tea club would convene as the Sergeants or Inspector came in from patrol, and sometimes we were joined by the oldest men on the shift who had a certain licence to hang about the place. That's when they began to reminisce, doubtless for my benefit as there's nothing like a fresh, attentive audience to encourage story-telling, and enthralling it was too.

A certain amount, of course, was rubbish, particularly when they drifted off into telling stretchers about when they were young studs about Cairo or

Singapore or wherever they had done their National Service. Real *Virgin Soldiers* stuff. To hear some of them you would have thought that half the indigenous population of North Africa and the Far East was half-breed Coatbridge as a result of their passing through. Mainly, though, they regaled me with colourful tales of policing in a hard town when complaints against the police were unknown and a more or less fair system of summary justice saved the courts unnecessary time and expense. As a point of interest, the now long-discontinued practice of making up your own legislation as you went along and enforcing it on the spot may help explain the apparent rise in reported crime in recent years. The other reason of course is that hardly anybody had a phone to report street crime and disorder so the only events reported were the ones the cops found themselves, or were eventually reported after someone trekked around the town until a working call box was located. Also, as everything's done by the book these days everything goes on record. Understandably, nobody recorded incidents where deserving riff-raff were put in their place using the Not By The Book method or banned from the town centre for a week as a sort of unofficial fixed penalty.

Those were the transition years, you see, between Old Policing, which hadn't changed in essence since the streets had gas lamps, and New Policing with which we are blessed today and which represents the expectations of modern society, or at least the sector of modern society which purports to represent us all. The old school really became obsolete in the period immediately following 1975 when the County and City forces joined and became Regional. It also coincided with things like Sexual Equality and Equal Opportunities, lawyers who realised that there was money in writing Legal Aid-funded letters of complaint about the police on behalf of their clients who would hitherto never have dreamed of doing such a thing, and the coming of age of the computer, still a nebulous idea in 1970. The occasional visionaries who maintained that not only did such things actually exist outside the world of science fiction but would someday be introduced across the police service were viewed as harmless cranks, but cranks or not the eventual introduction of computerised management did wonders for more than a few careers as the Seventies progressed, of which more later.

It saw the demise of the old Burgh Courts, which had been run along the lines of the one established by Judge Roy Bean in the Wild West, and the establishment of the District Court, where the magistrate, although still a lay person, was guided by a legally qualified Clerk of Court who maintained a certain order and decorum by reminding over-enthusiastic magistrates, when necessary, that flogging and transportation were no longer in vogue. Novelties like rules of evidence and even occasional verdicts of Not Guilty were introduced to an astonished audience of accused persons, cronies of accused persons, police witnesses and other local faces who hung about the place. The days were suddenly over where magistrates automatically found the town toerags guilty on the tried and tested principle that if they, the accused, hadn't been up to something the police wouldn't have arrested them, then subjected the worthless wretches to blasts of judicial wrath from the bench before passing sentence. Amazingly, there was no route of appeal to a higher court, no doubt on the principle that the rubbish which passed through wasn't worth anyone else's time. Judge Jeffreys, had he been transported from the hanging assizes he ran with such enthusiasm in the 17th Century, would have felt instantly at home in one of the Burgh Courts.

They are long gone now, but in 1970 these august institutions were still in business and dispensing their more or less unique version of justice. The equivalent in the county areas was the Justice of the Peace – or more simply JP – Court and although I never attended a performance in one I understand there was little to choose between them and the burgh variety. The same, of course, could be said of the annual Christmas pantomimes at the Glasgow Pavilion, in that the main members of the cast shouted Oh Yes You Did, Oh No I Didn't at each other to give the audience a good laugh before the villain got his just desserts in the last scene.

Management theories stolen from the world of business, and usually quite irrelevant to running a police force, were being bandied about and certain senior officers were re-assessing their practice of spending the day engrossed in the Glasgow Herald or entertaining visitors over a glass of whisky before slipping out to the golf club, realising that they were now meant to be Managers. The police service of 1970 was, by today's standards, an anachronism and I realise that had I been born just a few years later I would have missed out on the passing of an age. You may think that I exaggerate, but I don't. The police service of the period up to the early Seventies, while possibly right for its time, would be as appropriate to the demands of today as resurrecting the Bow Street Runners, but anyone who came through it, even just towards the end as I did, must occasionally miss it and mourn its passing. If nothing else, it was a damned sight more colourful.

I also saw my first real prisoners. A few had passed through during the day, but these tended to be warrants destined for the Burgh Court, which convened in the upstairs part of our building, or the odd drunk who didn't differentiate between day and night. The backshift offenders were a different story, especially on a Friday or Saturday evening. The vast majority of arrests were for Breach of the Peace, the vaguely defined and thus wonderfully adaptable Common Law charge which covered pretty well any form of drunken or disruptive conduct, or indeed anything else the arresting officers didn't like, and which had always been the saviour of the Scottish police. I understand it has now been replaced by a statute which must be inconvenient.

On that subject, the office cleaner was Betty, an absolute gem of a woman and one of the few members of the cast at Coatbridge I never heard a word said against. You may wonder where the cleaner fits in, these estimable ladies not usually being regarded as key figures in the world of policing, but the fact is that she was responsible for feeding the prisoners. Each office had evolved its own system for providing the guests with sustenance and at Coatbridge the system was Betty. On the arrival of a prisoner who seemed likely to be with us for a while, a meal would be ordered by the simple method of shouting on Betty if she was working or phoning her at home if she wasn't. Betty would then go home, cook a dinner or dinners as required and one of the van crews would collect it. Unlike some offices where the cats and dogs were better fed, Betty took a pride in what she served up and said that she wouldn't provide a meal unless it was of a standard to serve her own family. Her family must have done pretty well on the food front because every meal Betty supplied was a Sunday dinner fit for a king and the poor woman must have been out of pocket given the miserly fixed allowance she was paid. Unfortunately, although Betty provided first class grub in all good faith, the van crews, bar officers and anyone else hanging about felt obliged to sample the offerings, doubtless to protect the prisoners from food poisoning or assassination attempts, and the quantity tended to drop quickly. If a few prisoners were in and a good pile of plates sitting on the charge bar waiting to be delivered, it didn't matter too much. One dinner, however, could only go so many ways, despite Biblical precedent to the contrary, and Betty would have been horrified to hear prisoners complaining loud and long about the measly portions on the plate. On the other hand, meals were sometimes consumed by the bar staff legitimately. A prisoner had to be offered a meal, irrespective of what state he was in, but if the dinner guest was completely comatose through drink or if he answered the call to dine by advising the bar officer to stick it up his arse, the dinner was going begging.

Going back briefly to the Burgh Court in the upper part of our building, I heard several versions of the same, no doubt apocryphal, story concerning its use as a night court, an idea I thought had only been taken up in the USA. It seems that one night a local nuisance had been jailed for some misdemeanour or other and, as usual, kicked up an unseemly row before being flung into a cell, whereupon he dropped into a drunken sleep. He awoke later to find himself in a shadowy courtroom occupied by shadowy court officials who informed him that he had just been tried for murder and sentenced to death, a revelation which led to his immediate relapse into unconsciousness. When next he awoke and cautiously opened an eye he was back in his cell being prodded in the ribs by the bar officer's toecap and advised that it was time to go home, a much more familiar and reassuring scenario. Apart from a vague memory of someone shouting *Oh fuck he's dead* and the sound of running feet, the other details of his drink-fuelled nightmare have escaped him and are now just another mystery which will never be resolved. Amazing how stories get about.

Drunken shouting in the street, wrecking pubs and stand-up fights are no longer the nightly diversion they once were on the backshift. The loosening of licensing laws later in the Seventies were to blame, as they did away with the nonsensical closing time of 10 pm and so did away with the mad rush from about 9.30 to down as much alcohol in the next thirty minutes as humanly possible. This tradition of frantic binge-drinking led to alcohol-crazed idiots pouring onto the streets from about ten fifteen onward, there to be met by the representatives of law and order who could almost set their watches by the first sounds of smashing glass and screams of anguish.

From about that time the tranquillity of our office would be shattered by the swing doors crashing open and a mass of fighting bodies pouring through as the rowdy elements of the burgh were jailed for the night. Strangely, the prisoners' access was the same as the public's and your old grandmother could be standing at the public bar as a mass of fighting prisoners was shoved past her. Even stranger, the frosted glass inserts in the swing doors, which had been battered daily for generations, were still intact.

It wasn't only after ten, of course, as at weekends the town started to light up much earlier, but the heavy concentration was definitely related to closing time. Despite the violence, however, and the tendency of the cops to throw themselves into the spirit of the thing by returning like for like, complaints by neds were almost unknown. The once-in-a-lifetime offender away from parental supervision for the evening and making the most of it might be outraged when his Hooray-Henry attack on the police was met with an unexpected return volley, noticeable lacking the forbearance and good humour set out in the training manuals, but the philosophy among the regulars was that if you were daft enough to fight with the "Polis" you deserved everything you got.

The same reprobates, still sporting wounds from their arrest, would chat happily with the arresting cops on the following day, sometimes on a first name basis, or put up a drink for them in the pub knowing full well that on the next Friday the same fixture would be replayed, more than likely with the same result. It would be misleading to imply that they were all bosom buddies, because they weren't, but they did spend a lot of time in each other's company one way or another and they also knew that there was no real animosity on either side. Life was so much simpler, and mutually agreeable to all parties. There was also the possibility of getting locked up again for trying to lodge a complaint, a not unknown occurrence.

The professional complaint against the police, in later years an almost automatic part of every arrest and investigated to its bitter end, changed the whole relationship between the police and the petty offender, and everybody lost through it. Ned gets arrested and kicks up a fuss in the heat of the moment which leads to being dealt with in a manner which instigates the complaints procedure, and next day the ned and cop are passing the time of day at the cross while the investigation creaks into action in the background, its origins completely forgotten by all concerned. In some ways the prolonged official enquiries over hot-tempered allegations are like children falling out. While their parents are still at war, the children are playing together again.

Chapter 5

Came the great day. I arrived for earlyshift to find several brown paper parcels lying in a corner of the control room. Needless to say, as they obviously contained items of uniform or equipment, they had been opened and rifled. Just as obviously, the scavengers had taken one look at the contents and put them back.

I was now the proud possessor of a uniform tunic and one pair of trousers, despite having been assured of getting two. This, together with the hat, coat, gloves, belt, ties, whistle and chain and shirts – plus collars of course – constituted my working clothes for the foreseeable future. I had already purchased a suitable pair of black boots and organised a room by room search of my Grannie's house until she located an old set of collar studs in a tin. I often wonder how people without a Grannie managed, because for a certainty these things hadn't been seen in a shop for years. Resisting the temptation to try my new gear on in the office, I taped the parcels together and set them aside to try on later.

On arriving home I immediately laid all the kit out on my bed and did a quick change, while the family waited expectantly downstairs. They were in for a wait. The shirts were roughly the right size, allowing for the fact that, irrespective of collar size, the manufacturers assumed we all had fifty-inch stomachs and shaped the shirts accordingly. The trousers were still on the short side although they had been pulled in at the waist by about six inches. Not tailored, of course, just pulled in at the waist. The collar, after some experiment, was attached via the studs to the shirt and the tie knotted. I slipped into the bathroom for a quick look in the mirror. Apart from a tendency to look like a parcel where everything was pulled in at the middle, the impression so far was acceptable, and frankly as smart as most of my new colleagues in the office. The tunic almost made me cry.

When the storeman had been tugging at the back, I had realised that a fair amount of alteration was going to be necessary, but assumed that some attempt would be made to remodel it along the lines of the human frame rather than just cutting a chunk out and re-sewing it. Wrong. The jacket, I found from a faded and much laundered label inside, had once been issued to none other than my old friend the Training Department Chief Inspector in the days when he was still a constable, which must have been about the time of Gladstone. Even allowing for him having been a shade slimmer when wearing a standard constable's tunic, there was still a long way between his build and mine. A very, very long way.

The length was fine, but the alteration had been made by cutting about an acre of cloth from the back and re-joining what was left. The front pockets, supposedly covering the centre of the chest, had been pulled back so far as to be under the armpits, and the waist had been similarly butchered so that a loose flap of cloth protruded over the belt. The bottom section, supposed to flare out slightly from the waist, hung like a kilt. I buttoned it up and took another look in the mirror. I looked more suitably dressed for going round the doors on Halloween than reporting for police duty and more to the point I was expected to appear in public dressed like that, in broad daylight, while en route to the station. I presented myself downstairs for inspection expecting to be met with hoots of laughter. I was correct, and quickly took the lot off again. As you can imagine, I was looking forward to showing myself in the light of day next morning.

Next morning duly came and the uniformed scarecrow, a sort of Worzel Gummidge in blue, reported for duty having made the pleasant discovery that a uniformed police officer, even a cadet, merited free bus travel. I had suspected this was the case but had nevertheless made a token try at fishing about in my pocket until the conductress shook her head impatiently and walked on. Nobody saw the tunic at first, as I travelled in my raincoat and was greeted by an embarrassing cheer from a passing panda crew as I marched along the Main Street on my way to the office. They didn't stop to give me a lift, of course, just shouted. No doubt the coat itself was cause for amusement, being one of the old-fashioned rubberised variety, as once sported by school janitors, which hung almost to the ankles and smelled like a wet dog in the rain. As a matter of fact, they were a sight more waterproof than the nylon rubbish we were subsequently issued within the period prior to the advent of Goretex and similar materials, but it would have helped if mine had fitted. The storeman had promised that it would fit but I had naively assumed that he meant it would fit me.

Being a mere cadet I didn't at that stage get a greatcoat, another ex-military relic which had survived extinction by being adopted as police uniform. It was the school jannie's raincoat or nothing, but for cold days there was a liner to be worn under it. This object, a sleeveless quilted affair which hung over the tunic and made the wearer look like one of Genghis Khan's archers, was to be worn under the coat and in wintry weather contributed precisely nothing to keeping warm. A T-shirt under the shirt or a jumper under the tunic worked much better and the quilted object landed in the bin. I was told on supposedly good authority that a greatcoat would arrive later, the delay being probably to stop me getting over-excited.

On arrival, I managed to remove the tunic and coat in one quick manoeuvre and hung the offending garments behind the door while the bar officer looked me up and down over his specs and grunted his disapproval. He would have grunted disapproval at the Sermon on the Mount, of course, but he really would have had something to grunt about if he'd seen the tunic. I ignored his droll comments about my appearance, being unimpressed by the opinion of someone who sported braces over shirt sleeve order and apparently slept in his uniform trousers. Most days he looked like he'd fallen in the Monkland Canal and dried out in the sun.

In truth, my uniform looked passable, from a distance at least, but like most new recruits to a uniformed organisation I felt acutely self-conscious when wearing it in public. It wasn't perfect, but neither was anyone else's, all of them coming from the same source and all hacked to size with the same finicky attention to detail. I toyed with the idea of leaving it in the office and travelling in my normal clothes, but that would have entailed paying for my bus fares. Free bus travel was, and possibly even still is, a perk allowed to uniformed police officers although things have changed completely now and cops travelling to work won't even wear identifiable police uniform in their own cars if they can help it. Very wise too, in my opinion, as I found myself in a few potentially tricky situations on the way home at night without a radio to call up the cavalry. Blue hatband or not, Joe Public expects someone in a police uniform to deal with anything that crops up. At that time, however, as many cops used public transport as owned their own cars. Free-travelling police officers sitting on the bus was commonplace and very much welcomed by bus staff, especially late at night. In my case, like most of the others, a natural reluctance to spend money on what I could get for nothing, rather than any wish to ensure the wellbeing of bus conductors, won the day.

I had been building myself up to 2 pm when I would be obliged to exhibit myself to the public on the way home, when the bar officer shouted that I was to present myself upstairs where the Superintendent awaited. The urgent summons was to visit the corner shop for forty Senior Service, rather than any professional duties, but nonetheless I had to go out following a quick dip in the sweetie drawer.

I walked out of the office, turned right and was asked directions. I hadn't a clue, of course, knowing no more about the town topography than the route between the office and my bus stop and it was with some shame that on the occasion of my first brush with the public I had to direct them to the door of the office to seek assistance. I didn't waste much time collecting the Super's fags and getting safely back behind the bar. Suddenly, the cops who spent their day wandering the streets at the mercy of every nosey old biddy who couldn't find her way about unaided seemed more impressive than before.

It has never ceased to amaze me the range of questions a police officer, walking about minding his own business, is expected to answer. Simple local directions are one thing, but when you are expected to give precise directions from a street corner in Coatbridge to some obscure cul-de-sac in the West End of Glasgow, indicating street names and bus routes – and no doubt tourist attractions – in between, it is easy to see why so many cops creep around their beats avoiding eye contact with passers-by.

One particularly obnoxious ratepayer stopped two of us a short time later and enquired as to what number of bus she should get from the Main Street to Sauchiehall Street in Glasgow City Centre. Needless to say neither of us had a clue. I didn't know where Sauchiehall Street was beyond agreeing that it was probably somewhere in Glasgow City Centre and my mentor, a dyed-in-the-wool burgh man who would have had his teeth drawn before admitting to knowing anything at all about Glasgow, shrugged in a rather Latin gesture of indifference. The old dear, obviously annoyed, went on at some length about having spent twenty minutes trying to find a policeman only to be fobbed off by a rude one when she located him. My leader, having better things to do with his time, suggested that she might have spent her time more profitably looking for a bus inspector and left her to it. If he wanted to be nagged at by some old bag with an attitude problem he could do so in the comfort of his own home, as he quite sensibly put it.

Apart from coming to work I had no real need to know bus routes. I felt, and for that matter still feel, that if people use public transport, it's a damned sight easier for them to look up their own route in a timetable than rely on the police to memorise the numbers and times of every bus service in the West of Scotland. Personally, I had better things to do with my time. I felt much the same about delivery drivers and the like who wouldn't spend a couple of pounds on an A to Z street map and it wouldn't be the first time some ill-advised motorist, summoning a police officer by a whistle or cry of "Oi you, come here", had found himself half-way to Inverness before realising that the officer, while delighted to oblige, had inadvertently misdirected him. Sat-navs and Google Earth, of course, have largely consigned this to history, but it was a daily occurrence then.

Next day brought another summons to don my hat and coat in preparation for an outing. What was it this time, I wondered tetchily. Sandwiches for the Inspector? A pound of dog mince for the strays? In fact, I was to rendezvous with Tam the Main Street man and spend the rest of the day with him. Whoopee! I donned hat and coat and grabbed a spare radio, then raced from the office before anyone changed his mind and decided the kettle needed filling. The bar officer groused about being left to cope on his own which, in translation, meant that he would have to get off his chair occasionally.

I was about half way down the hill from the office when I realised that I didn't know where to meet my new neighbour, Tam. In my innocence I presumed that he would be readily visible, patrolling his beat with an ever-vigilant eye peeled for wrongdoers or otherwise making himself available to members of the public seeking his assistance. Ah, dear me. It was immediately obvious on arrival that the Main Street was a Tam-free zone and I wandered around the shops for some time, thankfully without anyone feeling the need to ask me anything. I could, of course, have radioed in to find out where he was but I was loath to do so as it would have drawn attention to the fact that Tam wasn't where he should have been, that is to say visible and available in the town centre, and even at that stage I knew better.

I would have been wasting my time in any case, for Tam's location at any given time was a source of puzzlement to even the most seasoned Sergeants, and had the bar officer stirred himself to radio for a location, it would have been completely out of character for Tam to have answered it. For all that the Main Street beat was fairly small, the infamous Tam could lose himself in it as readily as a fox goes to earth in the woods. Better men than me had tried to track him down and failed, and the general opinion was that finding Tam was a quest akin to searching for the Holy Grail or the source of the Nile.

I later learned that if I was to meet up with him, an arrangement to his liking had to be made in advance as there was no point in going about looking for him. Even among beat men who were notorious for their disappearing acts, Tam stood alone and it was widely believed that even if a cordon had been placed around the police office, nobody would have seen this latter-day Houdini leave or re-enter. He seemed to vanish after muster and re-appear to go off duty, yet a sighting of Tam actually walking the streets, and thus being available for police work, was as likely as sighting a unicorn. When it did happen, people talked about it and may have dined out on the story for all I know.

He must have had more notice of our meeting than I had, however. As I passed a narrow doorway on my second or third sweep of the town centre, he appeared like a genie and indicated by gesture that I should follow him. I did so without a word being spoken while he weaved in and out of back lanes and narrow passages and eventually arrived at a part of the town centre I had never seen before. Later, when I became more familiar with the layout of the town centre, I would have sworn we should have crossed several streets, but somehow we didn't. Maybe I was mistaken again. We entered a low doorway and found ourselves in the back room of a cafe. A head appeared briefly from the front shop, recognised Tam, and without further ado two mugs of tea and a plate of Penguin chocolate biscuits were produced, setting the pace for how we would spend the remainder of the shift. Up to this point Tam hadn't uttered a word. I wondered again if all the older cops had speech impediments for to date they had been invariably silent in my presence, except for the office-bound variety who spent the day whining for tea and complaining about modern youth, specifically me. The younger ones were chatty enough, but the old brigade, of which Tam was one, didn't say much at all. Not at first anyway.

It was a habit some of the older ones had, although not all of them of course, that they didn't talk to you or acknowledge your presence unless you had about five years' service. If a group of these old codgers was seated round a table playing cards, and a new start like myself entered, they would go quiet and stare until you took the hint and left or at least sat somewhere else. Maybe it was shyness, or maybe it was just their way of showing their superiority as old campaigners. Maybe they were just ignorant and ill-mannered, I don't know. Fortunately that's another habit which died the death many years ago.

In Tam's case it wasn't any of these. Tam, I soon learned, had an original and free-spirited approach to beat duties and how he should most profitably spend his day which was, unfortunately, at odds with how his supervisors saw things. The shift Sergeants and Inspectors felt, unaccountably, that he should be engaged in police duties while Tam, in a word, didn't. He was more into, as he carefully put it, liaising with the public rather than prosecuting them which roughly translated meant visiting acquaintances and accepting their hospitality all day, every day. As a result he was wary of who he took out and about with him. He had a couple of trusted cronies who had been through the mill with him and operated in much the same way as he did, or near enough. Keen young cops out to make a name for themselves and clean up the town were definitely not welcome, as that would have entailed Tam getting involved in police duties, which he seemed to regard as a serious misuse of his time. Sergeants and Inspectors looking for someone to walk about with for an hour or so were even less welcome and had about as much chance of successfully latching onto Tam as they had of getting him to investigate beat crime.

Funnily enough, I was accepted after he finally spoke and subjected me to another inquisition. He had been briefed by the bar officer, of course, but had to confirm it for himself. I had seen him about the office once or twice, but due to his forbidding appearance had never exchanged words. He was big and well-built, being somewhere about forty but not one of your youthful forties. You could have struck matches on his face. He had passing resemblance to Chic Murray, the well-known Scottish comedian, although it was as much due to his deadpan humour and mannerisms as in his actual appearance. A lot of people affected Chic Murray's mannerisms in those days although he's largely forgotten today, which is a sad loss. Like Murray, Tam's subtle humour took time to catch on to but once on his wavelength you realised he had a very sharp, incisive mind which was totally wasted in his daily activities.

He was noted for being as hard as nails, which I fully believed by looking at him, and may I point out that in the circles Tam moved you had to be very hard indeed to be noted for it. There are some people you just know not to mess with and Tam was one, although I never found him anything but congenial company. Over the years I would meet a number of old cops like him, affable and easy going on the surface yet with an unmistakeable aura of restrained menace which cleared a wide path as they approached.

I also found out that he had a morbid fear of being stuck with the son of a senior police officer, this having happened to him once before, some years ago, when supervisors were still trying to involve him in police work. He had taken the new probationer around for the best part of a week before realising that his activities were being reported in all innocence to the high-ranking father. Having established to his satisfaction that I was not related to a serving police officer of any rank whatsoever, or to any prominent member of the local authority or of the press, Parliament or Reuters News Agency, he loosened up.

I wasn't a threat to him, of course. I wasn't a keen new probationary constable expecting to start drumming up cases which would involve him, not that any Sergeant in his right mind would now have paired a new cop off with him unless there was absolutely nobody else about that day. I wasn't a rival from another beat who might later start poaching on his territory once its mysteries had been revealed. I was just the office cadet who would tag along and, once Tam had sussed out my character, be trusted to keep quiet about anything I saw.

It was amazing with hindsight that these leery old veterans all assumed I was safe. Of all the people in the station, a sixteen-year-old cadet was the one most likely to burst if questioned closely by higher authority. Then again, it didn't seem to occur to higher authority to use me as a double agent so maybe Tam was even sharper than I gave him credit for. In many ways I was like the fly on the wall. Nobody took me seriously enough to notice I was there with the result that I saw and heard more than anyone else in the office. I also had the good sense to keep it to myself which was probably a clever move on my part. The Tams of this world, although first rate support in a bad place, are for the same reasons the wrong people to irritate.

Some of the old beat cops of that generation and earlier were fearsome characters. The neds, who would occasionally take liberties with younger, fitter officers who should have been more of a deterrent, knew to behave when confronted by these old campaigners with their beer bellies and their forty-a-day coughs. They operated what nowadays we call zero tolerance and didn't hold back, and a cheeky remark from some mouthy toerag produced instant retribution as surely as pressing a button. Nobody expected them to treat low-life hooligans with forbearance, courtesy or professional restraint or to apply absolute minimum force when arresting them. They should have, of course, it's just that nobody actually expected it, the hooligans included. They decided what was and was not acceptable on their beat, and the ned who thought he could run the town learned differently.

It wasn't just the neds who did as they were told either. Coatbridge had a civic monument, The Fountain, which was a huge granite and marble Victorian edifice which sat at the convergence of several main thoroughfares and which in any other town would have been known as The Cross. Coatbridge didn't have a Cross, it had a Fountain. Large, imposing and frankly an eyesore, it was nonetheless a local institution and universally known landmark. It was also, unfortunately, sited on a spot which had been suitable in the days of horse-drawn carts but was beginning to cause a traffic bottleneck and so one day some burgh workmen in a lorry turned up to demolish it. Or, rather, they would have done if an old and venerable Sergeant of Police hadn't been taking the air on the Main Street and seen the desecration about to commence. The workers were instructed to desist immediately and take themselves elsewhere. The foreman understandably protested, pointing out that they were under orders from the council to carry out demolition work, a matter out with the remit of the local police. The Sergeant pointed out that he, and not the council or its employees, would decide what was or was not within his remit and a lively exchange took place. The debating point which carried the day was the one where the workmen were given the choice of leaving in their lorry voluntarily or leaving in their lorry with their picks and shovels protruding from various bodily orifices. The Fountain, as you may have guessed already, is still standing to this day although a few years later the council carefully moved it over by a few yards to allow the junction to be re-modelled.

The philosophy of that long-gone generation of cops was that terrorising the streets was an official police function to be used against selected deserving cases and the neds, fully aware of it, made themselves scarce whether or not they were actually doing anything wrong. Better safe than sorry summed up their policy. Rather like the town marshals of Hollywood western fame, the beat cop decided who was welcome on his streets and who was not. Totally without legal backing, of course, but when Two-Gun Tam, The Fastest Baton in Texas, walked down Main Street, the outlaws wisely got on their horses and left town. Two-Gun Tam would have sorted out even more outlaws if he'd spent less time propping up the bar in the saloons, but that's another matter.

Being on their side I didn't see the scary side of them very often, of course, although it was an education when I did. In the spirit of fairness, the ned would be given one warning then the sky would fall on him. Sometimes the warning stage was omitted for convenience if the ned was a regular. Tam and a few others like him, once they had tested the water, adopted me like genial if slightly disreputable uncles, and from them I learned the craft of the beat cop as they saw it. Their philosophy was simple and, in contrast to long-winded official pronouncements on policing initiatives, could have been written the back of a fag packet. They were there to keep the peace on their streets and keep the neds firmly under their thumbs. End of story. They didn't see any need to waste time submitting Road Traffic cases or involving themselves in social initiatives, nor did they feel the urge to go looking for any unnecessary work. Tam wasn't even keen on necessary work. They weren't detectives, they weren't Traffic cops and they weren't social workers. They were beat cops and that was that. When something needed doing it was done – mostly, and if they had nothing else on at the time – but if nothing was happening they were quite happy to leave it at that and find other ways to fill their day.

They would, perversely, adopt responsibilities which were really nothing to do with them at all. They would sort out domestic abuse cases and teenage nuisances who were making their parents' lives a misery by delivering a short, pointed sermon followed by some smiting of the unrighteous if the transgressor failed to take heed. They should, of course, have simply taken statements and reported the case, always assuming that sufficient evidence existed, but often elected to deal with it summarily and usually more effectively. They would also, however, spot two drivers wrangling over a trivial bump and melt into the shadows, refusing thereafter to answer their radios until the drivers had gone.

Some would say they were lazy, and many of them were. Just as many, in fairness, weren't and simply got on with their work. Tam certainly was, much as I feel disloyal in saying so. They wouldn't last long today, but they fulfilled the simpler expectations of the time and when all's said and done, that's what they were getting paid for in 1970. I for one would still be happy to live in a street where Tam or someone like him was the local beat man, because if you want to get rid of rats, give an old battle-scarred tomcat the run of the place, even if you have to accept its less agreeable habits. It might not be very presentable, but you won't be bothered by vermin either.

Their collective wisdom was wasted on me, however, because when my time came to hit the streets as a fully-fledged cop, I realised that what was accepted from Tam and his ilk was definitely not going to be tolerated from the likes of me. The old brigade were beyond redemption and would be allowed to die out in peace, but times they were changing. As that generation passed on, so did their ways, and they won't come back. They had a lot in common with the Scottish front-line regiments in some ways. An unwanted nuisance in peacetime barrack towns, but first in demand when a war starts.

As you may have already guessed, Tam was to be the first of the carefully selected mentors I touched on earlier and, yes, we will be hearing more of him shortly.

Chapter 6

It wasn't all beer and skittles, however. Much as I would have been perfectly happy to hang around the office or go out wandering with the beat cops, the powers that be in the Recruiting and Training Department had other ideas. They couldn't just leave us alone but were forever dreaming up a series of developmental programmes which I understand were intended to make us more rounded human beings and not become insular and narrow minded. All good and well, of course, but how we were supposed to have become set in our ways after a few weeks or months in the job was a mystery to me, although I could have suggested a few others who would have benefited from it. I understood that learning to be police officers was supposed to be the whole idea. Nevertheless, developed we would be, like it or not.

Development took many forms. Some activities and courses, particularly residential ones entailing a few weeks living away, were good stuff, in that it gave me and a good few like me our first taste of life away from the parental home, with the subsequent freedom to try out hangovers and other forms of loose living without constraint. Others weren't so good, often being no more than free labour for someone who had the ear of the training staff or some other boss. Call me bolshie if you will, and you won't be the first if you do, but I felt that if I wanted to use my own time in the evenings after a long day at work to rattle collection cans round some rainswept council housing estate, or housing scheme as we call them in central Scotland, and generally do good works about the community, that was for me and nobody else to decide. If Lanarkshire Constabulary wanted me to work extra hours, they could pay overtime. I don't recall having seeing our lords and masters in the training staff out and about at night supporting the good works, beyond making sure we had turned up and warning us to behave.

I felt the same about an adult education centre where I was sent to work for a few weeks. I mean no disrespect to the staff or those unfortunate souls who attended it, but four weeks watching a row of people, all much older than me and afflicted with what we now call learning difficulties, making wire coat hangers was not my idea of learning to be a police officer. I didn't even do anything, just sat and watched and tried to look interested until it was time to hop on the grey council bus which took them home, thus getting myself a free lift.

As a matter of interest, and to my eternal discredit, I stopped taking advantage of the free lift home when I saw two or three of our neighbours staring at me and talking behind their hands as the bus pulled away and the remaining passengers shouted and waved with happy abandon. No doubt I shouldn't have let it annoy me, but at seventeen I was still embarrassed by things like that. With hindsight, I should have played up to it and really set the street talking, but I doubt if my mother would have seen the funny side of it when the neighbours started asking pointed questions about what I was doing with myself since I left school.

I see up to a point where it might be beneficial to remember that not everyone has life easy, but a visit for the afternoon would have done the job and wouldn't have set the street talking about me either. Poor boy, but come to think of it he never did look the full shilling, did he?

And some of it was a complete turn-off, not least being sent to Motherwell Technical College on day, then later block, release to further our education. As can be imagined, the news of being sent to college after eleven years of school wasn't the most enticing prospect in the world when all any of us wanted to do was get out there and learn our new jobs. Had we felt any differently at that stage, there would have been something far wrong. I still feel it was unfair in that I already had two Highers and a batch of O-levels and the idea of going to college was apparently to allow anyone who hadn't managed to pass anything while at school, and there were one or two in that position, the opportunity to upgrade their education. However, it seems it was one in, all in.

The development agenda was spread out over the year, interspersed with visits to the home station if there was nothing else happening. Needless to say, we missed out on any holidays when the college term was on, being expected to turn up at our offices on the odd days when other students were lying in bed, but that was at least good practice for the unsociable working hours we would have to get used to. I don't know why we weren't just given the day off. The bar staff and shift supervisors at Coatbridge never seemed to know I was expected, although it's entirely possible that the Superintendent knew but didn't trouble to tell anyone else. That would have been a perfectly normal situation.

I did, however, become reasonably adept at three-card brag and on the second stint some time later, which was full-time rather than day release, started smoking. The connection between card playing and smoking may not be immediately obvious, so I'll explain. One of the lecturers, the Scots Law man, had the twin qualities of being a chain smoker and a thoroughly decent character who knew perfectly well we had no wish whatsoever to be there. Personally, I'd sooner have spent the day lancing boils. As he was so addicted to the weed that he had to leave the class every twenty minutes or so for a smoke, he kindly allowed smoking students the same facility. As the sole alternative to his mind-numbing lectures on Scottish civil law, the opportunity of nipping out to the toilets for a fag and staying for a hand of cards was irresistible. As this perk was only open to smokers, I took up smoking. Clever, eh?

We also had periodic reminders that we were not really expected to incur expenses, despite being entitled to them. Fortnightly visits from the staff at the Training Department accompanied the issue of expenses forms, all pre-printed with the name of the claimant. Why this was the case instead of using blank forms I don't know as there was no way of getting a replacement if you made a mistake or lost it. You also had a problem if you ran out of space, which confirmed my suspicion that you weren't really expected to use them. The character who brought them insisted that they had to be presented perfectly, without the slightest flaw, which entailed writing which met the margin with mathematical precision and finished with a diagonal line to close off the unused section so that nothing further could be craftily inserted once countersigned. If the line missed the corner of the page by so much as a hairsbreadth, the Training man rejected the claim with a malicious smile. He also rejected it if the content of the claim wasn't presented word perfect using the stilted, outmoded jargon insisted on in any and every police report, and despite the fact that we'd never been shown the right way of doing it. In other words, you got one shot at it every two weeks and tough luck if you got it wrong. On the rare occasions when, after meticulous scrutiny, the form was found to be acceptable, the claim was grudgingly authorised as if some kind of pea-and-thimble trick had been pulled on him but he couldn't prove it. One would have thought that the Chief Constable had to dig into his own pocket to pay up and was in constant danger of bankruptcy. That was certainly the impression given.

As to the rest of the college stint, the only other aspect worth a mention was playing against engineering apprentices at five-a-side football where fine ball skills took a poor second place to the noble art of fouling. All good stuff and probably the only worthwhile part of the week, and the rest I'll pass over as an utter waste of time and the taxpayers' money.

Sometimes a day out would turn up which was actually worth going to. I was amazed to be told that in the company of about a dozen other cadets dug out of various offices forcewide, I was to be used during a Royal visit to Hamilton. Must really be shorthanded to need us, was my first reaction, but apparently the Royal Personage, in those innocent days before terrorism reached these sceptred isles, didn't like to be seen being guarded by the police. Obviously that wasn't on, even during an era when our bosses still took the view that It Couldn't Happen Here, so a compromise was reached. There would be plenty of real cops just out of sight and ready to fix bayonets if the natives decided to hold an uprising, but on the surface the crowds would be controlled by young, smiling cadets and one or two young, smiling policewomen who were apparently just as acceptable to HRH. We did the crowd control such as it was, nobody misbehaved or committed treasonable acts and we were even allowed to go into the County Buildings canteen after the VIPs had gone where the remains of a rather extravagant buffet lunch awaited. To our delight it included copious quantities of red wine, and while nobody said we could drink it, nobody actually said we couldn't, so after some debate we used our initiative.

After the dignitaries had gone and we stood down, one of the gleaming black limousines, earlier used to carry the Lord Lieutenant of the County in his uniformed splendour, was returning to the town centre funeral parlour from where it had been hired. Two of us had the splendid idea of cadging a lift as far as the bus station, which would have been fine in itself, but were unfortunately spotted by some officious senior officer while lolling about in the back seat, waving graciously at passers-by and trying to pass for Royalty. Amusingly, some of the public must have thought we were the real thing and encouraged their children to wave little Union Jack flags back at us. Less amusingly, we were roasted by the Training Department staff for acting the fool while in uniform and bringing Lanarkshire Constabulary into disrepute. If they thought that was bringing the Force into disrepute, it's just as well they didn't visit us at our stations while under the tutelage of our handpicked mentors. Both of us had the presence of mind to nod solemnly in agreement and refrain from blaming our scandalous behaviour on the free wine, probably a subject best avoided.

News of my first real attachment came through dispatches one fine day. I was to present myself to Coathill Hospital, Coatbridge on the next Monday morning for a four-week period to undertake duties which characteristically were not made clear. They were great ones for giving lots of notice and time to prepare, our leaders. The only explanatory note was to say that uniform should not be worn but that a suitable standard of dress was nonetheless required. Casual dress, even among plainclothes officers expected to mix with all sorts of lowlife, was still frowned upon at that time, and a collar and tie was required in any and all circumstances. That period wasn't too far removed from an era when police officers were required to answer their front doors or even dig their gardens wearing a shirt and tie, hilarious as it now sounds. I even saw an order one time for an official funeral parade which specified that CID would wear hats, although it didn't specify where they were supposed to get them from, and it may be that a few cowboy outfits from Christmas were raided for imitation Stetsons. I suspect that certain members of the Training Department would have had us wearing white-tie evening dress while lying on a holiday beach if they could have made it stick, but there was certainly no leeway given on duty. I was also advised that as meals would be provided free of charge in the hospital canteen, I needn't try to claim expenses from the impoverished Chief Constable, and as I normally worked in Coatbridge anyway, I needn't think of claiming bus fares either. Perish the thought.

I knew that Coathill Hospital was in Coatbridge and fairly near the main bus route, so travelling wouldn't be a problem, but had little knowledge of the place beyond that. On enquiring about it, I was told by my cantankerous bar officer that it was a geriatric hospital. What exactly was meant by the term geriatric, I asked, as wise as before. It meant that the patients were old and wet the bed, he explained with some relish, and added darkly that it was the very place for me in that I would undoubtedly find my true niche in life. He seemed suspiciously pleased about the whole thing but refused to be drawn further.

Having gained in confidence by this time, and being capable of giving as good as I got in these exchanges, I asked if I was likely to meet him there as an outpatient. No, I wasn't, he replied and indicated that, now he thought about it, the casualty ward was where I was more likely to find myself if I didn't get the kettle on and start showing more respect for my elders and betters. He hadn't fought the Germans – single-handed apparently – just to take lip from the likes of me. I asked him if he'd won, which he didn't think much of, and on that happy note I took myself off home. I believe he complained to the shift Inspector about cheeky cadets and might as well have saved his breath. With hindsight, that most highly developed of all police management skills, my last remark was uncalled for he'd actually served in the dreaded Russian convoys in the North Atlantic campaign and as such was due a bit of respect, cranky or not.

If nobody in Lanarkshire Constabulary had explained my duties at Coathill, the nursing staff wasted no time about it. On my arrival at seven am, they welcomed me to the ward, handed me a white coat which didn't fit by about six sizes and pointed to the dozen or so beds where the male patients lay. They were mine. Great, says I, and what does that mean? It meant that I was to get them up, washed, dressed, shaved and taken to the toilet. All of them. I must have looked a bit taken aback because the nurse hastened to reassure me that she meant one at a time before she nipped off, sniggering.

Being game to try anything whether I had the foggiest idea of what to do or not, I approached the first bed. It being a geriatric ward, and given what I had been told, I expected the all the patients to be of advanced years and senile. In fact, they were mainly Multiple Sclerosis sufferers, most of them in pretty advanced stages of the disease and more or less immobile, but not at all elderly. Far from being senile or subdued, they were for the most part alert and interested in what was going on around them with a spirit and keen sense of humour which I found hard to accept or understand at first. I also discovered that they looked forward to the periodic visits of police cadets as a welcome change in their routine. There were one or two real old codgers who sat in their private little worlds, but as they didn't say or do much, they didn't somehow feel part of the gang. Alert or not, however, they were all still a handful to get up and dressed for the day. One thing puzzled me, though. Being unable to move, how did they do the necessary in the toilet and even more to the point, how did they manage afterwards? Toilet paper like everyone else, said one of the nurses with a wide smile. Still unsure, but with a growing sense of foreboding, I asked who wielded the toilet paper. An even wider smile gave me my answer. While I digested this piece of information, she added that by the time I had finished all the patients, some of whom were showing pressing signs of needing my ministrations, breakfast would be served in the staff canteen.

I won't go into detail which I'm sure you can work out for yourself, but suffice it to say that when a patient is permanently bedridden and unable to move about, his bowels need some pretty powerful stimulation to move regularly. I don't know what kind of medication was administered to that end, and the nursing staff probably needed an explosives licence to handle it, but after a few patients thus afflicted had passed through the toilet, it's a wonder the tiles were still stuck to the walls. Distinctly green about the gills, and making my way to the door for some urgently needed fresh air, I was reminded that breakfast awaited in the canteen. Yummy.

I would never have believed that I could have faced a breakfast after that, but like most teenagers I had an appetite like a horse. I told myself that if I put the previous horrors out of my mind, I could probably manage a bowl of corn flakes or maybe pick at a piece of dry toast, and took myself over to the canteen where the biggest and greasiest fried breakfast in the world was waiting for me. I say the biggest, and it possibly was, but the cause of this was that the canteen trainee appeared, for reasons best known to herself, to have taken an instant shine to me and begun an amorous campaign based on the admirable theory that the way to a man's heart is through his stomach. Whether it's true in the broader sense, I couldn't say but it works for me. I took a deep breath, put toilets out of my mind and went at it.

After day one, I adapted quickly to my new responsibilities and in fact took to it like a duck to water, never again having the slightest qualm about eating after morning latrine duty, provided the hands were well scrubbed before the nosebag went on. However, I am ashamed to say that, being on the shy side where young females were concerned, I never pursued my conquest and for the next few weeks studiously ignored the exasperated stares and clatterings as ladle after ladle of aromatic fried breakfast was loaded onto my plate. I may not have behaved like a gentleman and acknowledged her womanly charms, but I certainly didn't give her the idea that she was wasting her time either. I wasn't a complete fool.

The hospital staff, fully aware of the therapeutic effect of our visits, allowed us to liven the place up, within reason, whenever the opportunity arose. An arrangement would be made with the cadets in other wards who would each pick a suitable volunteer from among his patients and, weather permitting, a row of well-clad competitors, securely strapped into their wheelchairs, would line up for the Great Coathill

Wheelchair Rally. Volunteers weren't hard to come by as understandably there wasn't much in the way of daredevil sport laid on in the average geriatric ward, and as I've already said a surprising number of the patients were mentally full of beans.

The cottage-style hospital was laid out with individual wards connected by paths and driveways, and a suitable route would be agreed. Making sure that the event was well clear of visiting hours, so as to avoid relatives who might not see the funny side of it, the contestants would be lined up while their co-drivers in white coats manned the wheelchair handles. The flag – or at least somebody's hanky - dropped and the race would commence. What the other residents and staff of the hospital made of it I don't know, but our patients loved it, careering around the twisting paths of the grounds at breakneck speed, often up on one wheel, and completely at the mercy of a few irresponsible idiots in flapping white coats who had no more idea of the roadholding limitations of a wheelchair than they had of space flight.

I'm happy to report that nobody was killed and the merits of the various teams, including fighting talk of cheating and race-fixing, were the main topic of conversation in the ward for days afterwards. During afternoons when female patients from the next ward were wheeled through to join the males in group therapy activities, the dashing blades of the race track would recount their glories to an admiring audience. It was all good, harmless fun provided we undertook to avoid fatal crashes and brought them back in time for their medication.

On other occasions we brightened up the patients' days by surreptitiously smearing tomato ketchup on towels while shaving them, then allowing them a quick glimpse in the mirror while we stammered out horror-stricken apologies. That usually went down a treat, especially when we then swore the patient to secrecy so as not to spoil the trick for the next one, thus involving him in the fun. Provided we were careful not to try it on any of the older ones, whose hearts were liable to give out at the sight of their apparently severed jugulars, it was considered the height of humour by all concerned.

Personally, I still don't know how they managed to raise a laugh at anything, given their medical conditions and I doubt if I could have mustered up half their spirit in their place. They did, though, and if we managed to give them a lift with our adolescent nonsense, the visits were worthwhile for that alone. One patient, sadly, had a habit of asking every few days if I would mind putting a pillow over his face and ending it all for him. Apparently he asked everyone that, and I was assured that he meant it, but he never took a refusal to heart and would carry on the conversation as if the subject had never come up. That aside, I enjoyed working there so much that I seriously considered resigning from Lanarkshire Constabulary and taking up nursing as a serious career, as opposed to organising wheelchair derbies and mock chainsaw massacres. If I remember correctly, the wages in nursing were even more desperate than ours, and I didn't pursue it. I still wonder if I should have.

Chapter 7

Back on the mean streets, Tam was going through a bad patch, a periodic event, having been caught on his beat under the influence and "done" for it. Again.

To put it in perspective, it has to be realised that casual drinking on duty was a way of life in those days and widely indulged in. In fairness, many didn't touch the stuff at work at all. Free drink was readily available and a couple over the course of the shift wasn't really considered drinking as such, and so was largely ignored. To be "done for the drink", as the saying went, it had to be pretty bad and usually involved attempting to swim the breaststroke while lying on the pavement in full view of passers-by, or becoming riotous. If the public wasn't present the culprit was just as likely to be thrown into a van and dropped off at home, which of course didn't count.

The option to dismiss, nowadays a virtual certainty, was seldom if ever used, the standard punishment after being hauled up before the Chief Constable being reduction of a grade of pay for one year. Knowing Lanarkshire Constabulary it was probably seen as a useful revenue-generating exercise. Habitual offenders like Tam often had several overlapping fines running concurrently and apparently it was not unknown for a senior cop with a serious thirst to be clearing less take-home pay than a new probationer. The effect of that, however, was a vicious circle which left them short of off-duty drinking money which meant that they drank more at work where the indelicate question of payment was never raised. What their wives made of it all I don't know.

Tam, however, had hit an all-time low, his shift inspector having decided that enough was enough and mounted a campaign to keep him on the straight and narrow. Consequently, a police notebook had been fixed to the charge bar by a length of string and a tack and Tam was required to present himself every hour on the hour and sign the book. The book then had to be countersigned by a supervisory officer, having first ascertained that Tam was capable of standing upright and answering simple questions. Nobody realistically expected him to stop drinking completely, of course, and he didn't. He just had to moderate it.

The theory was that if he had to make his way from the Main Street to the office and back within each hour, his free time would be drastically curtailed and no doubt the unaccustomed fresh air and exercise would clear his head and do him a bit of good. Whether it did or not is open to debate, but he was certainly more presentable than normal, though far from amused by the arrangement. It also helped me, in that I didn't have to get the bloodhounds out to find him when it was time to go on patrol, but could hang around the bar with my hat on waiting for the parolee to turn up for his hourly book-signing.

Amazingly enough, it still didn't seem to occur to anyone in authority that Tam wasn't the ideal tutor for an impressionable cadet. One of the more sensible and responsible bar officers on another shift shook his head and muttered under his breath when I mentioned who had been showing me round the parish, but must have felt it wasn't his place to comment or interfere. Another well-wisher, a policewoman this time, concerned that I was being led into evil ways, gave me a well-meant lecture on avoiding bad company and picking up their habits. She was horrified when I mentioned some of the places I'd been and implored me on my life never to go in when Tam wasn't with me, not that I was ever allowed out beyond the shop at the end of the street. I've no idea what she thought went on, but I suspect that someone had being feeding her tall tales and I certainly never saw anything untoward if you don't count Tam quenching his thirst like a camel stocking up for a trip across the Sahara, or switching off his radio and going to sleep.

I was actually extremely flattered at being the subject of her attention. She was about thirty or so and the office pin-up, widely admired and openly lusted after by every red-blooded male in the building including a few whose red blood hadn't been stirred in many a year. Even the old Super himself drew in his gut and smiled gallantly as she passed and the very drunks in the cells used to call out their undying love as the door slammed shut on them. Nice as it would be to imply that there were romantic undercurrents involved, I won't waste my time. Firstly, nobody would believe it and secondly, sad to say, it wasn't true. I think she was genuinely shocked at the idea of innocent youth being corrupted by the town scoundrels and wanted to save me from a bad end. One thing I did learn, however, was to keep quiet about where I went and who I went with. The idea was beginning to dawn that Tam wasn't quite the stuff recruiting posters are made of.

Nor were the supervisory officers much better in some cases. It was widely known that certain licensed establishments were the exclusive haunts of the "gaffers" and should be avoided by the rank and file. To be found in one of them was to be subjected to vile abuse and threats of disciplinary action, although what section of the Discipline Code was contravened by getting to the sergeant's drink before he did was never clarified. Once the trespassers had been castigated and sent on their way, of course, the sergeant and inspector would invariably remove their hats and eye the spirits gantry expectantly. In fairness, I never saw a supervisor under the weather – not at that stage of my career, anyway – and had everybody kept their intake to such moderate levels, drink would never have become an issue.

A situation had arisen where both Sergeants on the one shift had fallen out and were no longer on speaking terms. Consequently, instead of going out together for a walk about the town, as they normally did, one of them had latched onto me. If I was present, he had an excuse for avoiding his unwanted colleague as walking in pairs is normal, but walking in threes isn't. A bellow rent the air to the effect that I should find my hat and coat and do it a damned sight quicker than I normally moved, and I was taken out for my first walk with a Sergeant. The conversation was stilted, he having nothing much to say to a sixteen-year-old and I being terrified to say anything which might incriminate anyone, as almost everything I had seen so far was incriminating to somebody. I was the custodian of all the dark secrets, remember, and under standing orders never to breathe a word about them, especially to Sergeants.

As a supervisor he should no doubt have been taking the opportunity to chat with me and impart wisdom, or at least try to pry information out of me, but he clearly couldn't be bothered and was just as clearly in a foul mood. It didn't take much working out that I was there under sufferance to keep his other half at bay and that was all. Wisely, I kept quiet and dogged his tracks, wishing it was home time.

We approached a small pub, one of the old-fashioned ones with a single entrance branching left and right to a bar and lounge respectively. He asked if I'd ever been inside, to which I quickly replied no, and what was a pub anyway? He gave me a look, but said nothing. He stuck his head into the bar which was fairly busy and grunted in annoyance but the lounge, or snug, on the other hand was more to his liking. One old lad sat in a corner reading the racing page, the rest of the room being empty. The old boy was summarily ejected and once he had scuttled off the door was closed and bolted, ensuring privacy. At this point I still assumed that he was in on some official business, but of course he wasn't. He leaned over the bar and roared for someone called Mary, who duly appeared with shouts and cries of delight on seeing him. He ordered a half pint and a whisky, the famous "half and a beer", and asked me what my poison was. I wasn't falling for that old gag of course, and loudly proclaimed that being only sixteen I wasn't even allowed to drink off-duty, let alone at work, and that the stuff had never passed my lips although I hoped to try it some day when I was much older. What was its name again? Lager?

Utter eyewash, of course, as certain pubs in Bellshill ran a policy that if you were able to reach the counter with your money you were old enough to be served, and like most sixteen year olds I had already taken full advantage of it, memorably on the occasion of the last school dance I attended when the only reason I got past the old witch on guard at the door was by filling my mouth with mints and sneaking in, albeit with some assistance, while she was shouting at someone else who had collapsed on the doorstep and was being violently ill.

My supervisor obviously knew the score as well as I did and, not being in the most patient of moods, growled at me to stop talking shite – I quote the great man verbatim – and tell the woman what I wanted. I hesitantly indicated a preference for a pint of lager and was told by this leader of men that a half pint would do me. Mary dispensed the restoratives then left us to it.

I was advised that if I breathed a word about it he would personally break my legs and I suspect he meant it literally. He was certainly capable of it, being even bigger and heavier than Tam. He took off his hat and relaxed, toasting my health, then asked how things were going with me. I tentatively replied that things seemed to be going fine and took the liberty of wishing him good health too. That was obviously the correct response as he raised his glass and explained solemnly that at my age a half pint at a time was quite enough on duty but that someday I would be allowed to take pints and spirits, all this of course depending on whether I kept my nose clean and worked hard. Incredible, I'll grant you, but true.

Suitably refreshed, and in my case inspired by his unique lecture on career development, we left and spent the remainder of the shift patrolling the town centre, the Sergeant shouting and swearing at neds and ordering them to get off the streets for no particular reason while I hung about in the background with my thumbs hooked in my belt and trying to look tough, a forlorn hope. I also noted that we never saw so much as a trace of the numerous beat cops we should have been bumping into over the day. Old cops and Sergeants apparently acted like opposing magnets, repelling each other and almost impossible to unite. During the patrol he slandered the character, appearance and personality of everyone from the Chief Superintendent down, and in particular the other shift Sergeant whose failings he dwelled on at some length. As one of the inner circle, initiated by having taken drink with him, I was now considered to be safe. How he had the brass neck to chase Tam and a few others like him around the town and roar at them for hanging about pubs was beyond me, but there you are. Interesting times.

Came the festive season and I was asked if I wanted to work an earlyshift on Christmas Day. The shift strength was usually at rock bottom on public holidays, largely due to the cost of paying them double time to come out, and I was a cheap alternative. In fact, I was a free alternative, there being no administrative provision for paying me overtime money at all. There was some vague talk of time off in lieu of payment, an arrangement which I never for a moment expected to transpire and of course never did. Naturally I said yes, being fully aware that it was the expected reply, and surprise, surprise, was sent out with Tam.

Being part of the official shift strength that day, instead of the usual supernumerary, I attended muster with the troops at the start of the shift and heard for the first time a pre-shift briefing which amounted to nothing more than the Sergeant handing out mail and allocating beats for the day, which were mostly the same as every other day, and running through the contents of the Station Log Book, a large volume containing handwritten entries on everything which had come to the police attention since the previous shift. He also mumbled his way through a nationwide list of stolen cars which nobody paid the least attention to, and flipped through an assortment of teleprinter messages before deciding to ignore them because it was Christmas Day and nobody was all that interested anyway.

All sorts of tripe was religiously read out at muster, my personal favourite being board and lodging frauds from places as far afield as Brighton and Torquay. The idea that someone who toured English holiday resorts fleecing landladies might turn up in Coatbridge was about as likely as Tam renouncing drink or submitting police reports. Nonetheless, if someone took the easy option and put an all-stations message on the teleprinter system, rather than taking the trouble to specify relevant destinations, out it duly went and nobody ever took it upon themselves to weed out the rubbish as it came in.

After nodding through muster like a seasoned veteran, I had the pleasure of joining the shift at the charge bar and enthusiastically joined in the shouting of abuse at the bar officer for his tardiness in dispensing radios before we took to the street. Tam and I left the office to the sounds of whining about boys out playing themselves while senior men stayed indoors and did all the work.

If Tam "socialised" during the course of a normal day, his performance on Christmas morning was epic. The day passed in a round of visits through every open premises in the town centre, of which there was a surprising number although entry was often by back door only, followed by calls at houses where Tam was greeted as a martyr forced to work when others were at home. I think each host imagined that his was Tam's only stop on an otherwise miserable Christmas Day and plied him with festive cheer irrespective of the earliness of the hour. This followed breakfast shortly after the start of the shift, where we both had a hefty fry-up washed down with a large whisky. Something to line your stomach, as Tam put it.

He was mainly a whisky man, although on a warm day he would graciously accept beer which he normally dismissed as a soft drink, something for the kiddies. He felt the same about gin, vodka and all wines, liqueurs and cocktails which he collectively regarded as effeminate rubbish best kept for ladies' nights out. He didn't seem to have anything against rum and brandy as such, but as whisky, the love of his life, was readily available it didn't really matter. He poured whisky down his throat at a prodigious rate, but told of a legendary police figure from his own early days, this one more of a beer enthusiast, who could down pints quicker than he, Tam, could lower a whisky. This man among men had obviously been Tam's role model in the formative stages of his career and must have been something to see in action. I had already met the legendary one, having bumped into him on the Main Street about a week before, although Tam hadn't introduced him on that occasion as his career inspiration. I remember a big, broad man in his sixties built roughly on the same lines as Tam except for a beer belly like an airship, which is possibly another reason why Tam stuck to spirits. A few months before, I would have assumed that legendary figures in the police service would be glamorous, crime-fighting detectives who cut swathes through the ungodly of the burgh, but I was learning better by the day. Not that there weren't good detectives and conscientious beat men out there, of course, it's just that the element I was mixing with had their own ideas of what constituted legendary behaviour and police work didn't necessarily come into it.

Like a fool, I thought that I could keep up with Tam as he downed the festive cheer by the gallon, and found, inevitably, that I couldn't. I began feeling distinctly seedy by ten when we should have returned to the office for our break. That would have been a waste of valuable socialising time, however, and we carried on without pause, probably visiting as many houses as Santa Claus had managed during the night. Like Santa, Tam and his little elf found a glass of something laid out at every stop.

By two pm and finishing time I was a sorry sight and not by any stretch of the imagination fit to be seen in the office, or indeed anywhere else. He, of course, looked much the same as he had at start of play, despite having drunk enough to put a rhinoceros on its back. It made me marvel at what he must have been putting away on the days when he was considered unfit for duty, but his main consideration for the moment was what to do with a cadet who had begun to develop a distinct list to port. It was clearly impractical for me to be propped up against the charge bar, eyes revolving like a fruit machine, while the radios were handed in and heads counted, and just as clearly my absence would be noted if I failed to show up. A compromise was reached, and I was placed in the small mortuary adjacent to the front door where I was told to stay put and not make a noise. What did he think I was going to do – sit on the slab singing Christmas carols?

A less cheery place to spend Christmas Day couldn't have been found, the mortuary being nothing more than a narrow, cold room with white tiles all over and the marble slab in the middle. While clean enough, being hosed out regularly, there was still an air of death and decay about the place which all the disinfectant in the world would never clear. Tam concocted a story about sending me off early to catch one of the handful of buses running that day and handed my radio in on my behalf. The story was obviously swallowed, probably due to lack of interest as much as anything else, as Tam stuck his head round the doorway a short time later and told me that I could safely vacate the crypt and find my way home. It being after two by then, he could no longer be held responsible for me or anything which happened to me.

The line about the bus shortage wasn't untrue, as it happened, and I wound up walking home, a considerable distance, in full uniform. Needless to say, not a single police vehicle was to be seen which might have taken me at least some of the way. On the other hand, my head was more or less clear by the time I arrived home, nearly two hours later, and my stomach back in trim for Christmas dinner.

I gathered from Tam the next day that the drink he had knocked back had been in the way of a light aperitif prior to going home and getting down to it seriously. I took malicious pleasure in watching him creep about with the mother and father of all hangovers, being myself fully recovered after my bracing walk home, but by eleven he was back on form, taking the hair of the dog like it was going out of fashion and swearing by it. You couldn't help but admire his stamina.

I don't know if somebody in authority got wind of what had been going on, and nothing was said, but I found myself confined to barracks for weeks after that, making myself useful in the bar and getting a feel for the place. I also began to realise that there was more to the bar officers than met the eye, nothing and nobody being a problem they couldn't deal with. They were all senior men, the bar officers, a pattern I found repeated in other offices, with a lifetime of experience in dealing with the world's ills.

A few of them in various offices I visited over the years, I regret to say, were office-bound because they couldn't be trusted outdoors. Tam, for obvious reasons, would have been a prime candidate for the office but they didn't trust him indoors either. An attempt had been made some time ago to ease him into office duties, but he'd left such a trail of havoc behind him – I suspect intentionally – that the experiment had never been repeated.

They were worth listening to, for all that, although it took some time to realise that what I had initially taken to be dreary reminiscences were actually what I should be listening to and taking note of. Many of them had interesting pasts too, having in many cases seen military service in World War Two, Malaya and Korea.

I also twigged that although they were, in some cases, elderly men for their rank killing time until the pension came around, they had often been good men on the street and still well respected by all, a status not acquired or retained lightly. Many a quiet backshift was spent sitting at the feet of the masters while they told me strange and incredible tales which I soaked up like sponge. Even in 1971, their ways were outmoded and they themselves living on borrowed time, but I almost felt sorry for the neds of a bygone age who had tried to cross swords with them. Come to that, any neds who ventured into the office still took care to be civil if they knew what was good for them.

I recall sitting in the control room one evening, snoozing gently, when the bar officer rose to his feet and ambled through to greet a caller at the public bar. That in itself was worthy of remark as the normal procedure was to poke the idle cadet in the ribs and point at the outer office. There was a low murmuring for a minute or so then a series of sharp howls and scuffling sounds. I peered out to see the bar officer climbing back over the counter with a smile of grim satisfaction on his face.

This seemed a novel approach to dealing with the public and I was intrigued to learn more, having been brought up as a child to believe that when in trouble the surest bet was to approach a policeman who would, figuratively speaking, clasp you to his bosom and make the nasty problems go away. It seemed like I might have been given false information. When I enquired who the caller had been, I found that the gentleman had called in to report vandalism to his expensive car. I couldn't see a problem with this and suggested that even if we had been busy, which we weren't, there must have been a more tactful way of getting rid of him. Quite right too, I was told piously, manners maketh the man.

Getting to the truth of the matter was obviously going to be like drawing teeth, but I persevered and to cut a long story short it turned out that the posh car in question was used by the departed visitor to entice small boys into going for a drive which invariably ended up in his darkened garage, a fact well known to the bar officer but as yet unproved in court. He obviously felt that vandalising a pervert's car didn't come into the category of reportable crime, being more of a public service, and had said so, following it up by assisting the owner safely off the premises with the toe of his boot. A quite reasonable attitude, when you think of it, but not really as laid out in the training manual.

In the quieter evenings I began to explore the building, finding much which hadn't changed since Victoria was on the throne. The building had been erected sometime in the latter half of the nineteenth century and, given the traditional reluctance among police management to make innovations, nothing had ever been thrown out. Nothing at all. The archive in the top floor contained files which hailed back to the earliest days and held cases, personnel files, standing orders and all the general rubbish produced by any official body which has a procedure for everything except clearing it out. They didn't bin any of it and nobody would take it upon himself to declare anything obsolete. You never know, was the invariable answer.

The front office contained what was left of the Burgh Criminal Records Office, by then superseded by the new one at Lanarkshire Headquarters. It was, and probably always had been, no more than a series of rusting green metal filing cabinets filled with cards containing the personal details and criminal records of known offenders who either lived in the burgh or had been caught while visiting it. The card usually, although not invariably, had a black and white photograph of the subject. These were hilariously out of date, showing the shambling drunks of 1971 as young spivs, Teddy Boys and occasionally army deserters in their prime. One, believe it or not, had been photographed in an army uniform from the First World War. Some poor soul had survived the Somme just to get the jail in Coatbridge.

Possibly these rogues of yesteryear were still active or potentially so, but some of the pictures were so old as to be period pieces. The Burgh retained the cards of offenders who couldn't possibly be alive, let alone a threat to anyone, with dates of birth far back in the mists of the 19th century. Some of them had sepia photos of men in bowler hats and rat-faced youths who might have been supporting actors in *Oliver*.

I found two in bowler hats who could have passed for Butch Cassidy and the Sundance Kid, which made me wonder if the famous outlaws hadn't been shot in Bolivia after all but had relocated in Coatbridge under assumed names. Cassidy was a good old-fashioned Coatbridge-Irish name but I think Sundance would have occasioned remark. Still, as there wasn't an accepted system for weeding such rubbish from the file, or perhaps that an official assumption existed that criminals over 100 years old could still be active, there they stayed. If I'd ferreted far enough no doubt I'd have located criminal intelligence files on highwaymen.

Similarly, I found and nicked – or liberated as I prefer to think about it – an order from the Chief Constable of the Burgh Police, dated about 1911, which I kept for years. In immaculate copperplate writing, under a splendid letterhead like a South American bearer bond, it advised all officers that the Burgh Council in its munificent generosity had provided two specially designed wheelbarrows for the purpose of conveying drunks to the police station. The location of these contraptions was specified, together with instructions for their usage, and concluded with a stern warning that the system known as the Frogs March was to be discontinued forthwith. State of the art equipment for those days, obviously, and no doubt a source of municipal pride and speeches on their arrival. I'm sorry to say that I lost the order, as it would certainly be a treasure nowadays.

On the same subject, I later saw a similar gem in another old office penned by the Chief Constable of Lanark County, a long-forgotten functionary who rejoiced in the name of Captain Despard, to the effect that nightshift officers were to refrain from shining their lamps in horses' eyes as it "made them shy". That office also contained Station Log Books going back to 1888, and gave a daily account of life and crime in the area during that period. Not surprisingly, the names of the offenders and habitual criminals were recognisable as those of their errant great-grandchildren of nearly a century later. Strong on old family traditions, some of them, and such exalted positions as town drunk were apparently guarded jealously and passed from father to son.

The value of these books became particularly relevant a few years later when the early computerised incident logging system came in and the retrieval of an incident further back than the day before yesterday became like one of the Twelve Labours of Hercules. Naturally, the obvious conclusion was frowned upon and it was an instant career-stopper to suggest that the new technology, which sundry mid-ranking officers were pinning their prospects on, might be in some respect flawed. Then again, if nothing had ever changed we'd still have been carrying muskets and calling out the hours on night patrol.

In 1975, the newly fledged Strathclyde Police ordered a trawl of the offices and the ancient relics – not the human ones of course, although some of them were distinctly obsolete by that time – were removed by the vanload. Some are to be found in the Force Museum in

Glasgow, but I feel certain that tons of fascinating material disappeared forever and was probably incinerated in case sensitive personal information on crimes and criminals from the previous century fell into the wrong hands. Hopefully, some of it has found its way illegally into private collections and may come to light in the future.

Chapter 8

The first residential course was intimated by the usual terse note from the Training Department, indicating that I was to present myself at Headquarters with enough clothing and personal effects to survive for two weeks at the prestigious Inverclyde Sports Centre in the sleepy coastal resort of Largs. There, I learned, I would join several cadets from my own and other forces as supervisors of a large party of schoolchildren from somewhere in Glasgow as they were introduced to sports, hillwalking and other physically and mentally stimulating activities. Under the eye of the full-time staff in residence, we would be responsible for their activities and general well-being. Naturally, nothing more in the way of a briefing was forthcoming although I had picked up enough snippets from other cadets to have an idea what was in store, and had the foresight to pack necessities like training shoes, t-shirts and drinking money. Predictably, it was pointed out that as we would be fed and watered in the centre there was no question of expenses being paid, the Chief Constable being one step from debtors' prison again.

On arrival at Headquarters I found myself with three other Lanarkshire cadets, none of whom I had ever met before. One of the training staff, the same one who took such pains with our expenses forms when at college, showed us into an unmarked car, an Austin A60 Cambridge if I remember correctly, and we set off. At least we set off on the first leg of the journey, which in total should have taken about an hour and a half, traffic permitting. Ten minutes later we stopped outside a house, presumably his, and were left without a word of explanation while he disappeared inside. Almost an hour later he reappeared, having apparently enjoyed a late breakfast by his own fireside while we sat in the car, and we continued the trip.

A few encouraging words or some sort of briefing might have been expected, but the journey was concluded in silence, our escort having made it clear that he didn't feel like engaging us in conversation of any kind. This from a member of the training staff responsible for us, mind. After a long, silent trip we were dropped off at the Centre, advised that we would be collected a week come Friday, warned to behave and left to it. Management techniques have come on a long way since then.

The staff at the centre were more welcoming and actually gave the impression of being pleased to see us, which was a new experience in itself. The children we were to supervise were to be fifty or so females in the fourteen to sixteen age group from the Springburn area of Glasgow. For those of us not familiar with the area, we were advised that Springburn was not absolutely the most upmarket part of town with the result that some of the girls would have deprived backgrounds and possibly occasional behavioural problems. Some did and some didn't, of course, but the idea was to take them beyond their limited life experience, restricted wholly to inner city life, and show them a wider range of activities than they would normally get to try.

We were also reminded that, despite the possibility that some of us would have girlfriends around the same age – we hadn't – we were on no account to get amorous ideas or encourage the young ladies to. As it subsequently turned out, most of them were a sight more advanced in that respect than we were and a few, from their general demeanour and appearance, had probably been entertaining the troops from an early age. Nonetheless, in our capacity as adults, being responsible sixteen or seventeen-year-old police cadets, it was our duty to look after them and become their guides and role models for the next two weeks.

As it was residential, we were expected to be about at all times, with the exception that two of us would be allowed out each evening in rotation to enjoy the fleshpots of Largs. If you've ever been to the seaside resort of Largs, you'll agree that it's not exactly the Barbary Coast, having about as much potential for wild living as a care home tea dance. It's a nice old place where nice old people retire for the quiet life, and the last event of interest was in 1263 when a fleet of hostile Vikings turned up on the beach to sort out their differences with the King of Scotland. They're still talking about it.

We would eat with our charges, one of us to each table, and take our own groups for organised sports and outings as directed by the staff. A timetable of events was passed round and we were shown to our rooms to unpack and make ready for the arrival of the schoolgirls. The fact that that none of us were in the least qualified to teach anyone anything about sports didn't seem to be an issue. Again, I wondered if our perceived need for developmental courses matching up to someone else's need for cheap labour was entirely coincidental.

I think the scriptwriter who created the St Trinians films must have spent time in a school in Springburn and been inspired by it. We had no sooner unpacked and presented ourselves in the main lounge, than two coaches pulled up outside and a mob of screaming, gum-chewing females erupted into the yard, fighting over luggage and cursing like drunken whalers on shore leave. A few were partially civilised, and stood out from the others, but not many. Their schoolteachers, or keepers or whatever, herded them indoors, lined them up in the hall, counted heads and vanished with obvious relief. The staff made the mutual introductions, then left us to get to know each other, while we stared at them with growing apprehension and they glowered menacingly back at us. A quick run through the names established who would be in whose groups, and therefore what table we would sit at for meals, then they were taken by a female staff member to be allocated their dorms prior to reconvening for lunch. We looked at each other silently, there not really being much we could say, and slunk back into the staff lounge, wondering what we had gotten ourselves into. We would find out shortly.

Over lunch, it became obvious that the tactic when confronted with authority figures, particularly ones as young and obviously green as us, was to stare constantly and ask embarrassing questions. It was made clear that they didn't think much of the police, and especially not cadets who weren't much older than they were. It was further pointed out that if we did some simple arithmetic we would find out that they outnumbered us about eight to one, and to keep the fact in mind if we wanted to survive the experience in one piece. It made you wonder what these courses were like when it was the boys' turn to have their horizons broadened. Much the same, I was later told by someone who had come through it, although dealing with them was more straightforward and had fewer potential pitfalls.

This lot also managed to find out within a short time what our status was as regarded experience with the opposite sex, and were delighted to discover that by and large it wasn't very much. By the end of the first lunchtime, we were heavily on the defensive while they were gearing themselves up for a fortnight of malicious fun at our expense and planning strategies. If successful leadership depends on the assertion of the leaders' authority from the start, we should have packed up at that point and headed for home. Being gluttons for punishment, and not knowing how to get home from Largs anyway, we decided to stick it out. It had the makings of a long two weeks.

As it turned out, none of us appealed to the flower of Springburn society, probably because we sported obviously short police haircuts, then very unfashionable, and also because we were, after all, part of the hated enemy. The Glasgow Police, we found, were held in especially low esteem in that part of the city, doubtless with some fault on both sides.

Such romantic attachments as were formed were directed at one of the full-time staff, a trainee sports instructor doing a rather longer attachment than us. Jimmy, as I'll call him, was neither one thing or another, having sports qualifications but still being, like us, subject to evaluation by the permanent staff and expected to be about at all hours. Unlike us he had long hair, absolutely essential during the dying throes of the Hippie era, and was a couple of years older than we were, therefore carrying a certain maturity and worldliness sorely lacking in the rest of us. It became obvious that he had either been warned off, as we had, or simply didn't fancy any of them which was just as likely. Either way, he made it clear that he was above their juvenile level and unfortunately made a point of addressing them in sarcastic tones as if they were aged about five and mentally retarded, which didn't go down too well and was unfair. They were all much older than five. From regarding him as an object of schoolgirl desire, they immediately moved to active dislike with the result that their pranks and practical jokes which might have become directed at all of us became concentrated on the unfortunate trainee.

His first mistake was trying to assert his authority. He formed up a group of about twenty in a semi-circle and told them that they would be going for a healthy run into the hills. The group, none of whom were given to energetic pursuits beyond doing their nails or shoplifting, demurred and advised him that they would prefer to learn badminton, which seemed a nice, gentle activity and one which the inhabitants of Springburn associated with the gentry. A dispute ensued. He began to shout at them and made ill-considered comments about their beloved Springburn, uncivilised slum dwellers, offspring of jailbirds and so forth, which didn't go down at all well. As a group, and exhibiting a commendable grasp of teamwork, they pulled him to the floor and piled onto him. They didn't say or do anything else, just sat on him for a few minutes until his struggles subsided, then allowed him up. They reformed their semi-circle without a word and waited for him to begin again, this time hopefully using a more agreeable tone. He obviously wasn't too quick on the uptake and made his next mistake by redoubling the personal abuse and threatening them with being reported to the management. They exchanged glances then fell on him again, this time being less restrained and he collected more than a few good kicks and punches under the scrum. His muffled cries rent the air for some time before the mob parted and he crawled out, his face red and his clothing dishevelled. He decided to let them play badminton, to our intense amusement.

Naturally his authority was in shreds from the word go and when we left he was heading for a very poor assessment indeed, largely based on his failure to read the signs and see trouble coming. You can be sure we took note and learned from his mistakes. Now that he was the bad guy, we became the good guys and had little or no trouble from the young ladies. Nonetheless we took care to work the groups in pairs and made a point of not being found alone in any quiet areas, having been advised that malicious allegations by children of this ilk were not unknown and that a witness was always a good thing to have. Good advice of course, and an excellent way of way of avoiding any such allegations being made in the first place.

The incident, much as we found it entertaining, didn't help us much at the time, having in one stroke destroyed any semblance of credibility the part-time staff carried with the rabble, which was another valuable lesson – it's easier to lose respect than it is to get it back. While we didn't get any trouble as such, we didn't get much respect either. Over the next two weeks we were treated to the spectacle of Jimmy being pursued through the grounds by a baying mob, Jimmy hobbling back to HQ with no shoes and Jimmy having his food openly plundered from his plate during mealtimes. How he put up with it is anyone's guess, but he kept the heat off us and that was fine. He also succeeded in having his evil way with one of the female members of staff, a girl on secondment from the Army if I remember correctly, which was more than any of us came close to doing, so he can't have been put off the opposite sex too much during his trials, and it made it even easier for us to take a malicious delight in his misery.

After two weeks of the Belles of Springburn, I would have cheerfully entered a monastery and never set eyes on another female again. They were always there, with hardly a respite from morning till lights out, and the pub on our rostered evenings off was the only escape. I'll skip over the awkward question of how old one has to be to be served hard liquor in licensed premises, especially in Largs where the average customer was about seventy. Even on the morning after, when one is not at one's absolute best and should be entitled to sit quietly contemplating the evils of drink, they were there, giggling and chattering like a flock of parakeets. One of the more obnoxious ones, an uncommonly well-developed young madam, had the habit of hanging over the meal table then sitting erect with a handful of chips or pieces of toast, depending on what meal it was, stuck to the front of her bulging pullover. Contrary to what you may think, it was far from an appealing sight and most certainly not one to be confronted with after a night whooping it up in downtown Largs.

It was particularly unpleasant on the morning after I had been seized with the splendid idea of calling into a seafront hotel and sampling something from every bottle behind the bar. A stomach awash with a hellish cocktail of wines, spirits and liqueurs, all washed down by pints of lager and no doubt the cleaners floor polish if we had been able to locate it, is not the ideal preparation for a day's leaping around a badminton court or leading bracing route-marches into the hills behind Largs. My room-mate, a kindred spirit called Al, had drawn the same evening off as I had and between us we decided that drink would wash our troubles away. In moderation it might have done just that, but at our age moderation in drink was a virtue still to be learned the hard way and we hit it like the Fleet arriving in port. They're probably trying to get the stains out of the bedroom carpet and walls of our room yet.

We also came close to getting the pokey from the local law. The way back to the centre was very simple as one had only to walk along the promenade until one saw a sign saying "Sports Centre" and turn right, which would have eventually led straight back to base. Naturally, having taken drink in excess, we were in a somewhat befuddled state – the expression rat-arsed comes to mind – and came up with a short cut which naturally got us well and truly lost. After wandering the streets for some time, the inevitable call of nature led to my leaning against a lamp post trying to find my zip, which was proving elusive, while Al opted for a convenient front garden full of rose bushes and for reasons never properly explained burst into song. At this point a light came on in the house, dogs began to bark and a police van turned into the street which led to two rubber-legged visions taking off like scalded cats into the night, one still serenading the street. Twenty seconds later would have found both of us in midstream, so to speak, and unable to run for it which might have been awkward. I very much doubt if our leaders in the Training Department would have seen us as representing the best traditions of Lanarkshire Constabulary when the inevitable terse interview took place on our return home. Capital offence material right up there with defiling the Sovereign's eldest daughter or claiming expenses, I daresay.

The rest of the visit drifted away in a haze of badminton, squash, volleyball and other games we didn't know how to play, let alone teach, invigorating hill walks in the rain and drink on three nights a week. On the plus side, however, the unaccustomed exercise kept the St Trinians lot too tired to reach their full antisocial potential, and they even lost interest in Jimmy a bit by the end of the second week, contenting themselves with occasionally spilling custard on him.

When our exalted leader turned up in the A60 to take us home again, it was none too soon, the novelty of being surrounded by females, albeit the shower we had been stuck with, having worn a bit thin. After a silent trip back, Al and I were dropped off near the steelworks in Motherwell for some unexplained reason. Unexplained because neither of us lived in Motherwell or worked there or had any conceivable reason for wanting to be there, so I can only assume that our driver had some reason of his own for tossing us out where he did. As he drove off, leaving us abandoned on a street corner with our bags like two illegal immigrants ejected from a lorry, his parting remark was to remind us to be back on duty sharp on Monday morning and not to try to claim expenses. The very thought.

I resisted the temptation to point out that I and two large bags would now have to find transport to Bellshill. Just as well I still had some bus fare left. Al lived at the other, rural, end of the county where I suspected they were still using stagecoaches. I would have thought myself that having been on duty for the whole of the last two weeks we might have been due a couple of extra days, but no, this was not part of the deal and for the record I have yet to be asked by anyone in authority how the course went or heard any feedback about how I performed. Just as well, now I think on it.

I arrived back at Coatbridge office on Monday morning, wondering if I was expected to report in on how the course had gone. Needless to say, nobody had even noticed that I was missing and why was I standing about in idleness when the bar officer was expiring from the want of refreshment? I remember pouring tea while gesturing rudely at his back and wondering how long I could have gotten away with lying in bed drawing wages before somebody came looking for me. Months, probably.

In fact the Super at Coatbridge, prince among men that he was, agreed that I was due a couple of days off and told me to take them on his direct instructions and if anyone – naming no names, mind – had anything to say about it I was to refer them to him for guidance. He actually put it more strongly than that, but you get the drift, and while I was naturally shocked to hear such commentary coming from an officer and a gentleman, I also learned a few interesting things that morning. Firstly, some bosses were good guys when the mood took them. Secondly, the cranky bar officer, bless his evil old heart, must have been interested enough in my welfare to have told our boss in the first place, which was a turn up. Thirdly, not all bosses liked each other which was an interesting slant for someone who had recently left school and was still used to seeing a united front from authority. Lastly, I was more or less surplus to requirements and if I got a couple of days off I wouldn't be missed.

The problem was, you see, that nobody really wanted cadets or knew what to do with them. We were punted about various offices and sent on courses from time to time, but if anyone in the organisation knew why, or what was being achieved by it, I never met him or heard from him. I still don't understand why they took us on in the first place. Police Cadets, in the Strathclyde area at any rate, were abolished some time later although subsequently resurrected for a few years. I have no doubt that under modern management they would be better looked after than we were and given some sort of meaningful career path. While not exactly perfect, and in some respects a step back from their forebears, the modern generation of managers at least show an interest in their underlings and know how to bolster the inexperienced by making them feel wanted. They also know how not to leave themselves liable to criticism by exposing impressionable youth to evil ways, which is possibly nearer the mark.

Compared to the support and active encouragement shown to today's probationary cops, it's a wonder any of us stayed the course. Then again, compared to the average well educated and motivated recruit today, maybe some of us weren't exactly the crème de la crème of the job market either.

Chapter 9

For those who don't remember life before Equal Opportunities, the role and status of the mythical and nowadays unmentionable being known as the Policewoman may be enlightening. Unlike today, a Policewoman – read Female Police Officer and think shame of yourself for being sexist – was not simply another member of the team who worked all shifts, patrolled dark streets alone on wet winter nights, attended battles in pubs, changed wheels in the rain, policed violent football matches and generally drew life's short straw as a daily matter of course. The Policewoman of yore, that is up to about 1975, was a privileged personage who seldom ventured into the elements unless the sun was shining and an early tan was required for the holidays. They didn't attend calls and certainly didn't get their hands dirty at any of the amusing little duties which fall to their modern counterparts. In Coatbridge at least, they didn't work nightshifts, being on call should anything crop up which needed the services of a female officer and couldn't wait until morning. At least one shift Inspector I remember didn't even allow on-call policewomen to drive in, preferring to send a van to the house to collect the little lady in question. How the little ladies themselves felt about the arrangement it is open to conjecture, but I suspect the arrangement was none of their making.

On the other hand, nobody expected them to do much beyond being about the office and making themselves useful until a female prisoner needed searching or a sex abuse case reared its head. The Policewomen's Department was an entity in itself, having restricted duties based on the quaint, old-fashioned notion that females are not suited to rolling about the streets engaged in mortal combat with drunks twice their size, and when confronted by a dangerous individual or crowd of dangerous individuals have as much chance of coming out on top as they have of being the next World Heavyweight Champion. At this juncture someone is sure to mention that the odd one or two could easily have passed as contenders for the World Heavyweight Championship, but contrary to popular myth such specimens were few and far between. Most were and are quite normal.

The legislators also forgot that whereas the police service can be coerced into being politically correct – up to a point at any rate – the riff-raff on the streets can't. Neds expected their cops to be big and ugly and to be able to exchange blows with them during weekend festivities. We now apparently live in enlightened times.

Policewomen were paid 90% of the salary of their male colleagues and if any of them were chaining themselves to railings and howling for full parity I don't remember noticing them. Strange as it may seem to the current generation of young female officers, most of the pre-1975 lot were perfectly content with things as they stood and which after all were the job conditions they signed up for. No doubt a few did harbour secret ambitions to play rugby, break wind in the locker room and generally prove that the female can do anything the male can, but a lot of the ones I remember listening to were, to say the least, less than enthralled when the new legislation turned them out for their first nightshift under the stars.

I don't blame them at all. If I had been given the chance to sit in the office making the Inspector's tea and listening to the rain battering against the window, as opposed to going out in it, I'd have taken it too even if it had meant smiling coyly at the old bugger and tittering at his off-colour jokes. No doubt there are now many from that period who maintain that they were all for equality and campaigned tirelessly, but if they did – and of course I don't doubt them for a minute – they were fairly quiet about it at the time. I recall reading that after France was safely liberated in 1944, there were suddenly thousands of hitherto unsuspected Resistance heroes swaggering around the streets of Paris and a certain parallel may be noted.

Before I become the target of threats and black spots through the post, let me make my views quite clear. Yes, we had our share of delicate exquisites who were quite happy to do next to nothing and smile winningly at the boss all day. Come to that we had more than our share of idle male personnel who also tried their damnedest to do as little as possible, albeit without the eyelash fluttering, so it's probably even. I would now add that many policewomen were and still are highly respected in their own right, the system of the day being none of their making.

The point is that today's generation of policewomen joined up to be fully rounded police officers, to take the rough with the smooth and did so with their eyes wide open, whereas their predecessors were recruited to carry out a specialised function within the police service and had the goalposts moved when they weren't looking. Some adapted well to the change, some didn't and some didn't see why they should, and so left. Some decided that their lifetime crusade would thereafter be proving that they were even better than the boys, but that's another matter and probably best left alone.

I heard a rumour at the time although, being at the bottom of the food chain, rumours reached me after passing through a lot of hands so I can't verify it, that the Police Service as a whole was quietly offered an exemption to the new legislation on safety grounds. These safety grounds were that females are in danger of being badly injured while trying to do work nature didn't intend them to do, but the offer was refused because the leadership didn't want to be seen to be getting preferential treatment. It may or may not be true, but has a certain ring of truth to it. When you think about it, females are advised to avoid dark, lonely streets and plan journeys carefully at night so as to avoid walking home alone. What does the police service do? They put young female police officers out to walk about on their own at all hours and send them to calls in multi-storey flats. No further comment there.

The top management of the time, of course, was largely comprised of middle-aged-to-ancient male officers in senior deskbound positions who weren't actually involved in outdoor policing and hadn't, in most cases, seen the light of day in years. On the odd occasion when they ventured forth it was like watching pit ponies being led into the sunlight. Naturally, they felt entitled to speak for the rank and file without consulting them and I recall that as my first exposure to management obsession with political correctness and the over-riding priority of "being seen to be doing" something. The actual doing of things, as opposed to be seen doing them, never figured very high with this style of manager, a breed which was just beginning to come to the fore about this time, but in my humble opinion they sold the policewomen down the river for no better cause than scoring a few Brownie points which nobody remembers any more.

The foregoing serves to explain why policewomen aren't mentioned over much in this narrative. In the early Seventies, the police service was still a largely male-dominated organisation and my contact with the female part of it was virtually non-existent. That would change, but only at a later date. The fact that some female officers who came through that period still managed to attain high rank and go on to great things in later years speaks volumes for their tenacity and refusal to accept second best. It's just a pity that they weren't allowed to do it as women rather as the unisex creatures we all became on paper after 1975.

Another group I didn't see much of was CID. Oh, I saw them move about the place, coming and going, and spoke to them in the passing or ignored subtle hints to get my coat on and nip out for their fags but that was about all. They lived in a closed little world of their own and communicated with uniform types only when it suited them. I hasten to add it wasn't just me they didn't talk to which would have been perfectly understandable. I'm sure they felt they could manage just fine without my input, but they were like that with everyone, going quiet when approached and whispering furtively. One or two I remember had even cultivated the habit of talking from the side of their mouths after pulling you aside and looking about to make sure nobody was listening. They couldn't so much as ask the time without looking like a bookie's runner on a street corner. No doubt there were times when delicate matters involving informants and high-powered criminal intelligence were being discussed but I didn't and still don't believe that such was the case very often, and certainly not all day every day. I think it was simply that they enjoyed the exclusive air it gave them and used it to prevent too many people being privy to what they were doing, or not doing, at any given time. They brought their share of arrests in, of course, but no more than anyone else did.

This was in the period before Regan and Carter burst onto the silver screen in The Sweeney wearing trendy suits and racing around in big cars. The trilby hat or sometimes a deerstalker – no kidding – and long gabardine raincoats, worn in all weathers, were still in vogue among the older, more senior detectives while the underlings wore tatty blue anoraks with a row of pens in the top pocket, which rendered them instantly identifiable as CID. As they'd all been in the same town for years everyone knew them anyway so they'd have been as well staying in uniform.

The younger generation of cops hadn't yet been mesmerised by the supposed glamour of detective work and the chance to cut a dash at work in flash suits. It even became an embarrassment when one uniform man, an old cop of long experience and widely respected as such, was given a stint as CID aide, a preliminary move to being appointed Detective Constable at some later date, and found himself completely shut out of their affairs. He got fed up with it very quickly and, I was given to understand, made his feelings on the subject clear before going back to his shift. If you think that you're going to hear tales of detection and serious criminal work I'm sorry to say you're going to be disappointed as I never got so much as a sniff of it, although I was later involved, very much on the periphery, in a real, sho-nuff murder enquiry.

It was a cliché in the press and popular fiction at one time for every major crime enquiry to kick off with Grim-Faced Detectives Racing to the Scene. I regret to say that the only grim-faced ones I ever saw were the ones who were too late arriving at the scene to get involved by appending their signature to some minor piece of evidence which guaranteed a lucrative stint of overtime at a future sitting of the High Court of Justiciary. A murder enquiry and, hopefully, a subsequent High Court trial, was and presumably still is, a profitable business for all concerned, and very often the first faces involved stayed involved for the duration. Overtime was virtually unlimited while the enquiry was ongoing and, if a result was achieved, High Court trials were notorious for going on interminably, generating even more overtime, with every witness cited to attend.

Time, money and inconvenience were of no consequence to the courts system, especially in the higher end, and if you could get yourself roped in as witness number 199 or whatever in a murder trial you were onto a good thing unless the guest of honour was inconsiderate enough to plead guilty. You also hoped he was smart enough not to be caught too early on and shut down the overtime jamboree before the summer holidays were paid for.

At this juncture I should mention that we're talking about murders where one ned hits another ned too hard and an otherwise unremarkable weekend brawl hits the big time. Real murders, that is to say premeditated acts involving innocent people, children and such are a different thing completely and really do involve grim faces. Nobody's that cynical. Drugs were largely unknown and so-called gang slayings, now so common, were few and far between in those days. I'll let you decide for yourself where they would have fitted in.

It was well known among police control room staff that if you tried to find a detective officer to attend a routine crime scene during the night in normal circumstances you could try a while – and be well advised not to hold your breath waiting – but at the first whiff of a murder they were coming out of the woodwork and up through trapdoors, yapping excitedly and clutching pre-signed labels to attach to bloodstained clothing, weapons, dog-ends or anything else which might conceivably lead to a walk-on part in court. It was also astounding the distances they could cover in a matter of minutes when a murder call went up. Again, in normal circumstances, asking them to attend from further than the end of the street was like suggesting they undertake the voyages of Marco Polo, but mention the M word and detectives from the other end of the county would materialise as if they'd been beamed down from a spaceship, complete with Grim Faces and overtime forms. Such hasn't changed. What has been dispensed with, happily, is the feverish compulsion of everyone and anyone in authority to be seen, and ideally photographed by the press, at the scene of the crime.

Within a short time of a murder being discovered, the circus came to town. A seemingly endless mob of senior police officers, most of whom had nothing whatever to contribute to the enquiry, would mill about and nod their heads wisely, each trying to look more grim-faced than everyone else, until the front page pictures were safely taken and on their way for tomorrow's first edition. A bonus would be the arrival of the TV cameras, as you can imagine.

If you read one of these true crime books, currently so popular, and examine any old photograph where senior officers and Grim-Faced Detectives in long raincoats are hanging about at a murder scene posing for the press photographers, everyone concerned somehow contrives to look like he's the key man, which is handy for the memoirs later, and I believe I know how it's done. Look at any such group and they nearly all play one of two distinct roles. One is talking and pointing at things, which gives him the air of knowing what's going on and being more or less indispensable to the whole show. The other is listening solemnly, brow furrowed, which gives the impression that he's in charge and the others are reporting in to him or, at the very least, seeking his advice on what to do next. It all depends on how the caption's worded and everyone's a winner.

Had it remained an opportunity for senior officers to have their pictures taken and be seen by their wives and bowling club cronies on the teatime news, no great harm would have been done. Unfortunately, they couldn't content themselves with being seen in the street looking grim and pointing at things, but had to get involved and see the actual locus of the crime for themselves. That led to a constant procession of VIPs who trampled all over murder scenes, destroying who knows how much evidence in the process, and each one leaving with a stern warning to the uniform constable guarding the door to allow nobody else in. One noted wag reminded a departing Superintendent that if nobody at all could get in it would be a bit tricky to investigate the crime so perhaps an exception might be made for the CID. That went down like a lead balloon as you may imagine.

Nonetheless, uniformed officers would be positioned so as to prevent unauthorised persons getting through although, predictably, every Tom, Dick and Harry who turned up for a photo call imagined that he was the exception to the rule and insisted on being allowed access. To make it worse, as the day progressed the visitors became more and more senior. Apart from the fact that the Belle of the Ball always arrives fashionably late, the top brass had further to travel from Headquarters. Also, being of high rank, they consequently became harder to stop. How the handful of Detective Constables and Sergeants – who actually do the CID work at a murder enquiry – ever managed to put forensic evidence together is beyond me. They must have prayed for rain or a big match on television to shoo everyone back indoors.

There having been a bloodstained body discovered in a house, and the cop I happened to be out with that day being remiss enough to answer his radio, he and I became the custodians of a murder scene in a council house on the outskirts of town and at that point I noticed a strange phenomenon for the first time, although I would see it again over the years. As the inevitable crowd gathered to gape at proceedings and get their faces on TV by waving from behind a journalist, a small and rapidly-expanding fleet of ice-cream vans and mobile fast food vendors, ever alert for trade, gradually built up on the periphery to refresh the audience with fish and chips and bottles of Tizer. Nowadays they would probably sell kebabs and Ecstasy tablets. The whole street took on a carnival atmosphere with everyone enjoying the day out and hoping for a sight of the departed as he was removed to the mortuary, ideally with the wounds showing.

You may think I jest, but no. If you ever see a really messy road accident or a serious street assault on a Friday night you'll see the audience of respectable passers-by killing each other to get to the front so that they can wail in horror at the sight of blood, and taking some shifting once they get a ringside seat. No doubt in the old days public hangings brought out the best in people too.

We stood guard for the best part of five hours before the nightshift sent somebody along to relieve us. Much as I'd like to give the impression that we became the mainspring of the thing by doing something clever or detecting a clue which contributed to an early arrest, the truth is that we didn't do much at all except ask visiting senior officers to stay outside then step aside, nodding respectfully, as they ignored us and marched indoors to trample evidence into the carpet. Nobody took our photographs, we didn't appear on the evening news and we definitely didn't get on the report as witnesses. No High Court money for us, then.

My neighbour, who'd downed a few pints earlier, was now in desperate straits. Not to put too fine a point on it, his back teeth were floating which I reckoned was exactly what he deserved. Unlike the ever-sociable Tam, this one wouldn't allow an under-age cadet to drink on duty – the hypocrite – so I'd sat grumping over a bottle of cola while he hit the Guinness like it was Saint Patrick's Day in Cork. After much agitated shuffling, he eventually had to leave me at the door while he nipped inside to use the toilet, which was awkward as that was near where the body had been lying. He was roundly abused by a Detective Inspector who arrived at the wrong moment, avoiding my amateurish delaying tactics at the front door, and promised to have him hung, drawn and quartered if any forensic evidence had been disturbed.

Commendably, my elder and better didn't make matters worse by retorting that there can't have been much worth disturbing by that time, given the number and frequency of our distinguished visitors, and also refrained from mentioning that half the cigarette ends dutifully bagged and labelled by the CID had also been smoked and dropped by senior officers as they popped in and out showing their best profiles to the press. They had to do something to pass the time while they were inside, after all.

On a more positive note, one of the food vendors, anxious to foster good relations with the police and knowing it was only a matter of time before he had his ear bitten anyway, sent over two huge bags of fish and chips smothered in brown sauce which we ate inside the murder locus, no doubt leaving a nice trail of suspicious crumbs – and certainly a few fag ends of our own – for the dayshift CID to find and bag the next morning. Showing my ignorance of the finer points in crime detection, I begged leave to enquire if littering a supposedly sterile murder locus with chips and fag ends was absolutely correct police procedure. My guide and mentor considered the point then answered, quite reasonably in my view, that we could hardly eat our chips outside with the press watching, could we?

And that was about that as far as murders went.

Chapter 10

Every summer a sort of pagan ritual known as the Orange Walk is enacted in cities, towns and villages throughout the country but predominantly in Northern Ireland and the West of Scotland. The days when this takes place, invariably Saturdays on or as near the 12th of July as the calendar permits, are staggered a bit as participants from Ulster and Scotland like to visit each other and latch onto each other's parades without missing out on their own big day. The event, as I understand it, is to commemorate a military victory in 1690 on the banks of an Irish river called the Boyne. It seems that William of Orange and his troops – the good guys – gave King James and his pretenders to the throne – the bad guys – a damned good thrashing for some obscure historical reason which has escaped me, not being too well up on 17th Century Irish politics. Why this particular event should continue to stir the blood some centuries later is even less clear to the outside observer as our fair land has a long history of occasions when monarchs of foreign extraction, not excluding the current line, felt it appropriate to take over our throne. Nonetheless, significant it continues to be and apparently symbolises the main cause for dispute in Northern

Ireland to this day. Why this should be a hot topic in Scotland is, again, shrouded in mystery.

For anyone not fully tuned in to Irish politics, the nub of the matter appears to be that when Britain decided to decolonise Ireland and move out, the predominant trend in the 20th Century when the popular idea around the world seemed to be Throw The British Out, it partitioned the place as it did in various other former colonies before going, thus leaving a legacy of ongoing civil strife and sectarianism behind it. The difference between Ireland and, say, India was that we managed to leave ourselves as one of the warring factions instead of getting out completely as we usually did. Thus we stayed embroiled in the thing. In a nutshell, Ireland contained two factions. One, the predominantly Roman Catholic Republican movement, wanted a united Ireland while the other, the mainly Protestant Loyalist side and King Billy fans to a man, didn't and wanted to remain part of the UK. Obviously both couldn't get their own way and in the early Seventies neither side was showing much signs of wanting to compromise over it.

To keep the thing going, the Orange movement – as it still does – took to the streets every year for a series of parades or demonstrations culminating the Big Walk as near to July 12 as could be managed. There was one in Glasgow and one in Lanarkshire, the venue of the latter changing every year. No doubt there were others, but I was never involved with them.

Whatever town had the honour of hosting the thing was more or less cut off from the world for a day as thousands of official marchers and bandsmen from dozens of Lodges, plus countless spectators, filled the streets and the parade, often several miles long, wound its way through the town at a snail's pace stopping traffic and creating utter chaos. As you can imagine, there was a very large policing commitment involved and cops from all over were on duty both at the Big Walk venue itself and in every settlement of any size throughout the force area. The latter, for those not too familiar with the big day, is because every local band and lodge had to parade about its own locality before being bussed to the main event.

Naturally, as all of these peripheral parades and gatherings had to be policed too, a cop – or cadet – who happened to be stationed in Coatbridge could still find himself virtually anywhere in the Force area for the day as manning levels stretched to breaking point. Accordingly, even the dayshift Monday-To-Friday wallahs were dusted down, told to locate their hats and coats and led outdoors, shivering in the unaccustomed fresh air. Everyone who could put one foot in front of the other was dug out and of course that meant me too although there was naturally no question of payment. As with Christmas, there was vague talk of time off in lieu of payment which as usual never came to anything. And so it came to pass that I attended my first Orange Walk as a member of Lanarkshire Constabulary.

My previous experience of Orange Walks was turning out as a boy to watch them go past when the political and religious significance was mostly lost on me and it just seemed like a big, colourful, noisy and hugely entertaining parade. I knew of course that the whole thing was, apart from being fiercely Protestant, fiercely anti-Roman Catholic too, but never really gave it a thought, most people in Bellshill being strongly polarised one way or the other anyway and casual religious friction being the norm. Like everyone else I always enjoyed the bit where the bands stopped outside the RC chapels and gave of their best for the benefit of the parish priests lurking within. The stick twirler – no doubt he's got a proper title – at the head of the leading band danced and cavorted wildly, throwing his pole impossibly high in the air and catching it without fail while the big drum was pounded furiously, a substantial sum of money supposedly awaiting anyone who could actually burst one outside a chapel. The priests scowled from their windows, the police tried to move the bands on – eventually – and the crowds cheered wildly, particularly when a second drummer appeared from the crowd and both men, one facing forwards and one back, took turns at trying to make their drumsticks meet in the middle. On a good day the lamp posts were shaking. All good, clean fun and, I might add, enthusiastically followed by the Roman Catholic children in our street who were about as wise about the religious and political significance of it all as I was.

Sometimes the parades went off without much ado, apart from the inevitable human debris left lying on the streets after refreshing themselves a bit too much over the day. Other days, the town in question could resemble Rome after the Goths had passed through, with pubs wrecked, shop windows smashed and the very paving stones lifted as missiles. On those days the cells were full to bursting and the hospital casualty departments, now known as A & E, doing a roaring trade. Duty at an

Orange Walk, therefore, could turn out to be quite a lively day depending on where you landed.

I turned out at muster at about ten to seven and found a seat among the members of the early shift who were in the normal assorted states of tired, very tired and sound asleep (Tam). Having been on backshift the previous day with a different group and therefore not being involved in the briefing, I had no idea what I would be doing today or who I would be doing it with. It turned out that I would be staying put with a skeleton crew while the rest were transported to far-off parts to police the main walk. Said skeleton crew was augmented by a sprinkling of dayshift types from here and there, a fine body of men who shared certain common features found in all indoor nine-to-fivers. Their shiny trouser seats looked out of place compared to their brand-new hats and coats, never used since issued, and they wore the betrayed look of faithful old hounds, used to an easy life at the fireside, whose masters have suddenly kicked them out into the cold.

There was a further addition to the crew, namely Old Rab, a soul mate and erstwhile drinking buddy of Tam's who had long since been prised away from him and banished to another shift. Recently, however, he had been filling in as a Court Officer and so had been swept up with the other members of the dayshift gang and told to present himself for Orange Walk duty. Cunningly, he sat well away from Tam hoping that the shift Sergeant and Inspector would forget about their previous history of association and send them out somewhere together, whereupon a whale of a time would be had by all. At the very least they might be sent out individually and could surreptitiously meet up later.

Rab's optimism was ill-founded. The Inspector, spotting the two reprobates lying low in the crowd – Tam asleep and slipping down in his seat and the other half of the act upright but trying to avoid eye contact – made a quick change of plan and sent me out with Rab, an announcement which produced a few malicious sniggers from the shift and some blasphemous muttering from Rab himself which thankfully didn't reach the supervisory ears. Tam, newly nudged awake and still trying to work out where he was, missed it although he quickly focused his thoughts and realised his plans were up in the air. He was paired off with a brand new probationary policewoman, full of enthusiasm and raring to go, who waved from the far side of the room and smiled encouragingly at him. Like Rab, Tam's muttered response was probably best left unheard.

Having met Rab once or twice before, I had an idea how the day was likely to go if he had any say in it. He and Tam had been cast in the same mould, being in the same service bracket, and had similar views on what constituted a day's police work. He was known as Old Rab, despite being not much older than Tam – mid forties at most – but being one of those characters who look as if they were born old then led a hard life. Many years ago he had been seen while on duty at a summer gala day by a passing Superintendent, seated behind the refreshment tent with his feet steeping in a basin of water while he drank from a cooling can of beer. The Super, one of the old school, had assumed Rab to be an old cop well up in service who was feeling the heat of the day a bit and had discreetly walked on, smiling indulgently. Laughing, he had mentioned it to Rab's Sergeant who advised him that the ancient one was in fact a probationer with less than two years' service and was supposed to be directing traffic at the entrance. By the time the Super retraced his steps in a distinctly less indulgent mood than before the culprit was long gone. This, then, was to be my new guide and mentor for the day. Fortunately, Tam had already given him the wink that I was to be trusted which made things a bit easier. By the time we left the office, he had actually spoken to me.

Our first job of the morning, it transpired, was to escort one of the local Orange lodges to its bus embarkation point which sounds, on the face of it, a simple task. Traditionally, local lodges congregate outside the domicile of their Worthy Master, who is ceremoniously greeted and placed at the head of the procession which then marches, by as long and circuitous a route as can be managed and with an accompanying flute band making as much noise as possible, to the local Orange Hall where all concerned mill around for a time, ideally disrupting traffic, before climbing aboard buses and heading off for the town hosting the main event. This early morning fun generally kicks off just after seven so we had to get moving sharpish. Given half a chance Orange parades were liable to move off without a police presence, contriving to take up the whole roadway instead of just one side, and the Lord alone knew where they would have landed up without an escort. Belfast, probably.

On being dropped off at the house, a nondescript council dwelling, it was immediately obvious that despite the official letters sent out every year warning them to keep to schedule they were nowhere near ready to move off. The entire Lodge plus an accompanying band, complete with flutes and drums, stray dogs and small children were filling up the street and front gardens. The men were all in dark suits, although amusingly one or two wore black plimsolls which they fondly imagined matched their clothing. Some sported white gloves and Orange sashes and some had them hanging out of pockets. The ladies of the Lodge were glorious in crimplene suits, floppy white hats and precariously high heels. A few enquiries among the loyal masses revealed that the master and committee were still in the house and awaiting our arrival. At this point two or three office bearers, noticeable by their more elaborate regalia, appeared and solemnly advised Rab that the master would be obliged if we would step inside for a moment, the invitation accompanied by much eyebrow raising and winking. Rab's eyes lit up and he nodded at me to follow.

The inside of the house must have had more drink stacked around the walls than the local cash-and-carry. There was enough beer to fill Townhead Loch and bottles of spirits as far as the eye could see. The master, who was normally employed as a road worker with the council or some such thing, but was supremely dignified on this day of days, extended a long-winded and formal welcome to the representatives of Lanarkshire Constabulary while the committee shuffled their feet and edged nearer the refreshments. The welcoming ceremony over, it was a free for all and I found myself holding a can of lager while Rab accepted a tumbler of whisky which he downed in one. His glass was hurriedly refilled and he began a series of toasts to the health of the Worthy Master, the Worthy Master's good lady wife who was making bacon rolls in the kitchen, the Worthy Master's offspring, Her Majesty the Queen, King Billy, Ian Paisley and a series of increasingly obscure loyalist figures while the committee charged their glasses and roared approval. By the time I had started on my second can, Rab and the committee were hanging on each other's shoulders and singing sectarian songs while the master and his good lady wife circulated with food and drink, all this and it not yet 8.00am. I carefully backed into a corner and pretended to drink the lager. By the look of Rab it seemed a good idea if one of us stayed in possession of his wits.

The procession, when it finally got under way, looked more like a conga line at a New Year party than an Orange Walk and luckily there wasn't too much traffic about as Rab had insisted, in the face of wiser advice, on taking pole position at the front. He was doing better than I expected – I thought the committee would have to carry him. I brought up the rear, catching stragglers who were losing their bearings within two hundred yards of the starting grid and keeping them from falling under the wheels of passing cars.

One of the features of an Orange Parade of those days, now long gone, is the collection of lethal accessories carried by the marshals who walked alongside the parade, keeping order and disciplining any of their number who looked like bringing the lodge into disrepute through unseemly behaviour, and offering the same service to drunken stragglers who latched onto the parade and caused a nuisance. Nowadays you might see a furled umbrella or possibly a light walking stick being sported as a badge of office, but in those days the required equipment was an engraved ceremonial stick of similar size and weight to a Maori war club which the stewards applied freely when required. One distinct advantage was to the odd cop walking alongside the parade. He didn't have to do much at all, a quick word with the nearest marshal bringing the wrath of the lodge down on any unfortunate malefactor. If there was one thing the officials hated it was having their lodge brought into disrepute. The same could be said of any attempts to break the ranks and cross the road through a march. Woe to he who tried it and devil mend anyone who did, it being well known that it was taboo. You might as well have tried to walk through a Presidential parade and push the Secret Service out of the way.

A similarly outdated part of these affairs was the choice of music. In the early Seventies, anything still went and the most blatantly provocative sectarian tunes were happily rattled out and frequently sung along to by the unofficial followers who were, admittedly, no responsibility of the Lodge's. This has been stopped by mutual agreement with the authorities, and nowadays they can play anything at all as long as it falls within the limited musical range of flutes and drums and can be marched to. I have since seen Lodges marching to the theme music from *"The Green Berets"*, *"Colonel Bogey"* and, on one memorable occasion, *"The Lily of Laguna"* where the normally macho swagger of the marchers had a definite sway of the South Sea Islands about it. In those days, however, it was "*The Sash My Father Wore*", "*The Green Grassy Slopes Of The Boyne*" and "*The Orange Lily*" delivered at full volume and be damned to popery.

The police escort, of course, was necessary to prevent disturbances as a substantial faction of the public disapproved and outbreaks of trouble were entirely possible. I heard later of one dear old lady in Glasgow, apparently of Irish Catholic extraction, who hated Orange parades with a vengeance. Every year an officer had to be sent to sit with her in her upstairs tenement living room which overlooked the parade route. In previous years her practice had been to build up a cheery blaze in the fireplace then, as the parade passed by, scoop up the burning coals in a large shovel and fire them through the open window into the marching ranks below. All good, clean fun for the spectators provided they weren't too close but unlikely to help in maintaining the Queen's Peace, a fragile entity at the best of times in Glasgow. I'm sure you can imagine the reactions of the marchers as fiery missiles rained down on them from above, accompanied by senile screeching as the dear old soul waved the Irish Tricolour flag from the window and shouted abuse. Apparently when the police were in the house, however, she was as good as gold and plied them with tea and biscuits so the deployment of an officer to babysit her for half an hour was probably manpower well spent as an alternative to quelling a riot.

On another occasion a parade was due to pass a certain pub where the regulars were, to say the least, fiercely anti-Orange. As the parade grew closer the tightly-packed patrons boiled up their blood and downed copious quantities of firewater while making ready an arsenal of chairs, bottles, tumblers and sundry other missiles to launch on the parade's arrival. A wise and experienced old cop outside, seeing the Battle of the Boyne about to be re-enacted in the street, made an instant strategic decision. Instead of sending for reinforcements, which might or might not have been on time, he used his initiative and locked the crowd inside. Due to regular outbreaks of violence, the pub windows had been replaced by walls of glass brick so the one and only exit was via the front door. This our hero smartly sealed off by pulling the doors shut and dropping a bent four-inch nail through the padlock hasp. While the flutes and drums banged away happily as the parade passed, the enraged mob inside roared and screamed in fury, hammering on the doors and walls as if they were being burned alive instead of deprived of a few minutes' harmless fun. Once the sound of flutes and drums had gradually faded into the distance, the nail was removed. By then, the mood had passed anyway and the drinkers drifted back to the bar for much needed restoratives. In such small ways are disasters averted.

We wound our way through the town to the Orange Hall, flutes and drums rousing late sleepers and nightshift workers with a selection of loyalist melodies, and arrived more or less intact having lost hardly any stragglers. It helped that the pubs along the route weren't yet open at that time of the morning so nobody was tempted to break ranks and left wheel into a convenient oasis. On arrival at the hall the crowd milled about again, disrupting traffic for the requisite period, then the marshals and sundry other officials ushered everyone onto the waiting buses and they left. I know that Rab, in the words of the Inspector, had been told to see them safely away but I felt he took it just a bit too literally, standing in the middle of the roadway and waving till the buses were out of sight like a proud mother seeing the family off on a trip. That done, and his point well made that he was a fervent supporter of the cause, he made a beeline for the Orange Hall where the bar had been open since about six, and joined in another round of toasts with the committee members who had been left in charge. We stayed there until about ten, hitched a lift back to the office for breakfast then hung about the Orange Hall for the rest of the day, toasting the memory of King Billy and his merry men.

And that was the Orange Walk.

Chapter 11

Back at the office, I was now the master of the control room having become adept at the simultaneous operation of the switchboard and radios, logging stolen cars and providing a constant supply of tea for anyone senior to me – that is to say everybody – who decided to drop in, while occasionally running to the public bar to attend to passing trade. In fairness, not all bar officers were as hard going as the one I'd met on arrival. One or two were even known to make the tea by themselves when I was under pressure, albeit rarely and usually making such a song and dance about it that I wished they wouldn't bother.

The thought of relieving my pressure by doing some of the menial work themselves seldom occurred to them. When they did decide to play mother with the teapot, they told the story over and over with an air of virtuous martyrdom to everyone who passed through the office, then played on it for days, refusing to stir from their chairs while I ran around the office in a lather of activity, on the grounds that they had done their bit. Spoiled rotten I was, and didn't know when I was well off, I was told. Cadets having their tea made for them, indeed. Breakfast in bed would be the next thing.

One old sergeant, a decent enough character but one who tended to confuse police cadets with Victorian chimney boys, had to have the story of my life of decadence and luxury in the uniform bar repeated several times before he would believe it and thereafter regarded me as a dangerous radical bent on undermining the police service as a preliminary move towards the revolution. He was never unpleasant about it, but tended to stop and stare at me as if the ghost of Karl Marx had materialised in the uniform bar, then walk away shaking his head. Cadets would soon be asking for a second bowl of gruel if the rot wasn't stopped.

A few regulars were conspicuously absent. My old adversary, the Ancient Bar Officer, was off on holiday. Two weeks grave-robbing by the seaside no doubt. Tam, the master drink detector, was also absent on sick leave. I wondered if his liver had given out, but it was apparently a simple case of having fallen off a ladder while painting his upstairs window frames and he was now obliged to sit at home with his leg in plaster. Tam would be devastated at being off work, of course – it meant he'd have to pay for his own drink. On the other hand the pubs in the town centre would notice an upturn in profits.

My scheduled shifts had been altered for some reason or other and I found myself spending more time with other groups who had tended to be off duty or nightshift when I was about. I found that each group, or shift, had its own character and little ways. Usually, the tone was set by the senior cops. If the senior men were reasonably sober and conscientious – and many were - so was everyone else. It stood to reason as the old hands weren't going to do all the work then allow the boys to sit about dossing. On the other hand, if the old stagers were a crowd of piss-artists like Tam, the junior men tended to follow on. Such is life.

The shift supervisors had surprisingly little influence. They went out and about, going through the motions of searching for beat cops and ascertaining that they were alive, sober and more or less in the area of the town where they were supposed to be. Sober, incidentally, was a flexible term open to a wide range of interpretations. Generally speaking, sobriety was accepted as the ability to stand upright, possibly with assistance, and make a reasonable amount of sense when engaged in conversation. Provided the supervisors found their men during their rounds, they were generally satisfied. It also made life much easier if the ground troops made themselves available for inspection early on in the shift, which they would if there was no disadvantage to themselves in doing so. The alternative open to shift supervisors was to attempt the enforcement of Prohibition, a futile task which many had tried and few achieved and at the end of the day only resulted in an elaborate and time consuming game of hide and seek. It was in everyone's interests to maintain the time-honoured status quo, and when the occasional uniformed apparition was discovered in a condition once beautifully described in relation to a prominent politician as tired and emotional, as often as not the Tired and Emotional One was simply bundled into a van and dropped off at home.

The new shift I found myself working with were a comparatively sober, clean-living outfit. They spent their days off playing golf instead of lying about in low dives or appearing at disciplinary hearings. The bar officer was a cheerful, hardworking character and, like his shift sergeants, was young by the standards of the office, which meant that he hadn't actually seen war service under Haig.

Coatbridge, you see, was like most former burgh stations in that it hadn't really changed since the demise of the burgh police force two or three years before, which meant nothing had changed within living memory. Personnel hadn't moved on to any extent, job rotation as a matter of policy being some way off. When you eventually clawed your way into a job like bar officer, it was a job for life or as much of your life as was left by the time you got it. In effect, Coatbridge Burgh Police was still alive and well in all respects which meant recruitment and promotion into dead men's shoes. It also meant that there was no incentive to show ambition as everybody knew when the next retirement was due and whose turn it was next to move up. It still hadn't been recognised that a new regime was in power and that the system was already changing, albeit slowly.

Very few cops had passed the necessary promotion exams to qualify in any case, and for the handful who had it was a case of keeping your nose clean, not getting done for the drink and in the fullness of time being promoted. The concept of Accelerated Promotion schemes had been heard of, and rumoured to be operating elsewhere in the County – nobody even considered other forces which were as distant planets to them – but none of these exotic beings had ever, to my knowledge, darkened the door of our office and as a certainty nobody already there was going in for it. Some did reach high rank in later years and deservedly so, but I can't for the life of me work out how it came about. Barring unexpected deaths in service, outbreak of war or other imponderables nature took its course at a snail's pace so that in the normal course of events, if you kept your nose clean, you could expect to reach Chief Inspector rank when you had about a hundred and fifty years' service. The ones who reached the very top must have been as old as the Biblical patriarchs which, when you saw some of them, was entirely within the realms of possibility.

A sizeable influx of recruits in the immediate post-war years and a complete lack of movement since then had left us with an unusually large number of very senior cops in the same service bracket, none of whom were going anywhere or for that matter wanted to go anywhere. A young shift, therefore, was very much a relative term. Today, to someone on a shift where the senior beat cop is lucky to be out of his two-year probationary period, the personnel of our office in 1971 must sound like the cast of *Dad's Army*. Although some older men in the office sported war ribbons, my new shift were comparative boys. I think only about half were over forty.

Walking a beat with them, however, was a different proposition to my tours of the Coatbridge Whisky Trail when out with Tam. These men, while not necessarily setting the world on fire, did make some attempt to police their areas on a higher plane than visiting their cronies and molesting local toerags. Attempts were made to deal with traffic problems, standing complaints on the beat were given regular attention and a stab was made at investigating minor crimes rather than by submitting an illegible form to the CID and forgetting about it. They answered their radios and attended calls without being hounded overly much, and didn't see the requirement to work as an infringement of their human rights, unlike others who come to mind.

Certain similarities remained, however. I seldom saw the offer of liquid refreshment refused, although they seemed happy enough with a quick social drink and didn't build the rest of the day around it. Any ned who was cheeky or didn't take the hint to move on the first time was quickly put right and shown the error of his ways. They still, as a matter of principle as much as anything, declined to make themselves too readily available for supervisory visits, possibly feeling that the supervisors should do something to earn their keep. They also had as many secret hideaways as anyone else, although these were used more sparingly and visited after attending calls, not instead of.

Like Tam, they rightly recognised that the concept of walking about a small beat for eight hours a day is both unrealistic and soul-destroying, and ensured that they always had somewhere to go when things were quiet. Being realistic, they also knew, as did their sergeants if they were honest, that regular breaks off the street are necessary to keep the mind functioning.

Unlike Tam, they stayed out and about when the beat was busy and their presence was likely to fulfil some purpose, and didn't regard it as a serious loss of face to be seen engaged in police duties. Not only would Tam have been embarrassed to be seen with his notebook out,

I doubt if he even carried one at all. I certainly never saw one and if one did exist it was in pristine condition with little or nothing in it. In other words, I began to learn something about what beat policing was really supposed to be about. Needless to say, I was subjected to the same "What school did you say you went to again?" enquiries for a considerable time until I stopped being the new face.

I also noted that when we visited some stop-off my new colleagues were greeted with a subtle but unmistakeable difference in attitude from the one shown to Tam. On one hand they were shown more deference and respect, but on the other hand people were more guarded and less forthcoming in their conversation. I think that was because, at the end of the day, Tam didn't really care what people were getting up to and everyone knew it. Tam had a very limited view of the role of a beat cop, in that he was there to chase the neds out of sight and onto someone else's beat. He didn't see his job as following them up, he was just there to deal out instant justice, jail them if there was absolutely no alternative and be able to cast an eye over his Main Street and find a ned-free zone. The other cops, while happy to visit all and sundry and accept their hospitality would also have felt obliged to deal with any breach of the law they had found or, to be strictly accurate, they would have dealt with any breach of the law they personally disapproved of. Most experienced street cops have their own entrenched ideas about what constitutes right and wrong and these personal viewpoints don't necessarily correspond precisely to the law of the land.

Working beat cops, as opposed to career climbers, have their feet firmly planted on the ground. They see too much of real human problems, death, suffering and heartbreak every working day to take trivia seriously. Unlike fictitious cops on TV they don't make a drama out of what they see or demand counselling every time someone says boo to them. They just deal with it and forget it. I recall reading that some minor television personality had once been a police officer for about six months, which of course made him a renowned expert, and that he once, to his shock and horror, became involved in a street fight which he felt was just too much to bear. He obviously dined out on that one for a while and clearly regarded it as pretty desperate stuff, bless him. The fact is that old cops have seen too much and done too much in too short a time to be easily impressed, by anything or anyone at all, and very soon form their own sound opinions as to what justifies taking action and what is utter rubbish.

The fact that some legislator had decided arbitrarily that thou shalt not do such-and-such didn't cut much ice with them at all. They worked in the real world and dealt with it accordingly. For instance, the law of that time said that drinking in public houses had to stop at ten PM, a thoroughly unpopular and unnecessary enactment which is now, thankfully, ancient history. While the beat men would regularly visit the pubs at closing time and assist the staff to eject the unwilling patrons, that being expected by all concerned, they saw nothing wrong with the manager continuing to serve favoured customers behind locked doors as a private arrangement thereafter. Nor did they see any great harm in taking their hats off and joining them, which was just as much of a no-no and just as widely accepted.

The same ridiculous legislation decreed that only hotels serving bona fide travellers could be open for selling drink on Sundays. In theory, then, the inhabitants of town A would have to travel to town B to become genuine travellers in need of refreshment, at the same time passing the travellers from town B going in the opposite direction on a similar quest. Naturally, the whole thing was a farce and treated as such by everyone, particularly the regular drinkers who simply gave up their normal watering holes every Sunday and packed the bars of the local hotels, ready to profess themselves bona fide travellers from strange, faraway lands if asked. They never were, of course. Was it any wonder that beat officers seldom felt the need to enforce such idiotic rules and simply ignored them, being more likely to make the bona fide travellers feel welcome by joining them in a hospitable glass or two.

The police management of a few years later cracked down hard on these practices and eventually banned beat cops from entering licensed premises at all without solid justification and an entry in the official notebook, and for a time controversy raged about that as you may imagine. The beat cops loudly proclaimed that they had lost a major access to the grass roots of the community where all sorts of information and crime intelligence was to be found. By their way of it – if you listened to them – a network of publicans, petty criminals and taxi drivers with their collective ears to the ground and who socialised nightly with police officers in the pubs and clubs, were a valuable source of knowledge. The police management, on the other hand, expressed an element of doubt as to how much useful information was actually gathered and how much of that was ever acted on. They took the position that as the main objective of the visitations was free drink, no matter how hotly it was denied, and that the recipients of the hospitality might have a certain reluctance to bite the hands that fed them, the arrangement was worth dispensing with. There was probably a lot of truth in both sides of the argument.

It came to pass, therefore, that I was initiated into another side of beat policing and was disabused of my fast-growing impression that I had joined an organisation devoted entirely to the procurement and consumption of free drink interspersed with occasional violent attacks on known troublemakers. I now knew that these activities, while not in any real sense taboo, were supposed to be ancillary to the main job requirements and not the whole purpose of turning up at work. I decided that this novel approach had its merits and was very happy where I was. I must have been heard to say so, always a bad mistake, as I soon found myself on the move. The Training Department, obviously at a loose end and finding Devil's work for idle hands, had dreamed up my next career move which would entail my being uprooted.

Perhaps the timing was right as I was in the early stages of forming some very bad habits. I stayed long enough to realise that Tam, undoubtedly a wonderful character and the material of myth and legend, was not the typical beat cop I had imagined him to be. Just as well, really.

Digressing slightly, it was about that time, just before leaving Coatbridge, that I fell in love with the

Jaguar Mk.2 3.8 litre saloon, the best police car ever made, and still admire it although it has long since passed into memory. If you're unfamiliar with the model, it's the low, wide one used by Inspector Morse and, going back a bit further, chased around London by the Sweeney in their early Ford Granadas.

They looked fast even when standing still and a damned sight faster when they took off. For most of the Sixties they were the last word in police cars, the yardstick by which other makes and models were judged and usually found wanting.

The old Mk2s came in three engine sizes, the 2.4litre, the 3.4litre and the 3.8litre and all looked more or less identical except for the badges they sported. It is now usual to refer to the 2.4 as underpowered, sluggish and so on, and by today's standards for big cars they are. In the early to mid-Sixties, when in their prime, they were just as quick off their mark as the other big six-cylinder models from Humber, Wolseley and so on. So the 2.4 was more than adequate for the time and certainly powerful enough for the normal well-heeled motorist. The 3.4, in comparison, could shift a bit and see off many a sports car but the 3.8, as used by police forces as traffic cars, was the wonder of the age on its arrival, being at that time the fastest production saloon car in the world. Just as no film about English police forces was complete without the black Wolseley complete with jangling bell, the icon of Scottish forces was a white 3.8 Jag.

It had a 0-60 time of about 8.5 seconds if you're into that sort of thing. If numbers don't mean anything to you, it took off like a cat with a firework up its arse as one of the drivers elegantly put it. Moreover, it could hit 125mph if you listened to Jaguar and 130 if you listened to the Traffic crews who piloted them and presumably knew what they were talking about. No doubt if modern aerodynamics engineering had been available, the top speed would have been higher still. These kinds of figures may not seem too special now, but was mighty impressive stuff in Ye Olden Days if you were pottering along in your Hillman Minx and one of the Jags sucked the doors off as it roared past you.

In fact, unless you had access to something exotic like a Ferrari, the 3.8 Jag could make anything else on the road look like it was going backwards. One older cop I knew who had driven Jags for years said that whenever he parked up the Jag for the day and drove home in his own car, he had the sensation of someone having severed his accelerator cable. Similarly, when returning to it after, say, a fortnight's holiday, there was a distinct danger of putting the foot down and taking off through the town hall.

A lot of the traffic cops of the time were just as impressive, being more like seat-of-the-pants fighter pilots than drivers which was just as well because the Jags, like most high-performance cars of the time, were lethal in the hands of an amateur, combining big, powerful engines with suspension systems, tyres and brakes which nowadays wouldn't be allowed on a supermarket trolley. Add a heavy gear change and steering and you had quite a challenging drive in any circumstances, so when you hit a tight corner or a bad camber or a slippery patch at speed you had to be very, very good indeed to come out the right way up. Needless to say, you could forget girlie toys like traction control, anti-lock braking and, if my memory's correct, seat belts to stop you connecting with the solid wooden dashboard or the spear-like, non-collapsing steering column if it all went wrong on you. Modern high-performance cars have an incredible level of built-in technology which flatters the mediocre driver's ability, which is just as well for some of the idiots let loose in them. Cars from the Sixties, even top-drawer ones like the Jaguars, didn't and the driver had to get it right or it was goodnight and lights out. An expert could make them sing, but an amateur was on very dodgy ground indeed if he tried to show off, so in the event of the Jag encountering something even faster – a remote contingency in Sixties Lanarkshire where owning any kind of car was still a novelty – the driving skills of the police crews would probably make up for the difference.

One evening the bar officer and I were enjoying a quiet cup of tea during a lull and chanced to listen in to a car chase taking place somewhere in the Upper Ward. The Upper Ward, an archaic name for the rural south end of the county, was ideal car chase country with its long open roads and limited traffic to get in the way when the drivers really nailed it. Some fool in a stolen Cortina was trying to outrun one of the Jaguars and making a real pig's ear of it, the swerves and squealing brakes on the bends getting more and more desperate by the minute while the Jag simply sat on its tail and let nature take its course.

At that time both sides of the exchanges on the radio between control room and car were audible and made good listening, the passenger in the car crew who operated the radio keeping his audience enthralled with a running commentary which suggested the Traffic men were thoroughly enjoying themselves and in stitches at the ned's increasingly wild manoeuvres. Updates spiced with ribald humour flowed until the inevitable end when the stolen car failed to take a bend and threw a couple of spectacular somersaults before coming in to land, undercarriage up, in a field. The radio man let out a roar more suited to the announcement of a last-minute goal in a cup final while another voice, presumably the Jag driver, could be heard laughing heartily in the background. Now, whereas job satisfaction's undoubtedly a good thing, it should still be celebrated in moderation, in public at least. As half the inhabitants of Lanarkshire were probably listening in by their firesides at home, as anyone with a radio could in those days, a certain discretion in how messages were worded might have been more appropriate. It may be a coincidence but shortly afterwards the radio channels were doctored so that only the control room could be overheard by listeners and seekers after thrills had to go back to watching Z-Cars.

In 1970 when I came along the Jaguars were starting to look their age and were actually out of production, but the last models were still in service and much loved by their crews, cumbersome old brutes that they were. I refer to the cars and not the crews, of course, although as I remember one or two of them were looking their age a bit too.

The successors to the Jags were, for the most part, an inferior lot and it was a long time before more modern and capable traffic cars caught up with their sheer power and panache. Some traffic cops will talk with nostalgic admiration of other police cars like the early Ford Granada, the Volvo T5 and various BMWs which have enjoyed their moment in the sun, but there was only one 3.8 Jaguar. Nothing else was ever so far ahead of the opposition in its time.

One balmy summer's day, while walking along the open, uncongested end of Main Street near the old Sheriff Court, I heard the sound of something with a lot of engine approaching at speed and turned to see one of the Jags in full cry heading for Airdrie where a stolen car had been spotted. It must have been hitting ninety on the bend and accelerating hard, the King of the Road, and I never forgot the sight.

I also heard a possibly apocryphal tale that the acceleration was so brutal that the crews were known to offer unwary policewomen a seat in the front, drop into second gear, floor the accelerator while releasing the seatback, and watch with delight as the unfortunate young lady landed in the back with her skirt around her ears. Well, maybe. Another Traffic Department yarn was that old Jaguar men could be identified by previously broken thumbs, caused by the ferocious kickback from the steering wheel when their chariot was being driven in anger. Again, maybe.

I was, on one memorable occasion, fortunate enough to be given a lift in one when going over to the Training Department at Hamilton on some mission or other. I climbed into the car in a state of high excitement, hoping the driver would open it up a bit for the boy's benefit. Naturally, the miserable old sod declined and drove to

Hamilton like his maiden aunt, an act of malice I hope haunts him for the rest of his days.

Not long after this, the Jaguars completed their working lives and were put out to grass. Sadly, they languished as unloved bangers and expendable extras on film sets for a number of years before being rediscovered and elevated to the status of cherished classics, a position they still hold. I sometimes recall the one I saw flying through Coatbridge and wonder if I might have been privileged to see the last Jaguar car chase in Lanarkshire. Rather like witnessing the last cavalry charge in history, it would be nice to think so.

Chapter 12

It was about this time I was reminded that I was entitled to a holiday and that if I didn't arrange it by submitting an annual leave application form nobody else would either. I don't know whether the management at Coatbridge was showing concern for my welfare by making sure the young lad had a well-deserved break, or whether they wanted rid of me for a while to give everyone else a well-deserved break. I therefore arranged a couple of weeks off and found to my surprise that my drinking buddy Al from the Largs visit was scheduled to be off too. Since Largs I had bumped into him from time to time and found we had a few things in common, that is we disliked the same people, drank lots of beer and never seemed to learn from it.

Al, a man ahead of his time, was the proud possessor of a car, an extremely old Ford Popular which he had bought to learn to drive in. By this time I had passed my test and was a fully-fledged driver, in theory at any rate, albeit one without a car and unlikely to get one for some time. Combining our resources we came up with the package of a car, a learner driver and a qualified supervisor which made the world our oyster. Where to go was the burning issue. We already knew that it would have to be south of the border as the Scottish licensing laws were still in the stone age. Pubs opened at 11am, closed again at 2.30, re-opened at 5 and finally closed down at the dizzy hour of 10pm. On Sundays it was even worse as the pubs were shut completely and hotels – for bona fide travellers of course – were grudgingly permitted to open from 12.30 to 2.30 and, if I remember correctly, 6pm to 10. England, on the other hand, didn't treat pub goers as social lepers destined for the Fiery Pit and had much more liberal opening hours. By now you may be getting an idea of what sort of holiday we had in mind.

A quick look over a map revealed that Carlisle was the nearest port of call so Carlisle it was. Wiser counsel prevailed, however, when my parents heard that two seventeen-year-olds plus one rickety old banger were heading south. I was reminded that an Uncle and Aunt lived in Blackpool and would no doubt be happy to put us up for a day or two. That was quickly arranged and no doubt a sigh of relief went up in the family home when we agreed to go somewhere where an element of responsibility and common sense was to be found, it being fairly obvious that we wouldn't be taking any of our own with us. The banger was duly loaded up, the parents pretended to look happy as we rattled off into the unknown and we headed south. This was about 4 pm.

By about 5 pm we were safely on the main road to England at a fairly sustainable 40 mph – and thinking there was nobody like us – when the heavens opened and something akin to the monsoon season in India started to lash down, as it invariably does when British holidaymakers head for the seaside. It was about that time, with tears of uncontrollable laughter running down his cheeks, that Al revealed the first of what was to be series of amusing problems. The windscreen wipers didn't work. You might imagine that during a torrential downpour on the A74 that would have been a catastrophe, and in any normal car built after the time of Agincourt it certainly would have been. In these old heaps, however, the wiper mechanism was a simple moving bar arrangement attached to a small motor which could be reached under the black metal dash from the front passenger seat. The motor had long since corroded into retirement, but the sliding bar was intact. For the next fifty miles or so Al drove, sniggering from time to time, as I pushed and pulled the bar back and forth, operating the wipers.

I remarked that the car seemed to be slipping and sliding about the road quite a lot which brought forth more merriment and the admission that the tyres didn't actually have much tread left. In fact, were he to be completely honest, none at all, a definite problem when you're driving in a couple of inches of floodwater and you'd like the tyres to maintain contact with the road surface. Not only that, but one had a slow puncture and was probably beginning to flatten out by now although, being a responsible motorist, he had a foot pump in the boot to administer occasional first aid. He assured me that although we were currently aquaplaning over the water, as opposed to driving through it, and as such had virtually no steering control, once the roads dried out the tyres would be fine. He explained that racing cars run on treadless tyres when it's dry because they grip better. It seemed pointless to remind the fool that it wasn't dry, he wasn't Jackie Stewart and we certainly weren't in a Formula One Lotus. This with a journey of about 150 miles in the worst summer weather since Noah's time still ahead of us, plus a return trip if we survived that long. More hilarity at that.

The next challenge hit us not far from the border at Gretna. About this point the A74 became a motorway and as Al, a learner driver, couldn't legally drive on a motorway I had to take over at the first lay-by we came to. I noticed that he slowed down very, very gradually and eventually crept to a halt using his handbrake. Somehow, and I can only put it down to sheer stupidity, the penny didn't drop and after getting myself adjusted we took off with me at the helm. For the first mile or so I was completely engrossed in mastering the gearchange as this thing had one of those old three-speed affairs where the changing of gears requires the use of a complex technique known as the double de-clutch. To cut a long story short it involves matching the engine revs to the movement inside the gearbox and in fact, when you master it, gears can be changed without using the clutch pedal at all. Naturally, I didn't know how to do it at that time and neither did most people unless they'd been driving since the Thirties.

The old Ford, a product of the mid-Fifties, shouldn't have needed it either but the synchromesh on the gears had long since passed on to a better place and double de-clutching was the only way except for optimistic crashing and swearing and grinding away at it. It was one of those things where if you can persevere and ignore the death rattle of the gearbox you pick it up after a while and eventually get most changes about half right.

It was after a good few miles, therefore, that I first noticed that the footbrake didn't seem to work no matter how much I pumped at it. It transpired that the braking system had a leak which allowed precious brake fluid to drip away until the brakes no longer did anything. Keeping calm, and resisting the urge to take a wheelbrace to his head, I enquired of my co-pilot why he hadn't repaired it. He didn't need to, came the clever reply, as he topped up the fluid reservoir every day or so. Why not today, I asked, equally sharp. Because he'd run out of fluid and hadn't time to buy more, he replied happily. Ah well, so long as I knew.

As we coasted towards the village of Gretna it became obvious that it was one of those places which shuts for the day and rolls up the pavements about teatime. The Gretna area nowadays is quite a lively spot with new retail parks, service areas and so on. In 1971 it was the back of beyond, giving visitors the impression that the Pied Piper had passed through and taken everyone with him as he left.

Nobody was to be seen except the village idiot who is invariably the only person about when you're in need of assistance. I approached him and explained in the slow, loud voice we British use when addressing foreigners and village idiots that we needed a garage. He pondered the problem then told me we needed a garage, which seemed to exhaust his supply of helpful tips for the motorist. Thanking him anyway, just in case he was dangerous or we might need him to push-start us later, we looked around by ourselves and found that the only garage which seemed to be about the village was a small, old fashioned establishment with a single-door workshop and a hand-operated petrol pump, both padlocked. It looked as if it hadn't changed since motorists wore dustcoats and leather helmets. Noticing that the proprietor apparently lived above the shop and assuming that he'd see it as his duty to assist stranded motorists I knocked on the door until a face appeared at the upper window.

I've got to say I've seen more enthusiastic Samaritans, this one shouting that he was closed then disappearing from sight. Not to be deterred, and still assuming that once he realised we were distressed travellers he'd leap to the rescue, I started up the knocking again until the face reappeared and told us this time to fuck off in a rich borders accent. A third bout of knocking produced a whole body which appeared from the rear of the building looking less than happy about the whole thing. He was also accompanied by a large Alsatian which looked as sociable as its owner.

From the safe side of the old Popular we enquired if he could sell us some brake fluid which would allow us to carry on and leave him in peace. He hesitated for a moment, probably undecided whether to sell us brake fluid or find peace by setting the dog on us, then muttered to himself while he found the key to the padlock and opened up. He vanished into the workshop, still muttering darkly, and re-appeared with a can of the precious fluid which he sold us for a scandalous price before going back indoors, omitting to wish us God speed and a safe journey. The brake fluid was duly poured into the reservoir and after some pumping of the brake pedal normal service was resumed. Naturally, our friend the village idiot had to re-appear while we were negotiating with the owner and help things along by shouting that we'd found a garage. When nobody answered him, he shouted it again and was still shouting about it when we left. By this time the rain was off, the sky was clear albeit darkening rapidly, and things were looking good.

These days, you cut off the M6 and continue along another stretch of motorway until you drive straight into the heart of Blackpool. In those days the route was to turn off at a sign advertising somewhere called Garstang and drive for twenty-odd miles through unlit country roads until Blackpool itself came into sight. Now I think of it, I don't actually remember seeing anywhere called Garstang as we drove along the road, but I suppose it must have been there. Things were going fine for a few miles then the car stopped. I didn't brake, it just stopped which was a bit different from its usual trick of not stopping when I did brake. After much poking about under the bonnet to see if anything miraculous would happen, that being the extent of our mechanical knowledge, and a few kicks at the tyres which other people seemed to do when in doubt, it became apparent that we'd run out of petrol. Yes, I discovered when I asked the sixty-four thousand dollar question, the petrol gauge had gone home about the same time the wiper motor did. More collapsing about in helpless mirth from my travelling companion whose overall sanity I was starting to question quite seriously.

That put us in an interesting position. We were stranded on a deserted country road in some unknown part of Lancashire, it was completely dark by now, we weren't in the AA or the RAC and, to summarise, I hadn't the faintest idea of what to do next. Naturally there wasn't a phone box in sight and if there had been I hadn't had the foresight to take note of my uncle's number, difficult as that may be to believe. Even if we had managed to contact someone, there was also the problem that I didn't actually know where we were, having apparently left the main route at some unmarked junction further back. I did know that if we backtracked onto the M6 and travelled a mile or so further south there was a service area where petrol was to be had, but that didn't help a lot at the moment. The Ford Popular was quite a small car but I didn't rate our chances of carrying it back to the M6 very highly.

It was at this point that our saviour hove into view. Out of the gloom came a meandering figure clearly heading home from an evening in the local pub, although where that lay was anybody's guess as we certainly hadn't passed one. He stopped, demonstrated his powers of observation by telling us that we appeared to be broken down and asked if he could help at all. At first I thought we had found the Gretna village idiot's brother, and started looking around for something to throw at him. In fact it turned out that he was just a harmless reveller genuinely trying to be helpful. When he was advised that petrol was required he threw up his hands and said that we could rest easy. He had petrol. He also lived nearby and would be glad to oblige.

We followed him into the darkness, turned up a track and after stumbling about in potholes for some time and spending a minute or so looking at the sky while he relieved himself against a tree, came to his abode, a static caravan where he lived with a pack of snarling dogs in an assortment of sizes and shapes. He disappeared into the dark, singing happily, leaving us surrounded by the pack of hostile mongrels who obviously didn't take to strangers much and seemed to be building themselves up to doing something about it. It felt like hours later, but was probably much less, when he came back brandishing a milk bottle, which he assured us was full of petrol, and shooed the mutts away.

We refused his kindly meant offer to join him and his menagerie for drinks in the caravan and left, thanking him profusely. We found our way back to the car while trying to calculate how many miles a pint of petrol would take us. I'm happy to say that the pint of petrol was good for a slow drive to the service area where the tank was topped up properly and the journey continued.

The simple ending to the tale would be that we drove into Blackpool and arrived safely, and so we should have had I remembered what my uncle had told me on the phone before we left. We should have driven to the seafront, which was easy to recognise because that's where the land stopped and the water started and so couldn't really be missed, then followed a few simple directions. We didn't.

I thought I could save some time by cutting diagonally across the town, not fully realising that Blackpool is actually quite a big place. In fact it's a very big place and we got hopelessly lost, passing through Lytham St Anne's at one point which is miles away. I thought for a time that I could work out directions by taking a fix on Blackpool Tower, but every time I lost sight of it for a minute it reappeared where it shouldn't have been, suggesting that either the tower was driving around in circles or I was. I finally gave up, found my way to the seafront, took my bearings and fetched up at my destination at 2 am to find my uncle standing at the front door where he'd obviously been for some time. He feigned nonchalance and swore he'd had every faith in us, but a pile of cigarette ends about a foot deep on the step gave the game away. We had been on the road for almost ten hours, the journey should have taken about five, even in the Popular, and frantic phone calls had been passing up and down between Blackpool and Scotland for some time. However, all's well that ends well and so forth.

Blackpool was quite a decent break as it turned out. The pubs, hotels and clubs of one sort and another seemed to stay open all the time, which I felt was very hospitable of them. I discovered that the local beer known as bitter, a substance not available in Scotland in those days and which I had never tried before, was something of an acquired taste for someone used to good old Scottish beer like McEwan's Export and Younger's Tartan. For some reason it didn't occur to me to order lager which is much the same everywhere and which I normally liked just as well. It goes without saying that I quickly acquired the taste for bitter although the different beers from a multitude of local breweries took some sifting through, and while some of them turned out to be pretty good, others tasted like they had been drawn from a passing donkey on the beach.

While getting to grips with the watering holes of Blackpool I became aware of an annoying custom, widespread in Northern England but not well known in Scotland, where the locals ask strangers and friends alike if they are All Right. Everyone you met or even nudged against in a pub asked if you were All Right. Knock their drink over or lift their wallet and they'd probably ask if you were All Right. I think it may possibly have been a local form of saying how-do-you-do, but at the time I found it irritating. I wondered if they ever listened to an answer and tried it once or twice to see. Each time some gormless Lancashire pub-goer asked if I was All Right, I said no and described, in some detail, an imaginary rash which had broken out in an embarrassing place. That usually produced a blank stare and five minutes later the same voice would ask me if I was All Right, so I gathered they weren't really interested one way or the other.

The uncle and aunt, who were Scottish and didn't keep asking if we were All Right, had a very open minded view on seventeen year olds who swilled beer and the food was good, my aunt being a good cook who knew what size of platefuls to give hungry teenagers. Blackpool was very well served by public transport and taxis were found in abundance at all hours which made it easy to get about, again something not found in Scotland in those days. We were quartered in South Shore, a fairly easy hop from the town centre and the bright lights, so what possessed us to skip the buses and taxis and take the banger uptown of an evening when we knew a lively time was ahead I cannot say.

One sunny morning we wakened up to the sound of car horns and raised voices in the cul-de-sac where my uncle and aunt lived. We peered out to find a number of irate drivers trying to get to work and making a poor job of it. Some fool had left an old black Ford Popular sitting diagonally across the middle of the street with the doors wide open, neatly blocking it off. A local cop had arrived and was starting to knock on doors when we flew out into the street, flew back when we realised that the car keys were upstairs, flew back out again and moved the offending vehicle to the kerb. When the cop found out that we were police cadets from Bonnie Scotland he asked if we were All Right – to which we responded civilly by saying yes, and we trusted he was too – smiled understandingly and left.

That was Al's cue to drop his last bombshell. He told me we should think ourselves very lucky the cop hadn't checked the car documents, which to be frank he should have when he saw the state of the old Ford which looked like one of the wrecks they keep at the Scottish Police College for practical exercises in Road Traffic offences. I assumed he meant it was an MOT failure but no, apparently that wasn't strictly speaking the problem. On enquiring into this slightly evasive answer, I was advised that the main reason this mechanical nightmare hadn't failed its MOT was that he hadn't actually presented it for testing since the last one ran out. When was that? About two years ago, now he thought of it. He'd bought the thing which had been lying up on bricks in more or less scrap condition with the intention of doing it up to make it roadworthy for when he became age to drive, but hadn't got round to it yet. My suspicions were becoming more acute by the second and I enquired, feeling that I already knew the answer, about how he taxed it without an MOT and what about insurance? A burst of nervous laughter confirmed my worst fears.

What was done was done, but I still had to drive this contraption back to the border then sit as a knowing accomplice when he took over the wheel for the rest of the trip, piloting a wreck without a scrap of documentation in force. The sensible solution, of course, would to have had the thing towed to a scrap yard where it belonged and taken the train home. That bit of advanced logic was evidently beyond us at the time because we never even thought of it and the old Popular had a stay of execution.

To cut short this disgraceful saga, to which I can only plead ignorance in mitigation, we got home in one piece and without being stopped on the road which was very, very lucky indeed and doesn't say much for the powers of observation shown by the motorway patrols. Our trusty mechanical steed should have attracted every traffic crew in the four police forces we passed through. If we thought our elders and betters in the Training Department would have been horrified by our conduct in Largs, and moved to get the resignation forms out, their reaction had this episode come to light can only be imagined. The only aspect of our transport which was legal was that it wasn't stolen, although I didn't actually pursue that line of enquiry far. Fortunately the story never came to light and as you may imagine we took very good care to keep it that way.

Chapter 13

During one of our routine visits to the Training Department where we were lined up, inspected and invariably found wanting in some respect, it had been put to us that an outing to an establishment known as an Outward Bound School was in the offing. The details of who was due for this treat were kept dark but the older cadets, who had already been and so unlikely to be sent back, found the news the height of humour. So did the training staff, which struck me as even more sinister as certain members of that body didn't normally possess a sense of humour at all. Nobody was forthcoming with details beyond knowing smirks and nudges, but I quickly came to the conclusion that this was not going to be a good thing to be involved in. Good courses and placements were handed out grudgingly and with the impression given that we should be grateful to the bountiful generosity of the Chief Constable, it being rumoured that he funded everything from new shirts to new buildings from his own pocket. The nasties were announced with crocodile smiles and laborious jokes which we were expected to receive with hearty laughter and general good humour.

The final word from the training staff was that instructions would be sent out in the fullness of time to those concerned and that we would be going whether we liked it or not, another worrying comment. When I arrived back at Coatbridge office one fine afternoon shortly thereafter, having enjoyed a pleasant day roaming the town centre, I was handed an envelope containing a short note saying that I would be heading for the great outdoors on the following Monday and to break the news to the family that I would be absent from the hearth for one month. I was also to report to the Training Department next morning to be kitted out and briefed. The fact that tomorrow was due to be my day off naturally didn't enter into the equation at all, nor had anyone enquired whether or not I had any forthcoming commitments over the next month, like booked-up holidays, family weddings, medical appointments, funerals or the like. I hadn't, as it happened, not that it would have made the slightest difference. Anyone who thinks slavery and indentured labour were abolished never served as a police cadet in Lanarkshire Constabulary, an organisation which in many ways would have been more suited to the early 19th Century than the second half of the 20th.

On arrival at the Training Department we were ushered into a side room and, of course, abandoned for an hour while the staff made ready to brief us on our forthcoming adventure. When one of the training staff finally remembered we were there, it was announced that we were to be issued with certain items of mountaineering kit. Visions sprang to mind of cutting a dash dressed as latter-day Edmund Hillarys setting out to conquer Everest. We were apparently to be entrusted with suitable footwear, anoraks and rucksacks procured at great cost by the Chief Constable whose children were probably going unshod because of it, and which was to be returned intact and undamaged.

I remember thinking that He – the capital letter suggesting royalty or the deity is intentional – must have been a busy man, our Chief. Everything done, bought or issued in Lanarkshire was apparently financed by him in person. The unspoken but heavily hinted-at message was that He paid for it all from his own pocket and we should therefore be both grateful and careful with anything given to us. At that stage I hadn't met or even seen the man, although small framed photographs of Him adorned every room in Headquarters, doubtless as an inspiration to all who laboured within.

The great leader's generosity aside, we would be expected to provide any and all other items of clothing ourselves. Needless to say, when the door of the training department's store cupboard was thrown open for our wonderment, the "mountaineering kit" was something to behold.

The anoraks were a pile of faded, moth-eaten cotton garments which looked as if they had been plundered from the bodies of dead Japanese soldiers after the Burma campaign. The rucksacks of similar vintage were equally worn and so full of holes we decided that the Emperor's lads must have been machine-gunned, although on the positive side anything kept inside would be well aired. But the boots were the piece de resistance. You might have thought that a suitable selection of pukka hillwalking boots in appropriate sizes would have been purchased from an outdoor activities shop and in this, of course, you would have been mistaken. We were pointed towards an ill-smelling mound of scuffed, mouldy items of footwear which might have been many things but weren't by any stretch of the imagination hillwalking boots. Opinions varied as to their source. One view was that they had been looted from the same bodies as the anoraks, another that they had been left behind by a passing Roman Legion and found in diggings many years later. My own opinion was that they looked suspiciously like the old pit boots my grandfather wore in his coalmining days. In any case they were anything but authentic hillwalking kit.

The idea was to get in quick and try to find a matching pair of pit boots in the appropriate size, ideally a right and a left. I did find two the correct size, although it would be exaggerating to call them a matching pair as they were different colours. To be accurate, one was brownish and one had all the colour scuffed off, although both had a fair amount of tread left on the soles. At least they fitted and certainly wouldn't need breaking in. I was advised that I should take them without further ado as the training staff didn't have all day to wait on my convenience. In actual fact, they possibly did have all day as I never saw them doing much, but perhaps I called in at the wrong times.

Fully equipped, we returned to our little briefing room. The remainder of the visit was spent being briefed. We were advised to take several pairs of old police issue trousers, and enough socks, underwear and jumpers to last a month. Someone correctly pointed out that we had only two pairs of police issue trousers each and that these were expected to be worn when in uniform at our stations, be available with a razor-like crease for inspections and generally clothe us at all times. Someone else suggested that after a month in the hills they might be a bit the worse for wear and asked if we would get replacements.

No we wouldn't, came the answer, and it was up to us to look after our clothing issue. Did we think that the Chief Constable had a budget made of elastic to keep ungrateful cadets in finery? One imagined the poor Chief living on bowls of gruel in the parish workhouse after squandering the last of his assets and being declared insolvent. I eventually took two pairs of denim jeans, despite having been told that they were the very last things to wear outdoors. I didn't have much choice, my wardrobe being largely restricted to uniform and denim jeans plus one pair of Sunday-best trousers which would have been even more out of place, being flared in the embarrassing style of the time. Jeans were bad enough, but tramping the hills dressed like a refugee from *Sergeant Pepper* would have been even worse. We were advised that we would report to Headquarters at the crack of dawn on Monday and that no travelling expenses or other drains on the public purse would be entertained. On that happy note went home carrying a collection of clothing items more suited to going undercover as tramps.

Came the dawn and we mustered at headquarters as instructed. With an inevitability which we were coming to expect, we were left hanging around the front door like the poor relations until about nine-thirty when two members of the training staff appeared with the keys to the training van, an elderly minibus which was to be our transport to the outer reaches of Wester Ross, a far-flung and particularly scenic part of the Scottish Highlands. As the vehicle wasn't even fuelled up and the training staff had just arrived, it was a fair bet that despite their strict instructions to be early, our illustrious leaders had still been lying comfortably in bed when we were peering through the gloom outside headquarters.

Things deteriorated quickly. Our party leader was the same happy character who had driven us to Largs and made claiming expenses such a fun challenge at college, and his sidekick wasn't much better, apparently understudying him and set on learning his ways. It was made clear to us that we were expected to sit quietly, for no good reason, to refrain from smoking in the vehicle, which was fair enough although nobody usually bothered much about it in those days, and generally avoid spoiling a grand day out for the training staff.

As usual, there was nothing in the way of a briefing or any of the encouraging noises usually made for the benefit of the youngsters on their way to a new adventure, beyond the usual dire warning about trying to defraud the Chief Constable by claiming expenses. This, without a doubt, was the ultimate crime for cadets in Lanarkshire Constabulary and we had come to discover that extracting money, even legitimately, was like prising gold from a miser. The one relevant instruction was that when we stopped in Fort William for lunch, there would be no indulging in alcoholic drink whatsoever.

They were, predictably, as good as their word. We were escorted into a small hotel in Fort William after a completely uneventful trip where even a subdued clearing of the throat was met by icy stares in the rear-view mirror – we eventually arrived at Applecross without knowing each other's names. The menu, arranged in advance, was a reasonable enough set lunch to be accompanied by one soft drink of our choosing, and as members of the public would be sharing the dining room we were to refrain from coarse speech or eating with our mouths open.

Over the years I came to dislike the way senior officers expected us to treat members of the public like royalty simply because they were members of the public. It's not exactly an exclusive circle and come to that what did they think we were? Sometime later an arrogant nuisance in the Captain Mainwaring mould rapped the counter in the uniform bar and proclaimed himself as a member of the public. It's a small world, said I tactfully, which produced a letter of complaint to the Super a day or two later.

We enjoyed a lively little luncheon, listening to the clock ticking and trying not to put the public off their food. The restrictions on alcohol apparently didn't apply to the training staff who indulged themselves wildly on a small bottle of beer each. The meal having been consumed, we were given dispensation to wander around Fort William for an hour and not get into trouble, bearing in mind that we were representing Lanarkshire Constabulary. Who would be aware of our identity or be remotely interested anyway wasn't explained. Thirty seconds later we were in the nearest pub, happily downing pints on the principle that if our leaders had taken even one beer they would be incapable of detecting the smell of it on us. Working under Tam's inspired tutelage had its advantages.

That theory was, of course, nonsense as it wouldn't have taken much in the way of a trained eye to spot the glazed eyes and rubber-legged walk which follows the act of pouring several pints of beer down teenage gullets in a short time. Whether the training staff didn't care, whether they had deliberately allowed us to follow our instincts or whether they didn't want it to be known that we had hit the town while they sat in a hotel whooping it up on a bottle of pale ale each, I will never know. One way or another, they feigned ignorance of our condition and allowed us to climb aboard the minibus unchallenged. I would like to be charitable and think that they were secretly good guys who turned a blind eye to a bit of boyish high spirits, but I'd also like to think that there really is a Santa Claus and I suspect that one notion is as likely as the other. Fortunately, we retained enough presence of mind to visit the little boys' room before embarking on the long second leg of the journey. There wasn't much in the way of amenities ahead of us and the chances of our leaders granting a pit stop behind a hedge was probably slim to non-existent.

The second bit was a much more enjoyable experience than the first, and it was nothing to do with the drink or that our keepers had thawed in any way. For the first time in my life I was seeing the real scenery of my native land which really comes into its own as you travel up the west coast of Scotland. In seventeen years I'd never seen it. I was enthralled by the wildness and emptiness and realised for the first time how little I had seen of the big world beyond my home environment. In case you don't know Lanarkshire, the northern end where I lived is the grotty industrial bit to the east of Glasgow, lying in a kind of no-man's-land between the hills and farmland of southern Scotland and the picturesque Highlands. We didn't and still don't get many tourists, certainly not any who stop for long.

We were heading for an isolated coastal beauty spot called Applecross, a tiny coastal hamlet sitting in a hollow surrounded by high mountains. At that time it was accessible either by sea if you owned a small boat and didn't mind a long journey, or by the Pass of the Cattle which climbed perilously over the hilltops via hairpin bends and gradients which would have made a mountain goat think twice. There is now, I understand, a decent road round the coast, but at that time it was still in the early stages of construction.

In the winter, Applecross could frequently be cut off from the outside world, an event which probably went unnoticed on both sides of the pass, but luckily this was summer. The minibus rattled and coughed its way to the summit of the pass and showed us a view of the Western Isles which could have been used as an advert to sell whisky in Iran. Below us lay the tiny settlement of Applecross and I think we all silently thanked the Chief Constable, bless him, for sending us here to this most glorious corner of Scotland. We soaked up the atmosphere and for a few moments we were the sons of Rob Roy, William Wallace and Robert the Bruce none of whom, incidentally, had ever been any nearer Wester Ross than I had. It was a sentiment probably brought on by a mixture of immaturity, patriotism and alcohol and has been referred to as drinking on an empty head. I understand that the New York Irish suffer similarly from it on St Patrick's Day. We sat in the van gaping at our heritage and felt great to be alive. It didn't last long.

Chapter 14

In those films about prisoner of war camps, once so commonplace, the opening scene was usually one where the leading members of the cast disembark from a tarpaulin-covered lorry under the eye of silent camp guards and stand surveying the huts. They're met by the camp commandant who addresses them in an excruciating Ealing Studios German accent and makes them feel at home by listing all the prohibitions and restrictions in the camp rules. This was normally followed by a reminder that escape was impossible, they would be shot for trying, and so on.

At that point a British officer, sporting an RAF moustache, would announce in a stage whisper to the other featured actors that they'd have an escape committee up and running by tea time and a tunnel under the wire was only a matter of time. They'd throw their kit bags onto the bunks and take to making secret radios out of bent paper clips and fag ends. By the end of the first week they would possess a selection of home-made Wehrmacht uniforms, wads of German currency, official papers and a detailed map of Occupied Europe to get them home. By week two the ground under the camp would be riddled with tunnels like a Gruyere cheese and vaulting horses would be springing up like mushrooms to cover the subsidence.

Our introduction to the West Highland School of Adventure differed perhaps in detail, but was remarkably true to the spirit of *The Great Escape*. I admit to seeing myself in the Steve McQueen role and why not? It's my story after all.

We disembarked from the minibus and stared at our new home, dumping our bags on the ground like real POWs. We hadn't much choice, the training staff having been met by the character who ran the place and carried off inside for refreshments with cries of welcome and handshakes all round. We later realised that one reason why the place survived was the impression of jolly good fun and *Boys' Own* camaraderie given to visitors by the adventure school staff. Nobody thought to offer us the hospitality of the house, or even indicate where we might go to unload the lager, earlier taken on board at Fort William and now well overdue for recycling.

The building was, I believe, an old farmhouse vacated and given over to the military during World War 2 as a training establishment of sorts. Without actually saying so in so many words, the proprietor gave us to understand that the cream of British Special Forces had trained here prior to being sent out to give the Hun a damned good thrashing in desperate commando raids. He may even have been telling the truth as it's well known that these places sprang up all over the Scottish Highlands in the early Forties. At the back of the old house was a remarkably authentic assault course which comprised an assortment of steel cables and logs fixed between large trees at a height guaranteed to seriously injure or kill anyone falling off. It was just dilapidated and mossy enough to have been there since the start of the war which suggested that it was in fact the real thing. We also found an outbuilding, probably built as a piggery or cattle byre, which had been converted into a rudimentary form of communal shower. The plumbing, like the assault course, had that solid, utilitarian look of army issue and again could well have dated from circa 1940, when mounting pipes and shower heads onto a stone wall, while omitting to provide any form of heating for the water or the shivering occupants, was just the thing to give the troops. No doubt it sharpened them up smartly on the cold winter mornings. Someone started to make a half-hearted comment about fresh air and the great outdoors, then thought better of it. As a group we stood quietly, contemplating the forthcoming month.

After a short time, we were summoned back to the main entrance by the sound of the training van starting up, refreshments having been partaken, and arrived in time to see our leaders driving off. Nothing like a parting word or two of encouragement to help the young lads settle in. It was obviously time to meet the staff.

The commandant who referred to himself, and was to be addressed by everyone else, as Warden, had obviously misread the script which called for him to stamp around in jackboots and threaten to shoot escapees. He was, as he would tell us many, many times over the next few weeks, a retired RAF officer entitled to be addressed as Flight Lieutenant, and possibly was because he sported an RAF pilot's moustache and addressed us in an authentic RAF pilot's accent. His duffel coat was more *Cruel Sea* than *Dambusters* but still, I suppose, in the spirit of the thing. We were under his command for the next four weeks, apparently, and would without fail engage when ordered in a variety of energetic and character-building activities which were to commence at approximately 0530 hours and terminate when lights-out was announced, every day with no days off.

We would be provided with what he ominously chose to call "an adequate amount of good, wholesome food" at certain times of the day and as a result would not require anything else, so he would lighten our load by taking charge of all monies in our possession to be signed for and returned on leaving. He would also thank us to hand over the fags too, as no smoking was to be permitted during our stay, indoors or out, as his was a healthy establishment. Further, we would not be permitted near licensed premises because, firstly, it was not part of the programme and, secondly, because there was no such thing for miles around anyway. The smoking aspect didn't bother me at all, not having long started at that point and being some way from nail-biting addiction, but it seemed that those who were addicted were going to give up the nasty habit without the option. We all nodded solemnly and handed over a token amount of cash, carefully secreting the bulk of it because if this clown thought we had arrived on the back of a turnip trailer he was sadly mistaken.

He introduced the other staff, a motley selection of instructors specialising in sundry outdoor activities, most of whom seemed to be ex-forces like himself, albeit of the other-ranks level. Two of them lived in married quarters with wives and children who stayed well out of our way, while the other two appeared to be single. I also gathered that somewhere in the background there was a Mrs Warden – I assumed she wasn't entitled to be addressed as Wing Commander or Air Vice-Marshal or we'd have heard about it – whose duties were not unlike that of a matron in a residential school, being available on demand to dispense simple medicines and give a family atmosphere to the place.

The interior of the building was as unappealing as the outside. The bedrooms were more like miniature dormitories containing three or four double bunks crammed together. For storage we had the floor. The bunks tended to confirm the army connection, being made of dark green painted metal and marked with the War Department arrow. They were also from the right era, having obviously been made when materials were short and British conscripts even shorter. These beds were designed when the average malnourished British Tommy was about five feet two and suffered from rickets, and I doubt if even 1940 Tommy Atkins had enjoyed much in the way of stretching out in comfort. The mattresses, needless to say, were thin, lumpy and smelled as if they had been accommodating our brave lads since Dunkirk. We dumped our kit and were advised to muster downstairs in an hour, by which time other guests, transferred from Colditz in brown lorries probably, should have arrived to swell our ranks. Dinner, said the Warden with some relish, would be served shortly afterwards.

I won't dwell on the meals as I still find the memory painful. Warden insisted that we were being given an adequate ration of good food, but omitted to specify who it was adequate for. It might have passed without comment in time of famine, or as the daily rations for a workhouse in Oliver Twist's time, but to a group of hungry, active seventeen-year-olds used to good feeding at home it was starvation level. Frankly, it bordered on the criminally fraudulent by Warden who was charging our employers for full bed and board and knew perfectly well that there was no way in which we could get access to shops to supplement it. I'm sure he also knew full well that there was no realistic prospect of anything been done about it on our behalf. Nowadays, even new recruits would walk out or at least get on the phone to the Police Federation, whether Warden liked it or not, but as I have already mentioned we had the employment rights of plantation slaves and had we complained through official channels our careers would have been terminated when the next convenient excuse arose, cadets having absolutely no recourse to appeal if they were deemed "unlikely to become police officers".

We wouldn't have been sacked for calling the Federation, of course, just put on hold for a short time then quietly dumped. I will say now in all fairness that not all of our bosses or the staff in the Training Department were so inclined, and some of them were in fact first class, but certain ones and one in particular were definitely so inclined, and their names are still tucked away in the memories of their rapidly ageing former subordinates. Lanarkshire cadets and probationary constables of the early Seventies who pause to recollect will possibly conjure up the same faces as I do.

The rations, such as they were, were all we were getting so I decided to make the most of it. This entailed volunteering to clear up the tables after mealtimes so as to have first go at any leftovers. I discovered that if the combined breadcrumbs from twenty or so plates is carefully collected it can be compressed into a ball which is almost the equivalent of another slice of bread. I got away with it for almost a week before my ploy was rumbled and competition to clear up the plates became intense. Warden was overjoyed at how everyone was mucking in, although one of the instructors who missed nothing enquired if I had been diagnosed as having a tapeworm. I couldn't have cared less.

We also started to send home for food parcels which arrived in the fullness of time as even Warden wouldn't have dared to intercept the Royal Mail, and Mars Bars, Cadbury's Dairy Milk and Opal Fruits took on the currency value of jail tobacco. The most prized of all was Creamola Foam, a powdered substance which came in small tins and which, when added to water, produced coloured fizzy drinks in assorted fruity flavours. In the July heat there was nothing to compare with it after a day sweltering in the hills, although I tried it again years later and wished I hadn't bothered. At the time, however, and in the absence of anything better, it was prized like vintage Bollinger and not a few fights broke out over alleged pilfering of supplies. I can never watch scenes on the TV news showing Red Cross food being thrown out of lorries to hungry mobs without thinking of Applecross and tins of Creamola Foam.

Chapter 15

Warden had arranged a nice healthy regime of early rises and stimulating runs into the hills before even getting a sniff of breakfast, not that it was worth breaking sweat for, but the real fun didn't start for a day or two. He also had an amusing trick of playing stirring classical music over a loudspeaker to rouse the guests, possibly imagining that we would leap from our beds to greet the dawn and surge into the great open spaces inspired by the Ride of the Valkyries or the 1812 Overture. He was, of course, mistaken. On the day when the course got down to it seriously, we were gathered together in the yard and told that we would be going forth into the wilderness alone which caused some consternation before he relented and admitted that the instructors would join us for certain parts of the trips. Whether it was to make sure we didn't come to harm or to stop us throwing away the rucksacks and striking out for civilization wasn't made clear.

One of the instructors, a jovial ex-sailor who affected a *Treasure Island* accent and was immediately nicknamed Master Bates – look up the heated controversy over what Captain Pugwash's crew were really called – swore that instructors were empowered to shoot mutineers and deserters, ha har! I believe from what he said, and by the sound of him when he wasn't trying to impersonate Long John Silver, that he came from somewhere in the West Country and so probably spoke with a bit of a Jim Lad accent anyhow. Before leaving, however, we were informed by our seagoing friend that some toughening up was in order.

That was within the remit of a second instructor who had been, we were advised, a Royal Marine and presumably knew all about toughening up weedy recruits. He, unlike Master Bates, was one of the strong, silent types who said little but contented himself with walking around with the air of one about to carry out daring deeds. Having said that, if he really was an ex-marine he was probably quite capable of daring deeds so that was okay. He was nicknamed Action Man after the famous toy soldier which also looked permanently ready for daring deeds and didn't say much. There were a few other instructors about the place who always seemed to be repairing things but we didn't have much contact with them. I wondered if they worked on some kind of rota system, month on, month off, but wasn't interested enough to ask.

The toughening up process, as led by Action Man, involved being taken round behind the house and introduced to the assault course. Up close it was even rustier and mossier than it had seemed when we arrived, and looked as good a way of breaking a leg as any. No word of complaint was heard, however, as by this time we had worked out that falling off a cable suspended between two trees and sustaining some debilitating injury was preferable to completing the full tour of duty with all its attractions. Some temporary pain then the prospect of limping about gamely while shouting encouragement to the others from the safety of a plaster cast seemed a fair exchange. An injury suffered by an inmate on a previous course had resulted in his staying about the place in plaster, so there was no danger of being taken home and sent back at some later date.

The result was that we threw all caution to the winds and flew around the elevated assault course like howler monkeys, laughing in the face of danger while expecting at any moment to fall to the ground where we could roll about emitting suitably agonised cries. It didn't happen, of course, but the virtuoso performance had the effect of impressing Warden no end. Never seen such damn' enthusiasm, he was overheard to say, while Master Bates called us likely lads and swore we would have passed muster on the rigging of a tea clipper, splice me buttocks, although if he'd been any nearer a tea clipper than building an Airfix model of the Cutty Sark I was much mistaken. Action Man simply looked strong and silent as if he'd expected no less.

Our antics came back to haunt us later, however, when we had another go on the thing the day before we were due to go home. Nobody was prepared to take the slightest risk so close to freedom and so the former troupe of fearless acrobats clung to the upper branches of the trees in abject terror while Warden and Captain Birdseye stamped about below calling us shirkers and worse. Action Man shook his head in a strong, silent kind of way.

The falling-off-the-tree ploy having failed, another tactic was tried to get a day or two off. Mrs Warden, among other things, fulfilled the duties of a nurse or matron and for a time we harboured the notion that reporting sick would get us a couple of days off. A vision floated before me of lying in bed looking pale and brave while she sat at my bedside reading the scriptures to comfort the sick, and tempting my appetite with ice cream and other mouth-watering little delicacies. The imagination took wings and I envisaged myself tottering to the window on crutches like Tiny Tim and waving the lads away on some awful expedition prior to diving back into bed with a comic and a cup of tea. No, was the short answer to that idea when two of us appeared at sick parade after breakfast holding our little tummies and whining.

Mrs Warden, or whatever her name actually was, dispensed medicine when required, although I have no idea what, if any, her qualifications were, and had a small selection of simple cures for simple ailments, including diarrhoea and constipation. If the ailment wasn't treatable from her limited medicine chest, it didn't exist and wasn't acknowledged. I could see her treating multiple gunshot wounds with Germoline and recommending a brisk run in the fresh air.

As it happened, the change of water or air or whatever really had upset the tums a bit and I was more than a touch on the runny side, and about the same time discovered that another inmate was fairly solidly bunged up. We obtained the necessary cures from our resident apothecary and promptly swapped them with predictably lively results, on my part at least. Within a short time I was sprinting to the toilets in arse-clenching distress, while the other half of the act could barely walk, his bowels having solidified into rock, and whereas I could shit through the eye of a needle at fifty paces, he was asking around for a crowbar.

I had the best of it, though. While my condition was short lived, if exhausting, and treatable by not venturing too far from the latrines, my partner in crime became so constipated that it looked for a time as though Mrs Warden would have to add dynamite to her medicine chest. I missed the fun when the triple dose of laxatives she prescribed the invalid finally found its way through, although I gather it was spectacular and included a selection of fearsome sound effects which frightened the sheep for miles around. For the record we were not permitted to recover in bed, being advised that fresh air and exercise would do us much more good. I suspect the trick had been pulled before and long since rumbled by the staff.

We were to undertake two expeditions, a three-day one and a six-day one. Both would entail being out on the hills for three days, the second one throwing in another three days in an open boat for good measure. Part of the fun would be cooking for ourselves while away, which meant carrying the rations and cooking utensils in our rucksacks. Just to get into the spirit of the thing, there would be no mamby-pamby luxuries like meat but we would have the once-in-a-lifetime opportunity to subsist on the fare of our wartime predecessors. And what would that be, we begged leave to enquire? Powdered eggs mainly, came the gleeful reply, along with bread, jam and, er, more powdered eggs. Considering that bread and jam is fairly cheap, particularly when the allowance is about two slices per head per day, and that the powdered eggs were probably discovered in an outhouse when Warden took command, the exercise had the twin advantages of introducing us to authentic outdoor living and saving the cunning old bastard nine days' feeding costs. I can still close my eyes and smell powdered eggs boiling over a small camping stove, the aroma of paraffin being the most appetising part.

Another luxury to be omitted was toilet paper, an utter waste of rucksack space and an effeminate self-indulgence used by cissies from the big city anyway. When the obvious question was asked, we were advised by Warden that on the Applecross Peninsula nature supplied large, flat leaves in abundance which were soft and strong although, he regretted to say, not overly absorbent. They also grew alongside nettles and could be easily confused by the unwary, as one of our number from a northern force, where I thought they would have known all about such rural things, discovered on the first day out. To my dying day I will remember him settling down comfortably behind a boulder then, after about a minute or so of quiet contemplation, erupting from cover like a startled pheasant and running about in circles, screaming and clutching his backside. On the positive side, it's not a mistake you make twice so I'm sure he learned a valuable lesson from it. Everyone else certainly did.

On the other hand, my own fall from grace came shortly afterwards, so I wasn't able to take full advantage of his discomfort. We had been advised that the last thing in the world to wear in the hills is denim jeans, but having nothing else and never listening to advice anyway that's what I wore. While still in convulsions over the nettle episode I sat back on another rock, ripped a large triangular section out of the seat, and spent the rest of the four weeks going about with the right half of my arse exposed to the elements. The weather was exceptionally sunny that year, even for July, and when I went home I took three heavily tanned cheeks, not two.

I had always thought of hermits as wild, bearded creatures who lived in caves, not unlike the character who appeared every week in Monty Python's Flying Circus, then everyone's must-see TV programme of the week. Apparently there was another variety, and one of them named Duncan lived along the route of our three-day walk, specifically beside the spot picked out for our first overnight stop. Duncan, like all eccentrics, was the subject of dark rumours and it was loudly speculated among the staff at the centre that his relationship with his sheep had passed the stage of casual friendship some time ago. It was also put to us that, although he loved his sheep dearly, he was more than partial to playing away with teenage hillwalkers which suggested the exercise of great care on our part when entering and leaving the tents.

It seemed that our schedule would see us arrive outside his croft on Sunday evening when Duncan, a devout member of one of those strict religious sects found in the remote corners of Scotland, would be shut inside for the Sabbath and would stir outside for nothing short of his house burning down. He would, however, be up and about early next morning and we were advised to keep our boots inside the tent as he was likely to make off with them given half a chance. Sure enough, he refused to open the door or in any way acknowledge our presence even when someone did a supposedly seductive sheep impression under his window.

Next morning, true to form, he was up and moving at dawn and grinning expectantly at us as we emerged a bit warily from the tents. Disappointingly, he didn't look like the Monty Python man at all. He was dressed in a filthy old suit and flat cap and looked like Spike Milligan. He nodded ingratiatingly and eyed up our boots as we put them on then, realising he wasn't getting new footwear or anything else for that matter, disappeared back into his croft muttering darkly. We didn't see him again.

Who we did see was the postie. Having walked for a day and a half, seen not a living soul besides Duncan and his woolly harem and become convinced that we were so far from civilisation as to be about to fall off the end of the world, a merry tinkling was heard behind us and the local postman, ringing the bell on his bicycle and waving, shot past us and vanished over a rise. Where he had come from was anybody's guess as there was nothing but vast expanses of scraggy grass and heather to be seen for miles in any direction. The Lord alone knows where he went either, for like Duncan we never saw him again. Maybe he was one of those ghostly figures who appear to travellers on lonely roads.

Our next human contact, later the same day as we encountered the spectral postie, was the strangest yet. We had collapsed for a break in sight of two small stone crofts sitting together at the waterside. After a minute or so an old crofter accompanied by an even older collie wandered over and nodded amiably, pulling a tobacco pouch and pipe from his pocket. Once the pipe was smouldering to his satisfaction, the old man wished us a good day and settled down to be sociable.

No doubt passers-by were infrequent and an opportunity to meet someone from the outside world wasn't something to be rushed. A short chat revealed that he lived here with his wife and widowed sister and, as we had gathered, didn't see much company besides the odd hillwalkers like ourselves and presumably phantom postmen. Incredibly, he let slip that his wife was originally from the "big towns" like ourselves, specifically being a Coatbridge woman he'd married many moons ago and brought up here to live with him. Stole her on a sheep raid more like, but I didn't like to contradict him. What I did say was that I was a police cadet currently stationed at Coatbridge. He threw his arms in the air with delight and without further ado I was hauled over to the croft to be introduced.

The Americans would have bought it at any price and shipped it stone by stone to Missouri or Arizona or wherever they called home. Getting the occupants thrown in would have been a bonus. Tiny, cramped and from an age gone by it was with one tiny window just big enough to let the occupants see when it was daylight outside. A peat fire burned, even in July, and two rosy-cheeked old ladies in shawls sat on wooden chairs, knitting by the firelight while another collie, this one asleep, lay at their feet. Apart from the – relatively – modern clothing worn by the old people, this place hadn't changed since Culloden. If a fugitive Bonnie Prince Charlie had stepped out of the shadows to enquire how the Rebellion was coming along I wouldn't have turned a hair.

The wife of the house made a couple of tentative enquiries about Coatbridge. I think I would have been welcome in any case, but once I had named a couple of old timers who she remembered as bits of boys and established my credentials, she was all over me. Tea was made and large, warm, freshly made bannocks, a sort of outsize oatcake, with home churned butter were produced. The tea was strong, sweet and made with fresh milk. I was encouraged to eat up, which as you'll no doubt guess I did without being told twice, and only left with the greatest of reluctance when my compatriots outside started making impatient noises. I'll swear there were tears in the old lady's eyes, and there certainly were in mine when I thought of leaving that cosy fireside to wander the hills like a lost soul.

On the other hand, if she came from Coatbridge and knew the same old cops I did, she was probably used to police visitors eating her out of house and home and afraid I'd start dropping in regularly. To be on the safe side I didn't tell the others about the hospitality of the house until we were well away or she'd have had even more cuckoos in the nest.

Chapter 16

The next outing was another three-day hike, this one to be followed by the open boat thing taking a further three days. The hike passed without much happening, apart from our being sunburned and half-starved. Master Bates and Action Man had dropped us off from a minibus, handed over an Ordnance Survey map and a compass and pointed out the route and final destination, a small camping spot on the shore of Loch Torridon. They would meet us there in three days, although they would pop up every so often along the route, being in the advantageous position of having transport.

Knowing that these gung-ho military types set great store by initiative and original planning, I suggested that as we were all going to meet up three days later at Loch Torridon anyway, why not achieve the objective – good phrase that – by simply jumping in the back of the minibus and going with them. Fuck off, you idle bastard, came the gung-ho military reply, which was fair comment I suppose.

The trek was more or less uneventful. One of our number, a self-opinionated idiot from the Gas Board or the Water Board or some such thing in the Home Counties, was appointed team leader by Warden and given custody of the map and compass. I think it was because he had been the only one who stayed awake while the mysteries of map reading were explained to us. Not having an original thought in his head he followed the map religiously, insisting on going up and down a long series of small hills like some sort of giant fairground ride when anyone with half a brain could have spotted that exactly the same destination, a distinctive rock formation, was achievable by following the valley floor for about three straight miles and avoiding the puffing and wheezing part. You didn't even have to read a map – you could see the bloody thing in the distance.

Not only did he fail to work it out for himself, he refused to be diverted from his purpose even when it was explained to him in quite plain, pointed language. Several times, in fact. It had been emphasised earlier by the staff, however, that team leader meant just that and decisions would not be made by committee or who could shout loudest. So follow the leader it was, albeit against a background of rich, abusive commentary on his fitness for the post which even a navy man would have been proud of. He pulled this trick several times, refusing to be told, and effectively trebled the distance we had to cover. He was lucky to make it back alive.

At one point about half way through the march, I spotted the minibus at the top of a hill where a navigable track obviously lay concealed from intrepid hillwalkers. Master Bates, Action Man and one of the spare instructors were watching us in open-mouthed wonder as we marched up and down half the hilltops in Wester Ross, completely ignoring the nice flat path below.

Loch Torridon is a lovely area, very remote and very scenic. More to the point, it also had the Torridon Hotel, situated just across the water although about two miles round the loch on foot. On arrival at our rendezvous, the instructors had watched us erect our tents, always an amusing spectacle involving lots of confusion and swearing, then told us to get a nice early night.

If Master Bates and his jolly tars thought we were going for an early night while the Torridon Hotel sat beckoning to us from over the loch like some moonlit oasis he was much mistaken. We had, as I said earlier, kept some cash back from the clutches of Warden with no firm purpose in mind, but just as a standby. A firm purpose now came to mind.

Feigning sleep for a short time, the more adventurous among us then slunk out, did a large circle on hands and knees around the instructors' tents, and headed across country for the hotel. It took some time, but as we broke cover in the hotel car park, our clothing decorated in bits of heather and rabbit droppings, it felt well worth the effort. Strong drink by the long, refreshing glassful awaited. We arrived in the public bar rubbing our hands and shouting loudly for flagons of their finest ale and walked straight into Master Bates who was paying for three large whiskies, the crafty bastards having waited until we were nicely tucked up for the night before driving round. No wonder they parked the bus well away from the tents. He glanced at us and nodded matily, asking what had kept us so long, and advised us that his tipple was a large Glenmorangie malt, should anyone be interested. It was plain to see that while we'd wasted half the night crawling about the hills like poachers the leaders, wiser in the ways of the world, had been using the time to far better effect. Action Man was already having trouble making his glass line up with his open mouth.

Keen to maintain good diplomatic relations, we had a whip round for three Glenmorangies which Master Bates and the crew received with cries of well-feigned astonishment, and the beer, which flowed freely, was on fine form. I thought myself that a salty old sea dog like Master Bates would have been into the rum, but apparently not. He didn't care for it at all, he admitted after his third or fourth malt whisky at our expense, and confided that he had never been much of a one for cabin boys either which we appreciated hearing. Action Man, obviously relaxed by the liquid windfall, grinned at us in a manly, square-jawed kind of way for long enough that I'm still a bit uncertain about his attitude to cabin boys.

One thing puzzled them though, as Master Bates announced in the middle of restoring the anonymous third instructor to his chair from whence he had slid. Why the fuck were we marching up and down hills like the Seven Fucking Dwarfs when a perfectly good path lay below? They had half-expected us to start singing Hi Ho at any minute, he sniggered. We explained the dilemma we had found ourselves in with our fool of a team leader, proud of having followed orders to the letter in the face of adversity and expecting some word of praise for our professionalism. Should have thrown the prick off the top, came the professional military response from Action Man. Master Bates staggered unsteadily to his feet like one about to make a speech, looked at each of us solemnly, farted and sat down again. We moved on to other topics of interest.

Although the new-found good fellowship didn't extend to buying us a round in return, the instructors were good enough to run us back to the camp when the bar closed. I don't recall it too clearly, things having become a bit hazy after midnight, but it occurred sometime in the small hours of the morning in the best traditions of remote highland hotels where police visits are rare. I do remember one bit, where Action Man weaved over to the bar and enquired of Mine Host when they closed. October, came the reply.

We reached base safely, albeit after some hairy driving which entailed swerving about the road with a semi-conscious Action Man at the wheel, and the goody-goody members of our little party, including the Gas Board idiot who had refused to come with us, were suitably put out. We arrived together arm in arm, singing rude songs, tripping over guy ropes and generally spoiling their beauty sleep. I have to admit we were all a bit poorly in the morning but rallied well when we discovered that someone had filled the Pride of the Gas Board's boots with what I hoped was loch water.

The boating part of the outing was another gem. Apart from docking at some godforsaken spit of land in the evening to pitch tents and regale ourselves with powdered eggs *a la paraffin*, we plied back and forth visiting small islands and bits of mainland which shared the twin attractions of being uninhabited by anything beyond the odd sheep or two and looking the same as all the other bits we had visited. Only one, an island riddled with anthrax from wartime experiments and apparently off limits for the next thousand years or so, stood out as distinctive. As you'll guess we took good care not to confuse it with anywhere else and attempt a landing. Being seamen for a few days I half expected the standard diet to be replaced by something equally delectable like weevily biscuit or rancid salt pork like the lads in the old *Hornblower* stories enjoyed, but no. They obviously had a lot of powdered egg to get through.

Admittedly we did learn the rudiments of tacking small sailing boats into the wind, although the technical terms, largely meaningless to us even at the time, are now completely gone and forgotten. I do, though, remember the first lesson from Master Bates, the captain of my boat, as to why sensible sailor-men don't spit or otherwise deposit bodily fluids into the wind. Being a jolly tar with a keen sense of humour he kept that particular pearl of wisdom to himself until one of the students of seamanship had done just that.

I also remember snatches of conversation on the subject of belaying spinnakers and splicing bilges and other such maritime drivel, but I suspect that Master Bates was showing off in front of the landlubbers and making it up as he went along. All he needed was a crutch and a parrot. My own opinion was that as marine engines had been invented some years back, and were giving uniform satisfaction worldwide, it would seem more sensible to use them than ply back and forth at the mercy of the prevailing winds, being soaked by spray and ducking swinging booms or futtocks or whatever they were.

Rather more professional was Action Man. While it's all very well to have a naval man, and initially it sounds impressive, it occurred to me that service in the Royal Navy doesn't in itself confer any knowledge of small boat handling. The Royal Navy, like all navies since about the time of the Roman galleys, supplies its staff with nice big ships to play about in and the fact that someone worked as an engine room fitter on a 5000 ton destroyer or spent his naval service washing dishes on the Ark Royal doesn't necessarily mean that he knows the front end of a small boat from the back. He might, but then again he might not. Worryingly, Master Bates declined to be drawn on the subject and steadfastly refused to divulge the exact nature of his naval career.

Action Man, on the other hand, had to be good at it. Handling small boats in enemy waters is one of the things marines do on behalf of Her Majesty and it can be taken as read that competence in getting the small boat there and back in adverse conditions is part of the overall job description. It was noted too that his boat always seemed to be following a straighter course than ours, despite the loud nautical cries from our master and commander. From this we deduced that skill and experience was of more practical value than the ability to impersonate Robert Newton, good as it was.

The weather was mixed. It stayed sunny which meant we got progressively more sunburned, not having any shade or headgear of any kind, and somehow developed frighteningly swollen forearms from a combination of sun and salt spray. For a couple of days I looked like Popeye the Sailorman, which was at least appropriate, although the condition subsided quickly and with no lasting harm. It was also blustery out on the water which stirred up the waves and tossed our pathetic little boat about like a cork. No doubt experienced sailors and yachtsmen and such would have taken it all in their stride, exchanging hearty sailor jokes and calling for vittles and grog from the galley, but we city slickers felt as if we were tackling Cape Horn in a canoe.

Our entire crew was stricken by seasickness shortly into day one and stayed that way. In the mornings Master Bates, moving deftly from Long John Silver to Captain Bligh, was close to applying a rope's end to get us off dry land and back on the briny. I imagine the early African slaves climbed aboard ship with more enthusiasm. People may speak lightly of seasickness, but if you've never experienced it in a small boat with nowhere to go take it from me it's the horrors of Hell. Death begins to have an appeal. Within a very short time the green-faced crew were lying prone in the scuppers, as I believe the term is, emitting feeble groans and being drenched by cold seawater every time the boat dipped. We were past caring and personally I couldn't have raised my head clear of the water if a shark had been heading for it.

Master Bates, cursing and blaspheming as only a veteran of the Royal Navy can, wound up sailing the vessel himself but didn't do too badly out of it. He had noted our contraband chocolate bars early in the voyage and cadged them for himself by the simple ruse of suggesting that we might like one to eat as a cure for *mal-de-mere*, the sun having melted them into a nice gooey consistency. The very thought of warm, soggy Mars Bars made us retch over the side with renewed vigour so he kindly agreed to take the nasty things away where they couldn't upset us. I've never really taken to boating since then and the sight of a Mars Bar still brings back bad memories.

The expedition ended with us staggering back to base close to collapse. Having spent six very energetic days out in hot weather while living and sleeping in what we stood up in, a shower seemed a good idea. The instructor who met us at the gate agreed. We stripped off, dropped all clothing into a pile, and dived into the shower block. Sometime later we emerged, all clean, fresh and feeling more or less human again, and discovered that exposure to the sun had turned us an eye-catching mixture of brown, pink and white depending on how long various parts had been unclothed. We looked like a row of Neapolitan ice-creams. We also had a problem. The clothing, which had gone unnoticed while we were wearing it, had developed a distinctly fruity aroma and was no longer fit to be worn or even approached. Having no other means of doing so, we lifted the offending garments with long pieces of stick then, holding them at arm's length, ran back into the shower block and dropped them into the sinks to soak overnight, all this in the open without a stitch of clothing. Fortunately nobody else was about. Next day it all dried out in the sun and you can imagine how we looked when they had to be worn again. Personally, I tipped the lot into the bin when I got home.

Rock-climbing was another challenging wheeze somehow designed to prepare us for a life in the police service. It was certainly as relevant as three days vomiting into the sea. Rock-climbing was actually a misleading term, or at least it was to me. Being a townie with little idea of the great outdoors, I imagined rocks as largish boulders which we could carefully scramble up and down on, enjoying a pleasant day out while we did so. The so-called rock turned out to be something modelled by nature along the lines of the Matterhorn but without the easy, sloping bits. If the weather had been at all cloudy I don't think we'd have seen the top. My understanding was also that some form of foot and hand holds were part of the deal, thus giving us a sporting chance of getting up and down alive, but the large, vertical piece of Scotland facing us appeared to be more like an up-ended billiard table whose surface would have challenged the climbing skills of a lizard. On closer inspection there were in fact sundry holes and grooves but still nothing to get excited about.

I also noted, with a degree of foreboding, that the instructor supposed to be taking us, Action Man, had cried off with some ailment or other which seemed a bit disappointing for an action hero used to catching bullets in his teeth. He had been replaced by Master Bates himself, no doubt a master mariner who could shiver his timbers with the best of them but, accordingly, unlikely to be a seasoned mountaineer too. Seamen tend to stay at sea and don't, as a rule, climb enormous cliff faces which explains why the Navy, and of course the odd outward bound school, employs marines who are good at it. I was starting to wonder why they employed Master Bates at all.. But no, all was apparently well and he was fully qualified to lead as we were advised when the point was raised, although again the exact nature of his qualification remained shrouded in mystery. I have to admit to being far from convinced.

My doubts increased when our resident sea-dog grabbed some ropes, a handful of metal devices I discovered were called pitons and could be hammered into cracks in the rock to support said ropes, and a hammer. He told us to give him a few minutes start and come up behind him, which seemed a trifle odd, then disappeared into a long concealed crevice in a generally upward direction.

We sat for some time, feeling vaguely abandoned like small children whose nanny has suddenly put the brakes on the pram and nipped off with a soldier. There was, however, nothing else to do but sit there and listen to the faint metallic sounds as hammer hit steel, and louder seafaring oaths as hammer hit fingers, getting further away until they died out altogether.

I'm no expert in climbing, and in fact don't even rate as a novice, but I'm certain that his mountaineering techniques were, to say the least, original. My understanding of the idea is that the lead climber carefully makes his way up, securing himself as he goes by hammering pitons into the rock and running a rope through them, the theory being that if he falls he doesn't fall far. Once at the top, or at least at the top of the first planned stage of the climb, he passes down the rope, now firmly anchored, to the next man who uses it as a safety device as he ascends so that he too doesn't fall far. He does not, unless I've got the whole thing completely wrong, vanish into the peaks shouting Last Man Up's An Arsehole. Nor does he take his rope along while the beginners at the bottom catch up as best they can.

That, however, was his strategy and we followed on, trusting to our fingernails and some serious prayer in the absence of pre-fastened safety ropes or anything in the way of expert advice. Having made it to the first ledge, more by the hand of providence than anything else, I felt I had to offer some help to the next budding Sherpa who was still half-way up and dropped him a line which he fastened around his waist.

Not having a hammer or pitons, Master Bates having taken them all, and lacking anything else to use, I fastened the other end round my own waist, not really thinking through the implications and possible consequences of what I was doing. It became clear to me a moment later when the idiot below fell off and swung back and forth like a pendulum some twenty feet below me, but still about a hundred feet above ground, swearing horribly and emitting loud, watery farts which echoed around the mountains and indicated the level of his distress, by this time not much more than mine.

Luckily I was sitting with my legs wrapped around a small outcrop of rock and managed to take his weight, although I also admit to a certain loosening of the bowels and some terrified cries of my own. Eventually he managed to make his way up followed by the rest of the party and we huddled on the small ledge, eyes popping from their sockets and grasping little tufts of grass for support as we stared at the horrific view below.

When we finally crawled over the edge at the top and lay gasping and quivering like aspens, fingernails dug into the ground like grappling hooks, we discovered that Master Bates had eaten all the sandwiches and was in a foul mood for being kept waiting. He obviously had no concept of safety or danger, regarding others at any rate, and I doubt if he actually realised how close he had come to being star witness at a fatal accident enquiry. It also occurred to me that he had eaten all the sandwiches on the assumption that nobody else would make it to the top, a sobering thought.

I became convinced at that point that he was certifiable and should probably be in some sort of institution where he could see out the remainder of his days singing sea shanties and stealing chocolate from the other inmates. I wondered if he had been drinking salt water which is notorious for driving sailors mad, but decided that was unlikely at several hundred feet above sea level. The other possible explanation was that Lanarkshire Constabulary had slipped him a few quid and told him we were expendable, a status I had thought only applied in wartime, and that the whole thing was an elaborate plot to get rid of unsatisfactory cadets. I asked myself if my conduct and general performance to date had justified being officially liquidated, didn't like the answers I came up with and decided to be extremely careful until safely home.

What goes up must come down, and it occurred to me that if we wanted to get to the bottom in one piece it might be an idea to throw Master Bates off first and make our own way to ground level, relying on luck rather than his unique approach to mountaineering. He was in the middle of telling an unresponsive audience an amusing gag about how falling off a cliff didn't kill you, it was stopping at the bottom which did it, har-har, when one of the party rolled over and was sick, probably from sheer terror. Our very own Sherpa Tenzing, lost to all sense of decency – and, more to the point, quicker off his mark than I was – used the opportunity to relieve the invalid of some Cadbury's Chocolate Buttons and continued, with a complete disregard for his own life, to describe the delights of being airlifted from a mountain with a compound fracture of the leg.

He was getting closer by the second to flying lessons when the guardian angel of sailors inspired him to announce that the descent would be via a hillside behind the rockface rather than by reverse route, which eased tensions a bit and saved any awkward questions later.

We began our descent via a long sloping hillside composed of loose slate or scree or some such geological term which crunched and slipped and slid underfoot. We should probably have avoided it and stuck to a more permanent surface where grass was growing but our guide didn't bother to mention it. He seemed to take the view that learning the hard way was always best, and as I've said he was unhinged anyway. About half way down the whole lot started to move, gently at first then like a roaring avalanche. Some of the party were still on solid ground and rolled about with laughter but two of us found ourselves accelerating downhill like Olympic skiers at a velocity which seemed quite likely to embed us head first in solid rock at the bottom. Luckily the slide slowed down as quickly as it had started and we hopped off at the end, having come to no harm, which was amazing. We had travelled a hundred yards balancing on a bed of loose stones in about five seconds flat and if we had lost our balance and fallen over it would have taken a week to dig us out. These near-death experiences were starting to come along too often for my liking. Master Bates, ever solicitous of our welfare, roared at us to stop fucking about. And that was that.

If rock climbing had seemed a good way of achieving immortality by dying young, abseiling seemed even more likely and we were introduced to it the next day. To those readers unfamiliar with the term, abseiling is an utterly crazy way of getting from the top of a cliff to the bottom, being only marginally more sensible than diving off head first. It involves securing a rope to something solid at the top, feeding the same rope through and around the victim's pelvic area in a certain complex way and persuading said victim to leap backwards from a high place. I've no doubt a qualified outdoor instructor could put it much better, but that's the gist of the thing. Once having leapt backwards into the void, one bounces down, feeding the rope out as one goes and hopefully remembers to make sure that the boot-clad feet, rather than the head or the knees or the elbows are the appendages which do the bouncing against the cliff face.

You may notice that I speak lightly of leaping backwards into the void, but of course that was at the end of a lengthy session of persuasive argument from the instructor and terrified snivelling from the abseiling students. It wasn't helped along by our leader who made up for a lack of anything noticeable in the way of professional skill with a Micawber-like optimism. Abseiling doesn't seem all that hard until you're staring into the void listening to some lunatic telling you to jump backwards and the same lunatic has clearly forgotten how to loop the rope around you. You will no doubt by now have guessed who was still Chief Mountaineering Coach and his Give-Me-a-Minute-Till-I-Get-the-Hang-of-This routine as he tried various ways of securing an abseiling rope didn't somehow inspire confidence. I had visions of being hurled off the cliff with a sheepshank tied round my neck.

If you think a drop of thirty to forty feet isn't all that high, try it and see what you think when you're up there looking down and the odds of the rope being looped around you properly is about fifty-fifty, probably an optimistic estimate. I had no doubt that Master Bates was able to tie the rope to a secure anchoring point at the top, sailors usually being adept at knot tying, but that was as far as it went. When we eventually abseiled to the ground safely, squealing like pigs in an abattoir while he shouted encouraging abuse from above, I suspect he was as relieved as we were. One thing was certain, Mrs Warden didn't need to prescribe any more laxatives for a spell.

All good things come to an end, and happily so do the bad ones. The four-week stint was suddenly over one morning when the old training minibus hove into view. Even better, I was delighted to see that the driver was one of the good and deserving members of the department so the journey home would actually be a pleasant one.

Warden, incidentally, was no mug. Before leaving, the Training Department staff joined us for lunch which was quite a decent spread for a change, containing identifiable traces of real meat and covering most of the plate. It was Christmas Day in the Workhouse with the high-spirited orphans cheering and hallooing for second helpings, and getting them too. Warden sat with our staff, beaming like Mr Pickwick, while his jolly instructors circulated, smiling like conspirators and tempting the young scamps to just one more plateful of pudding.

Our leaders came away thinking what a marvellous place it was and wondering what all the fuss was about, or at least they pretended to. On the way back, of course, nobody complained. If we had to suffer it, so could the next lot.

Chapter 17

By now I was firmly settled into being part of the strength at Coatbridge and I have to confess that I had fallen into the classic trap of thinking, like the old settlers, that I would be there for life. I assumed, without thinking the thing through, that I would be left here to eventually become a cop, complete with chequered hatband, and work my way up the seniority ladder until I became a cantankerous old bar officer, and amuse myself in my declining years by wearing braces over my shirt and grumbling about every innovation conceived since the invention of the wheel. Such was not to be.

Another short note arrived in the internal mail advising me that with effect from a date two weeks hence I would be stationed at Motherwell, another large steel town, albeit one I was more familiar with. Like Coatbridge, it was only a shortish hop from home as the crow flies, but in the other direction. Also, the crow flew to Motherwell by bus on a fairly regular timetable, which it didn't to Coatbridge. Unlike Coatbridge, I had been visiting it since early childhood, Motherwell being in those days a fairly decent shopping centre and certainly a cut above Bellshill which wasn't a fairly decent anything.

Among other attractions it had the Dalziel Co-operative which had a rather good toy department and, at Christmas, a resident Santa Claus I was taken to see every year, or at least that was the arrangement when I was younger – I don't want to give the impression that at the age of 17 or 18 I was still sitting on Santa's knee specifying which Hornby model train I wanted that year. My father worked in Motherwell, in the Anderson Boyes engineering company, maker of world-renowned coal-cutting machinery and my mother shopped there on a Saturday. For some reason, Motherwell was considered a local trip from Bellshill while Coatbridge, a similar distance away, wasn't. I grew up with people in Bellshill who hadn't even heard of Coatbridge. Everybody I knew went to Motherwell, while Coatbridge was just a name and until recently all I had known about it was its filthy old canal with allegedly malarial mosquitoes. Motherwell, however, was more like home.

Motherwell was also a former burgh police office, being part of the old Burgh of Motherwell and Wishaw force. This comprised, funnily enough, the two adjacent towns of Motherwell and Wishaw, Motherwell always being the sort of senior partner in the arrangement, and a large council housing scheme in between called Craigneuk. Craigneuk police office also had the privilege of covering the huge Ravenscraig Steelworks, and at the time was noted for being the only police office in Lanarkshire which sent out a car crew comprising three men, two to go to the calls and one to guard the van against marauders, the vehicle being periodically overturned or set alight when left unattended.

Craigneuk police office itself was a small, huddled, bunker of a building with a steel-covered door, the result of an earlier petrol bomb attack by the savage tribes who inhabited the area. A further flavour of Craigneuk can be suggested by the fact that when the *Sunday Mail* ran a weekly article called Pub Spy, Craigneuk threw up the winning candidate for Worst Pub in Scotland. As you can imagine, it romped past the winning post ahead of some pretty heavy competition.

Motherwell, then, former capital city of the burgh and now headquarters of the Central Division in Lanarkshire – Coatbridge was in the Northern Division – was my new home. I arrived to much the same fanfare of trumpets as I had at Coatbridge, being directed to the control room adjacent to the bar and told to make myself useful until someone decided what to do with me. Again, if the upper management was aware of my arrival, and I'm not convinced they were, nobody made any effort to say hello and we're expecting great things of you, me boy. It goes without saying that it wasn't long before someone decided that tea-making would be as good a way of breaking the ice as any, and again it was assumed that when I answered the phones I knew who everyone in the building was and had an intimate familiarity with every street, shop, pub and face in Motherwell.

One major change awaited me, though. It transpired that whereas I was to spend the next week or so hanging around the office being useful, a specific remit awaited when a certain officer returned from annual leave. I was about to meet Big Bob the warrants man.

I have to say that I was expecting another Tam to appear, hung over and surly, having twigged within a day or so that the local law in Motherwell was as partial to refreshment as the last lot, and that the stations were largely mirror images of each other. Both covered big industrial towns with roughly similar populations, and had more or less the same size of police establishment. Nonetheless, there was a definite but hard to quantify difference in character, and you'd know immediately what station you were in when you sat with the shift at muster without ever being able to put your finger on what the difference was.

There was still the same old burgh mentality, of course, the same old faces still patrolling the same areas they had patrolled when the place was a self-contained police force, and the same disdain for anything not of their own corner of the world. Like Coatbridge there was still a burgh council in power, although it was on borrowed time, and in most respects, although it would never be admitted, there was little or nothing to choose between them. Bob, however, was a whole new experience.

A hangover from Motherwell Burgh was the post of warrants officer. This is not to be confused with the more modern counterpart who oversees a computerised system of storing, monitoring and executing warrants from an office in Headquarters. This was something else entirely. The police office had a filing cabinet in the uniform bar full of hard-copy paper court warrants in brown envelopes, these carrying the details of the offender, the type of warrant and space to record and update attempts to execute it. All shifts were supposed to take an active interest in finding the subjects and getting them into court, but it was usually neglected unless the subject happened to get the jail for something else, then the warrant was tacked onto the charge for good measure. Why should they bother when a warrants man was lying on his arse on a constant dayshift job, was the usual attitude, and you can see their point. Cops on rotating shift work, a dreadful thing, imagine or choose to imagine that other cops who have slipped into constant Monday to Friday dayshifts live in a sort of Lotus Land, peeling grapes and being waited on hand and foot by dusky maidens.

The Burgh of Motherwell and Wishaw had created the post of warrants officer, the incumbent being expected to be out and about locking up bad people as opposed to sitting in an office shuffling paper. Bob, who I had yet to meet, was the current one and had been for some years. He worked independently and was basically one of the supposedly despised, but in reality deeply envied, dayshift wallahs who took no part in any other police duties. That was one thing I found he had in common with my late guide and mentor Tam – he rarely answered his radio. He occasionally worked a backshift for appearances sake, just to look keen, but no more often than absolutely necessary and usually when he had an ulterior motive, a normal situation as we will see. As he told me later, neds didn't just exist at night. They had to be somewhere during daylight hours and they were just as easy to winkle out then as later.

It may even have been easier as they weren't so likely to be criminally active and therefore not on their guard when they saw us coming. For some reason, many neds had a strange mental block and couldn't fathom out why, long after getting clear of a crime scene untouched or failing to turn up at court, the polis could suddenly appear to arrest them. It never seemed to dawn on them that simply escaping detection at the time wasn't the end of it and that in the Motherwell area a bounty hunter named Bob was active. This entailed the said bounty hunter having a comprehensive local knowledge of all things and people criminal in the Motherwell and Wishaw area, their habits, known associates and relatives, coupled with the knack of ferreting out wanted toerags from the most unlikely hidey-holes. The post had lingered on into Lanarkshire, though I suspect unofficially, because it got results.

The warrants man, however, needed a number two as Scottish law requires a second, or corroborating, officer for virtually everything concerning the locking up of neds. It had been decided to allocate the office cadet to the warrants man when one was available, freeing the shifts from the obligation of supplying him with a colleague, or neighbour in the parlance, every time he went to execute a warrant. The theory was that the warrants man, with no other responsibilities or distractions, would clear up the warrants backlog and empty the overflowing filing cabinet, at which point he would presumably have done himself out of a good job and be returned to normal shift duties. That, of course, was where the theory started to fall apart. Although this had been the plan for many years it had never actually happened as somehow, no matter how assiduously Bob appeared to work, the level of brown envelopes, while never increasing, never seemed to go down either so he was never in any danger of being sent back to normal duties. For every warrant executed the courts enthusiastically supplied more and Bob paced himself carefully.

So, after I had spent a couple of tedious weeks around the office doing much the same as I'd done in Coatbridge, Bob returned and from that moment I became part of his exclusive little world. We were privileged as we didn't get the school crossings to do, or calls to attend or anything else to interfere in any way with our primary task, nay mission, of executing warrants. We would unstintingly devote our every waking moment to exhaustive enquiries, leaving no stone unturned or avenue unexplored, leading to the final, dramatic capture of our target of the day. It would be challenging, but rewarding, and I looked forward to seeing some serious policing at first hand for a change. By this time, of course, I really should have known better.

Bob had been a sort of embryonic community constable for many years in North Motherwell, one of a small group charged with policing this large part of the town where a sizeable proportion of Motherwell's crime and criminals were to be found. They largely worked independently, did their own thing and made, as I understand from various sources, a reasonably good job of it. They had, in all but name, the role of village cops with all the associated advantages. They even had their own office, a small brick shed of sorts situated on Logans Road and known, oddly enough, as the Logans Office.

This independent approach, however, was not without its critics, the feeling in management circles being that a self-contained unit which seemed able to function without their wise guidance and counsel was suspicious, radical and therefore dangerous. Something devious had to be going on, went the thinking, and there may even have been some truth in it.

It didn't dawn on the high and mighty that everyone else functioned without them too, the normal state of play being that cops policed the streets effectively in spite of management, rather than because of anything they contributed. The upper echelons, then as now, held meetings with each other and anyone else who would turn up, dreamed their dreams and told themselves how well things were going. The lower orders, that is up to about the rank of shift Inspector, kept their heads below the parapet, avoided contact with the high and mighty when humanly possible, humoured them when it wasn't possible and got on with their job.

While getting on with it, however, the fiction had to be maintained that their duties were being directed from on high, a charade the North Motherwell men must have neglected to keep up. Accordingly, North Motherwell as an entity was wound up and the cops allocated new duties. The fact that these individuals had amassed an incredible amount of local knowledge and crime information was skipped over, and indeed one of them finished his career a number of years later watering the plants in the new Divisional HQ for the want of anything better to do in the afternoons. Another found himself in a nebulously defined, jack-of-all-trades clerical job on the strength of being one of the few who could be relied on to do whatever was thrown at him without arguing back, moderate his language and refrain from breaking wind in the presence of female clerical staff. Only Bob came out of it on a good thing. He was made warrants man.

Bob's daily routine seldom changed. At 9 a.m. or thereabouts he strolled into the front office – Bob never rushed – and sifted through the warrants cabinet, noting changes to the contents since his previous day. It wouldn't do to arrest someone who had already been picked up and processed since his previous shift, comical as it might have been. He then hit the streets and began his twin activities of tracking down warrants and making money. Bob, you see, was in addition to his policing duties, an entrepreneur, having all sorts of sidelines which he successfully combined with warrant work.

He bought, repaired and sold caravans when they were still wooden framed and repairable by a competent handyman, which he was. He bought and sold old cars, again those needing work done on them. Like caravans, cars of this period were still simple enough to be worked on by a skilled amateur in his home garage. With a socket set, a trolley jack and a couple of screwdrivers Bob could repair almost anything on wheels. He bought and sold car radios at a time when car radios, in particular the new and much coveted push-button models, were still an expensive luxury. Being expensive, nobody wanted to buy them new so a brisk trade in used ones existed. Having the whole of Motherwell and Wishaw to roam, and automatic entry almost anywhere by virtue of the uniform, he was free to buy, sell and take orders on a satisfyingly grand scale.

He would appear in back street garages to the dismay of the proprietors and, after hanging about nonchalantly for a suitable length of time, make a great show of admiring a pile of car radios unwisely left in full view. If they weren't in full view he nosed around until he found them, most people in the motor trade at that time being into dealing in car radios to some extent. These were seldom fitted as standard by the manufacturer, unless you bought a top-of-the-range luxury model, but were widely sought after. The next step was to drop heavy hints that he was on the lookout for one, ideally a push-button Motorola which was the Rolls-Royce of in-car entertainment at the time, on behalf of a friend. If not immediately responded to, the next step was to repeat the hint and keep repeating it, refusing to be diverted or sidetracked on any pretext whatever. I fully believe that had the garage been burning down on his arrival and the smoke-blackened owner being carried out on a stretcher, Bob would have had a couple of push-button Motorolas out of him before the ambulance was allowed to leave.

These steps were of course well spread out and punctuated by casual conversation and long silences which he was never the first to break. He pointedly never enquired how a small back street garage came to be in possession of a pile of nearly-new car radios in the first place, but if he wasn't offered his pick at a knock-down price fairly early in the proceedings he would begin to take a keen interest in their serial numbers which generally produced a quick offer of sale. Not that Bob suspected the proprietor of knowing them to be dodgy, of course, but anyone dealing in used goods of any kind can never be one hundred percent sure of their provenance and would rather be on the safe side, as he well knew.

A certain amount of spirited haggling would then follow, everyone being allowed to save face, but Bob seldom failed to come out ahead in the deal. Sometimes he did have a customer waiting, other times the purchase was speculative, but one way or the other the radio would be off his hands by the end of the day at a nice profit.

The same routine was played out when he was doing up a car and needed components. A visit to a scrap yard would entail a certain amount of hedging about and ferreting through the piles of assorted parts until he got too near something the proprietor felt coy about, at which point Bob would be asked what he was looking for specifically. Confiding that he was looking for an A60 starter motor or an Anglia carburettor for an elderly friend, his wish was invariably granted and, unless it was something major like a complete engine and gearbox, supplied free of charge.

Bob, expressing surprise and delight at his good fortune, would then desist from digging around and leave, either carrying his prize if it was small enough to conceal on his person or arranging to uplift it later when he had transport. Sometimes the owner would offer to have it dropped off at Chez Bob, sparing himself another visit as he knew Bob's practice was to leave people alone for a while after they'd done him a favour. An old fuel pump or a silencer box guaranteed peace and quiet for a week or two. Also, the items being scrounged were always for friends, ideally old ladies of whom he seemed to know a suspiciously large number, and never for personal gain. The fiction was maintained by all concerned that Bob did car repair work and fitted radios as a sort of charitable work for the elderly and needy, rather than as a paying business.

The other way of getting rid of him was to supply some small titbit of information about someone else's dubious activities or whereabouts. While talking about something entirely unconnected with police work Bob might mention, as an aside, that he hadn't seen so-and-so for a while. In return, and after a suitable length of time had passed, the location of so-and-so would be casually dropped into the conversation. Bob, of course, never let on that he had picked up on it. It wasn't informing, heaven forbid, as nobody in Motherwell would actually tout to the police, but if one accidentally let something slip while one was passing the time of day, distracted by Bob nosing around where he wasn't wanted, it could hardly be helped, could it? Bob would then leave, having added to his store of criminal intelligence, and everyone parted happy. If he managed to trace some outstanding ned and pick up a bargain at the same time, he was especially happy. In such a fashion Bob combined policework with commerce.

Not all his visits were strictly business, private or public, and he often whiled away the idle hours by visiting dosses of which he had a multitude. Many of them were known only to him and quite often the people who owned or worked in them thought he was still the North Motherwell man. As the other old North Motherwell men were now confined to barracks he was the only one they saw. He didn't make anyone the wiser and up to a point he still was the local cop. Nobody could tell the difference anyway as he had always spent his days nosing about for bargains.

Incredibly, he didn't drink on or off duty so was never seen hanging about licensed premises, a practice which would have led to a keener interest being shown in him by supervisors who largely left him alone. Further, he didn't smoke or use strong language. In fact, he was a unique character in every respect.

If, I hasten to say, you're getting the idea that he was some sort of soft, clean-living type, wholly unsuited to the rough and tumble of policing, you are seriously mistaken. Apart from not smoking or – wonder of wonders – drinking he had been extremely fit in his younger day and was still a very capable man. Swimming and water polo were his sports like many in Motherwell when the burgh maintained a traditional pool with a fine history of swimming champions. It was next door to the police office and town hall and has, sadly, been replaced by a monstrosity with water slides for the kiddies.

The neds knew Bob well and treated him with a marked deference. He didn't need to shout and swear to get his way and had established his credentials long ago. It seems that when he was a new face in the burgh force, fresh from police college, a local worthy had stepped into his path, identified himself as a dangerous character and, in the best traditions of Western movies, suggested that Bob, in the interests of his health, should walk softly around him. Bob, being well-mannered even then, had given his own name in return before breaking the unfortunate worthy's jaw. These things get around quickly.

I also noticed as time went on that when Bob was lifting warrants nobody, even the most obstreperous neds in the town, elected to make a fight of it, that being quite a normal reaction to getting the jail at that time. Fighting with the Polis was a local tradition with war wounds exhibited proudly next day after release and no particular hard feelings on either side. Bob, however, was so well established among the criminal fraternity and so much a part of their everyday social circle that nobody gave a second thought to going off quietly with him, and Bob himself raised another interesting factor. As he was about six foot three and built in proportion there was no embarrassment or loss of face involved when the ned concerned had a reputation to consider. A smaller, less imposing cop trying the same arrest might have had a fight on his hands. In fact, things sometimes got so cosy when Bob was arresting and transporting bodies that he would come away with several good snippets of information, the unwitting passenger being completely oblivious to having told him anything.

Most of the day, of course, revolved around wheeling and dealing and visiting, but just as an observer would be coming to the understandable conclusion that we were employed as street traders, Bob would look at his watch then swoop down on some startled ned who would find himself being locked up on an outstanding warrant. Said ned, still baffled as to how it all came about – as I was myself – would be transported to the office, locked up and the paperwork completed in nice time for us to down tools and go home, having earned our keep for the day.

Sometimes we had access to a spare van and did the transporting ourselves, sometimes not. If on foot and far from home, Bob could generally conjure a wanted body out of nowhere, achieving the twin objectives of executing the daily warrant quota and getting us a lift back to the office. Had he been lost and dying of thirst in the desert, I feel certain he would have dug up a couple of wanted Arabs and arranged transport to the nearest town, no doubt fitting in some camel trading while he was at it. I subsequently met other characters who could outwit neds and bosses alike, cadge like a professional beggar and still get through the day without doing much in way of actual work while they did so, but I never met another one who made it into an art form.

Chapter 18

As you will have gathered from earlier comments, the standard of uniform as issued in Lanarkshire Constabulary was not the absolute last word in sartorial elegance, new starts like myself being provided with whatever could be dredged up in the basement clothing store and altered to an approximation of the wearer's size and shape. Every year, however, a force-wide event known as the Annual Uniform Issue took place.

The theory was that a central bank of data existed which held the relevant measurements and sizes of every member of the force. This was passed on to the currently favoured clothing manufacturer who was expected to provide uniforms made specifically for each officer. One pictured hundreds of little cross-legged hobbits in dark, satanic Glasgow sweatshops sewing and cutting away for months. In the fullness of time vanloads of brown paper parcels would turn up and, again in theory, everyone was handed a made-to-measure uniform.

"Occasional" misfittings would attend an arranged uniform parade where tailors from these establishments, and I use the word tailor in its loosest interpretation, would take measurements and complain that people kept putting on weight, losing weight, growing, shrinking or otherwise sabotaging production. This show of indignation was usually put on to excuse a uniform which seemed designed to fit some early pre-human biped resembling the wearer only in having the same number of arms and legs. In reality, almost everybody turned out at the misfit parade as the odds of getting a uniform which actually fitted were about the same as getting eight draws on Littlewoods Pools. The suppliers were kept busy.

There were, as I remember, two of these suppliers in Glasgow who got the contract in turn, one getting it when the quality being provided by the other reached such a low as to make a new supplier necessary. After perhaps two years of being sent reasonably good kit – remember that we're speaking in relative terms here – things would go back downhill until the contract had to revert to the first supplier. I was told that there were only two available to choose from, so things were unlikely to change, but it may have been more accurate to say that only two submitted tenders cheap enough to be considered by the ever parsimonious Lanarkshire Constabulary and its poverty-stricken Chief.

There had to be better ones out there. When I went to the Scottish Police College at a later date and saw recruits from other forces parading in smart, good-quality tailored uniforms which seemed cut to match the body inside them my suspicions were confirmed. Aberdeen City men in particular were turned out like the Brigade of Guards and Glasgow City, who definitely can't have been shopping where we went, were close behind them. Our uniforms looked like we'd run them up ourselves from horse blankets and black dye.

Bob, having been off for some reason on the day the misfit parade was held in the big hall at Motherwell Police office, had the problem of getting his issue changed. Someone with only the vaguest idea of human anatomy had sent out a tunic and trousers made for someone who had a forty-six inch chest, stood four feet high and had arms like an orangutan. Whoever had created this masterpiece had got the chest measurement about right and decided that he had done his bit for the day. As one wag explained when a line of similar garments was displayed at misfit parade to a chorus of choice comments on the tailors' skills and parentage, the Missing Link was alive and well and hiding out in Motherwell.

As a matter of interest, and just to round off the day's fun at these gatherings, the policewomen lined up with the lads and stood in silent mortification as their hip and waist measurements were called back and forth between the tailors. Predictably, their male colleagues exercised suitable tact and discretion by repeating the measurements in loud voices for the benefit of those at the back of the queue. I somehow doubt that it happens now.

The initial reaction from Authority when Bob reported the situation was that he would just have to wait until someone could see about it. This, translated, meant that the matter would be forgotten as soon as Bob left the office and he was expected to walk the streets dressed like a comic busker or continue to wear his current issue which, having been worn for a year already, was nearing the end of its useful life. The uniforms barely saw out a year if your duties entailed being out and about in all conditions, and by the end of year two wouldn't be fit for hanging on a scarecrow. Neither option was acceptable and Bob, who as we know went deaf when someone tried to divert him from his purpose, hung about and persisted until he was authorised to take a spare van and visit the supplier for a new outfit.

That, of course, set off a whole train of events, official and otherwise. Management, discovering that a vehicle was leaving the force area on an expedition to Glasgow city centre, a matter of some fifteen miles away, had to make a big production of it and dream up another job to justify the journey.

The attitude was still prevalent in Lanarkshire that Glasgow was a sort of Dark Continent with Here Be Dragons marked on the map as a warning to unwary travellers. Our leaders and their good ladies might go shopping in Glasgow every Saturday morning, but, when they went back to being leaders on Monday, reverted to form and would tie themselves in knots at the thought of their men crossing the frontier. I suspect that the attitude was a mixture of ingrained mistrust of other forces and an even more ingrained mistrust of their own troops, assuming that anyone allowed out of his own area and thus beyond the reach of supervision would be bound to get up to something. They may well have been right.

We were warned not to get lost or go anywhere we shouldn't and subjected to meaningful nods and raised eyebrows which implied unspoken temptations and dangers in wait, and I began to wonder which parts of Glasgow our leaders visited of a weekend. It was being made out as being some fabled destination which combined the attractions of Las Vegas and Transylvania.

Given that I was evidently about to enter the gates of Hell I wouldn't have been surprised if the Chief Inspector had stopped me to hang a crucifix round my neck as protection from evil spirits. If he had, he would have been about a year too late. Tam, doyen of Coatbridge beat men, had already introduced me to evil spirits, although his response when confronted was to drink them.

Bob the businessman, on the other hand, had just been given official sanction to extend his sphere of operations and immediately applied his agile mind to jobs of a different kind which he could undertake while in the big city, a place he obviously regarded as a modern version of Aladdin's Cave.

It was the accepted wisdom in the county that many if not all premises in Glasgow were an open house to uniformed visitors who could expect generous discounts or even handouts on virtually anything the recipient could walk out of the shop carrying. Bob shared this view and also felt certain that nobody would notice his Lanarkshire shoulder numerals which were of a slightly different pattern to Glasgow's, but not noticeably so. The upshot was that we left with a long shopping list, a small map of the city which conveniently appeared from an inner pocket – suggesting that this wasn't his first expedition on duty – and a prisoner in the back of the van, complete with paperwork, to be dropped off at Her Majesty's Prison, Barlinnie while we were passing.

The fact that the legendary Bar-L, while undeniably in Glasgow, is nowhere near the city centre was neither here nor there to the Chief Inspector but Bob, normally adept at ducking unwanted tasks, seemed oddly keen on the idea. When I pressed him about it he smiled at my innocence and explained that as it was well out of our way, a point he had laboured to the Chief Inspector, nobody would expect us back for hours. It was also my first opportunity to see the Bar-L from the residents' side of the wall.

The ned was duly produced from the cells and turned out to be a stranger, even to Bob. Our charge was an occasional visitor to Motherwell who had been unlucky enough to collect a Go To Jail Do Not Pass Go warrant as a result of succumbing to temptation while passing through. The correct term was an Extract Conviction Warrant, which allowed the Chief Constable to remove him directly to prison without passing through a court. The Chief Constable being busy that day, no doubt burning expenses claims, Bob and I had been delegated the run.

The ned was obviously from some area where the local law had a more tolerant attitude than in Motherwell as he emerged from the cell area making ill-considered remarks to the bar officer who had gone in to fetch him. The bar officer, who had a rich command of the English language himself, had replied in kind and was about to proceed to the next phase in the visitor's education when Bob reminded him that Bar-L might decline to sign for damaged goods. They possibly weren't above damaging the goods themselves when provoked, but accepting them as such might be a problem. The ned, who probably didn't realise how lucky he was, was marched out of the office and put in the back of the transport, a Mini-van of all things.

Bob had been considering his agenda for the trip to make the most of the time he could reasonably justify being out of touch. Clearly Barlinnie had to be first as we could hardly tour the retail attractions of Glasgow and the clothing suppliers trailing a prisoner behind us as we went, so the Bar-L it was. The prisoner, having gained in confidence by this time, continued his verbal abuse all the way and, incredibly, hadn't even the sense to pipe down once we had passed through the huge sliding gates of the prison. Bob, surprisingly, had said and done nothing throughout the journey which had encouraged our guest to new heights in profanity. Not only did Bob seem oblivious to the ranting in the back of the van, he had a look of smug satisfaction as if everything was going as planned. I soon realised why.

Barlinnie is one of those ancient prisons which I've been told hail back to the days of the Napoleonic Wars, providing its guests with all the cheerful, welcoming warmth of a medieval dungeon. The smell of urine, disinfectant and carbolic soap left by generations of Glaswegian recidivists permeated the reception area which was tastefully decorated in a theme of cracked wall tiles and tobacco-yellow ceilings, and fitted with dark wooden cubicles for the new arrivals to disrobe and be fumigated in. The whole place seemed to be lit by one forty-watt bulb working overtime against a layer of dead flies.

The warder who checked the paperwork and accepted the prisoner looked as if he too might have been there since Waterloo and was turned out in a brown dustcoat and a black uniform hat with the peak dropped to cover his nose, Guards style. Uniform hats in those days were frequently doctored by wearers who had either served in the guards or, more often, wanted to give the impression that they had. Some just thought it looked good, myself for one. Facially, he resembled one of those stone statues on Easter Island – the mystery of what they represent is now solved – and had the air about him of someone it would be wise to humour. Our ned, either not the most astute of individuals or harbouring some kind of death wish, transferred his resentment to this imposing personage and aimed a new selection of offensive remarks at the unmoving basilisk stare.

Bob caught my sleeve to stop me leaving too soon, just as a sharp crack and a piercing howl was heard and which echoed around the tiled walls for some time. The amusing comments dried up immediately as the prisoner suddenly remembered the correct protocol for addressing authority and a passing trustee, sweeping the floor, shook his head with the air of one who has seen it all before and called the new arrival a wanker. There's a moral there somewhere. We left at that, feeling that it was going to be a good day after all.

The clothing suppliers was three floors up in a large, smoke-blackened warehouse building in what is now the Merchant City of Glasgow, currently complete with Italian designer shops and trendy bars. It certainly wasn't trendy then, being more like a film set for Old Whitechapel in the days of Jack the Ripper. Access was gained via a decrepit, shaking elevator manned by a decrepit, shaking operator who smelled of chips and old ashtrays and sported what appeared to be a permanent, deep suntan, although I suspect it would have washed off had he ever tried the experiment. Glasgow must have been one of the last places in the world with lift attendants in shiny suits and hand-knitted pullovers who spent their days like troglodytes in the gloom of these ancient buildings, clanking up and down interminably yet somehow finding time to read their copy of the *Daily Record* which was always folded up beside them. I've never understood the point of them being there. Operating one these old lifts isn't exactly rocket science and by the time the operator gets in most of the space is gone. Bob and I squeezed in and held our breath while the lift made its way up, partly because there wasn't enough room to breathe normally and partly because the custodian of elevators seemed to have forgotten the deodorant that morning.

On emerging gratefully from the elevator – the operator had insisted on completing some drivelling story about his iniquitous working conditions while our faces grew redder and our cheeks puffed out further by the second – we arrived at the clothing supplier's lair. The reception area appeared to have been decorated by the same interior design team that did HMP Barlinnie and there was nothing in it beyond a long painted wooden counter covered in brown hardboard and a wooden bench should we feel the need to relax a bit.

The view beyond the counter was one of endless shelves filled with dark serge uniforms and, rather like the basement billiard room in Lanarkshire Headquarters, a heady mixture of dust and tobacco smoke did service in place of air. Whoever owned the place – there wasn't actually a sign that I could see identifying them – they clearly weren't aiming at cornering the top end of the clothing market. Savile Row was safe enough.

We stood around for a time being ignored by the staff until one, a thin, seedy character with a pencil behind his ear who might well have been the lift attendant's brother, sighed loudly and deigned to notice us. He had the self-important air of the minor functionary used to being wheedled and courted by generations of police officers trying to get their hands on a presentable uniform, an ambition which he had the power to grant or withhold as the mood took him although by the state of the stuff piled up on the shelves he probably didn't have much choice.

He examined the parcel of junk which Bob dropped on the counter and made some amusing remark to a passing colleague about being lucky to have the right number of arms in the jacket and where did these county polis think they were, Burton's? They both fell about laughing at this example of whimsical banter which had no doubt seen many an outing and waited expectantly for us to join in. We didn't. Bob, with a lot on his agenda, had better things to do than humour Glasgow's answer to Laurel and Hardy and I was too busy stepping back from the line of fire, not quite sure what was coming but very sure that something was.

I was treated to a privileged glimpse of what Bob must have been like in his young days. He didn't even waste his breath speaking. He slapped his hand down on the parcel, pushed it a few inches closer and treated the tailor to a deadpan stare. Charles Bronson could have taken lessons. The room was suddenly a couple of degrees chillier and I was glad to be standing to one side of Bob, not facing him. Evidently, so was the second tailor as he disappeared from sight like a startled rabbit.

There was a brief and not very successful attempt at returning the stare then the comedian, catching the drift of how his day was about to go, smartened himself up rapidly and set about digging out a selection of replacement garments with commendable speed and efficiency. So anxious was our man to help that Bob came out with an extra tunic and both of us left with new hats and gloves we hadn't even gone in for. Nothing was too much trouble for the storeman's new best pal. Bob, ever the psychologist and a great exponent of allowing the loser to lose with dignity, exchanged a few pleasantries with his new crony before they tore themselves away from each other.

I compared Bob's methods with how my old pal Tam would have dealt with it. Bob had reduced the storeman to jelly by simply staring at him, let him wriggle for a minute then allowed him to recover his lost dignity, thus coming out with more kit than he'd gone in for and guaranteeing himself first class service if he ever had to go back. All effortlessly done and the objective achieved without breaking sweat. Tam, had he even reached the stores and not inadvertently found his way into a nearby pub, would have kicked the comedian's arse up between his ears. We left the store feeling that things were definitely going well. We also decided to give the lift a miss and use the stairs, having absorbed enough authentic Glasgow atmosphere for one day.

The episode puzzled me slightly, as I couldn't imagine the average Glasgow cop putting up with much nonsense from these characters either. They must have come by the idea that "county polis" were made of softer material and fair game for wide city boys like themselves. I heard a similar view expressed years later from a civilian court flunky at Glasgow Sheriff Court, comparing county Sheriff Courts unfavourably with "his" court, busiest in Europe and so forth. Both views were, of course, mistaken.

I won't dwell in detail on the rest of the day which entailed my riding shotgun on the van while Bob nipped in and out of shops, warehouses and trade suppliers of all sorts. For a dyed in the wool burgh man he had a remarkable knowledge of Glasgow and where to root out bargains. He emerged from each stop laden with boxes and parcels, his smile getting wider by the visit, and topped it off with a visit to a scrapyard in the East End from where he obtained half a dozen Motorolas and a tyre. Incredibly, the proprietor seemed to know him. Needless to say, we stopped off at Bob's house to empty the van into his garage before reporting in. With hindsight, I should have offered to invest some of my meagre earnings with him. Even as the junior partner on sixty-forty at best, I would have come out well ahead, but that's just another example of life's missed opportunities.

The vehicle allocated to us for warrants work was invariably one of the Mini-vans still in use at Motherwell. These miniscule and largely unloved contraptions may have had their virtues, but suitability for general police duties certainly wasn't one of them. They were cramped in the extreme and heartbreakingly slow, being fitted with the cheapest 848cc engine option which, as one wit put it with the typically tasteful police humour of the day, wouldn't have pulled a soldier off your sister. Cheapness was almost certainly why they were purchased by Lanarkshire Constabulary who would have turned us out in rickshaws if they had been built in Britain. Shoehorn a couple of seventeen-stone cops and a prisoner or two inside one and it had trouble going up hills, despite the tortured screams from the engine which suggested that you were piloting a full-spec rally car. That didn't bother Bob a bit. Firstly, as nobody else wanted the things, we could usually get our hands on one without any trouble, and secondly Bob didn't drive fast. He was easily the slowest driver I had ever been out with, kerb crawling at all times and impeding the flow of traffic so that we always seemed to be at the head of a procession. We were frequently passed by more capable and enthusiastically driven police vehicles flying along at speed on their way to calls which initially caused me some embarrassment and frustration. I wanted to drive fast, sound sirens and flash blue lights of course, and was intensely disappointed by Bob who drove like an old lady going to church.

As usual, I should have had more faith in my elders. Bob pointed out that you could either drive fast or see what was going on around you, but not both. While the hotshot drivers were taking a month's wear out of the tyres and brakes every time they attended a routine call, we were cruising slightly above walking speed and missing nothing. On one occasion we even collared a warrant who had stepped out into the road to make a rude gesture at a rapidly disappearing blue light and who didn't see us creeping up behind him in the Mini.

That was about the only advantage the things had – they were fairly unobtrusive. Apart from a small blue light about the size of a jam jar on the roof, usually covered in dirt anyway, they were unmarked in any way as police vehicles. Also, as they were mostly spares with no regular drivers, nobody washed them unless they had reached the stage where you couldn't see out of them, then giving them nothing more than a quick run over with a hose and brush. Luxuries like soap and car wax were unheard of and the brush tended to lie about the yard near the petrol pump and oil dispenser. This naturally meant that it was always dirty and greasy and the cars were sometimes filthier after we'd done than when we started.

As an aside, we were supposed to be supplied with car shampoo, wax polish and cloths to keep the motors spic and span, but we never got a sniff of them. The Traffic Department, on the other hand, treated their vastly superior vehicles like babies and collared all the cleaning kit, making sure their own personal pride and joy wanted for nothing in the way of tender care and maintenance. The doting crews would shy away with expressions of horror at the thought of putting a drunk on their spotless upholstery which they'd spent half a Sunday shift cleaning. Unlike the Traffic's pampered cars which had components renewed at the drop of a hat and taken in for a full check-up if they had a touch of the mechanical sniffles, ours were run into the ground, which I might add didn't take long with Mini-vans.

They were kept until they reached the stage of being an embarrassment and spending more time laid up in the workshop than they did on the road. At that point, when they required daily artificial resuscitation in the form of push starts, often by prisoners who were supposed to be travelling inside them, they were taken to the car auction where the professional dealers fell about laughing at the idea of anyone buying them. I've read in motoring magazines that old police cars are a good buy as although they've got high mileages they're well maintained, which makes you wonder where motoring journalists get their inside information. Possibly some former Traffic cars, good ones with big engines which can take high mileage and had a loving daddy looking after them, might be worth risking a few pounds on, but that's about all. Ask anyone who was ever fool enough to part with money for one.

After a year or so of driving around the dirty streets of industrial Motherwell, the once-white bodywork of the Mini-vans were more of an ingrained light brown with rusty bits. The advantage was that hardly anybody saw them coming or noticed them sitting at the kerb. That meant that our Bob, who had a carefully nurtured contact inside the Social Security Office who supplied him with signing-on times, could lie in wait for his target of the day to turn up at the appointed hour. Strangely, the neds never seemed to realise that their signing-on times were being given out and at least once a week someone would walk into the net. They didn't take the sight of the dirty, decrepit Mini-van seriously either or wonder why it was sitting outside the Social. I don't think they could believe it was a real police car, although they must have had some inkling when they landed in the back of it or had to push start the thing.

Bad as they were, one thing was even slower and less desirable than a Mini-van and that was the three-wheel Reliant since made famous by the brothers Trotter in Fools and Horses. Unlike Del Boy's transport, the one figuring in this tale was a passenger version, not a van, which gave it a slightly higher social standing although not by much. I think it was called a Regal. The vehicle in question had been lying in the yard at the back of Motherwell Police office for so long that hardly anyone could remember it not being there.

It had been brought in as having an involvement in some long-forgotten crime or other and abandoned, a common situation where vehicles were impounded in a fit of enthusiasm then left to rot for years. Often, the rightful owner either couldn't be traced or if traced declined to come back for a worthless heap he was happier without, and many of the owners in question wouldn't have entered a police office voluntarily if a Bentley had been waiting for collection. Eventually, and after endless paperwork had been generated, a decision would be made to sell the thing and get rid of it.

Such was the case with this one. The accepted method was to invite offers from local traders, the first decent offer on letterheaded paper, indicating a bona fide business, being successful. If the vehicle was worthless, as many were after rusting away for years, the local scrap merchants rather than garages were contacted and if they weren't interested in buying it they were coerced into taking it away anyhow. Occasionally, some cop with a knack of repairing old bangers would arrange for a local motor trader to buy it on his behalf for a song, thus observing the proprieties and no real harm done.

The Reliant was a slightly different proposition. The big problem in cars of that period was that their bodywork rotted away before their engines gave out, but as the Reliant was constructed of fibreglass, and therefore not subject to normal corrosion, it could last for years. In other words it was still apparently a going concern despite having virtually zero market value. It had a tiny and easily repairable motorcycle engine and the perished tyres would cost next to nothing to replace. Someone with a bit of time and mechanical aptitude could get it back on the road for minimal financial outlay, particularly if that person had access to a cheap or even free supply of spare parts. As you may guess, I knew of such a person and he had been casting an acquisitive eye over the vehicle for some time.

Bob had decided that the Reliant would be ideal for his son, newly qualified to drive and needing cheap transport. The Reliant fitted the bill nicely, being economical on fuel, taxable as a motor cycle through a loophole in car tax legislation and being so slow as to discourage any rash driving by an overenthusiastic teenager. Unfortunately, the station Chief Inspector had come to the same conclusion and had also set his sights on it for himself.

Normally, the Chief Inspector would have had his way on the well-established police principle that an ace beats a king, but this was a delicate situation which required careful handling. Either would have had to use the services of a local motor trader to submit an offer on his behalf, an easily arranged ploy, but any suggestion of the Chief Inspector misusing his authority to rig the auction would have finished the whole scheme. Again, I knew someone who would have arranged for such a suggestion to be put forward.

Having said that, any obvious wrangling over the vehicle would have scuttled the deal for both of them, the fiction having to be maintained that real motor traders were involved, so they had to tread warily. An impasse had thus been reached and for some time the two would-be car dealers circled each other like rival dogs, hackles up and growling occasionally while they watched for openings in the other's defences.

The Chief Inspector tried to rush through a purchase while Bob was on a week's annual leave, not realising that Bob had an informant among the office typists who had to process the paperwork. Bob was in the office like a shot and the Chief Inspector, feigning innocence, binned the invoice and settled down to bide his time. Bob tried the old car market traders' trick of swapping spark plug leads around so that if the engine was started up using a spare battery, it missed and farted like an old horse, thus putting off other prospective buyers.

The Chief Inspector, who also hung about the car market and knew the trick too, switched them back. Both then purported to lose interest for a while, indicating that the car wasn't worth buying, and hoping the other would lose interest too. That didn't work either as one was as good a horse trader as the other and just as willing to settle down for a long stand-off, and so the rivalry dragged on and on, neither party taking his eye off the ball for a second or conceding an inch, each prepared to dig his heels in and wait the other out indefinitely. Both had also adopted the dog-in-the-manger philosophy, meaning that both would rather watch the thing lying in the yard forever than see it go to the other. And so the matter stood for some time.

The saga mercifully drew to a close when a stolen van being reversed into the yard by a tow truck collided with the Reliant which promptly collapsed, revealing serious and badly repaired accident damage. The thing had been a death trap all along.

Chapter 19

Being sent to the Motor Tax Office at Hamilton was one attachment nobody wanted at any price, but with a grim inevitability the customary short note appeared advising me that I was starting there on the next Monday. My tour of duty under the mentorship of the incredible Bob was up. Unwanted though this secondment was, however, it at least had a sound operational reason behind it instead of being somewhere to put us for a while with the vague aim of widening our horizons and knowledge of the world. On that subject, I sometimes wonder if a cadet had appeared in the Training Department expressing informed opinions on current affairs he'd have been allowed to get on with learning about his job in peace. The situation, to the best of my knowledge, never arose so we'll never know.

It's easy to forget that it's a fairly short time since the age of the computer dawned on society as a whole and on the police service in particular. When I first sat at the feet of the wise ones in Lanarkshire Constabulary receiving their pearls of wisdom, the idea of computers finding their way into the daily life of police work was one which brought forth gales of laughter and droll observations about how we'd have Mr Spock and Captain Kirk running the force next, ha ha!

Computers were the stuff of lurid fiction, being perceived as enormous, room-sized contraptions with flashing lights and whirring discs operated by mad scientists intent on world domination. One or two of the real fossils simply looked blank when the subject was raised, having no idea at all what a computer was and not caring much either. Never in our lifetime, went the refrain, and a common suggestion for using computers profitably was to put jackets on the things and send them out on the streets to lift neds. Very forward thinking, of course, and typical of the attitude found at all levels of the force except for a shrewd minority who peered into the future and planned their careers accordingly. The rest either laughed it off or didn't actually understand any of it in the first place, and I have to admit that if you took Lanarkshire in the early Seventies as a yardstick of contemporary policing standards there wasn't any obvious need for the silicon chip and all the good things it brings.

With hindsight, of course, we're all brilliant and if you suddenly jump to the present day you have the advantage of missing the awkward stage where computer technology was in its creakingly inefficient infancy and very few people knew enough about it to be patient while one Bill Gates and a few people like him transformed the world. You would also have to jump the other awkward stage where efficient microchip technology had become readily available but the police service, being the police service, was determined to get its money's worth out of the prehistoric junk they'd stocked up on initially.

It was an unfortunate period where rising junior and mid-ranking officers had grasped the possibilities of the new technology with both hands and could see the way ahead but the budget was still in the hands of the dinosaurs, many of whom still mistrusted anything with an electric plug on the end of it let alone computer systems. I genuinely believe that some of them thought it was a passing fad, just as many of the British General Staff refused to take tanks and aeroplanes seriously during the First World War and steadfastly predicted the return of horse cavalry till their dying day. Sadly, we still had the remnants of a breed of senior officer who had formed their style of management during War Service and honestly believed that nobody junior to them in rank could possibly know something they didn't, which was unfortunate when the subject of computers came up. They were therefore extremely resistant to change which would have taken them out of their comfort zone of knowing best about everything, an unthinkable situation. The introduction of the biro pen was still probably causing ripples.

To return to the computer-free days of the early Seventies, however, motor taxation offices across the land were huge paper depositories holding the file of every vehicle on the road by its place of initial registration. If a car was first registered in Lanarkshire, for instance, it would get a Lanarkshire number and its file would remain in Hamilton, filed alphabetically, forever.

How did that require a police cadet to be stationed there, you may well ask. Very simple, came the answer when I heard I was going and asked the same question. Each motor tax office got a stream of enquiries every day from police forces across the country in the days before the Police National Computer and DVLC computers in Swansea were set up and linked in the interests of instant police accessibility. Now, of course, any enquiry about vehicle ownership is but a quick computer transaction away but in those not so far off days, a phone call to the relevant motor tax office, followed by a hopefully thorough rummage in the files, was the only solution. After office hours you had to sit and wait, although in an emergency someone from the department would be dug out to open the place up.

The motor tax people, understandably, felt that answering police enquiries all day was a bit of an imposition so Lanarkshire Constabulary agreed to provide someone, specifically a police cadet as the member of staff least likely to be missed by anyone else, to sit by a phone extension and take calls. Realising that the incumbent might find himself loafing about in idleness during quiet intervals when the phone wasn't ringing , an unheard of thing which, if encouraged, might have led to the collapse of civilization, it was decided that he could keep busy doing routine filing work while waiting to be summoned. For most of the day he or she would be, in all but name, a junior filing clerk in Hamilton Motor Tax office, located in the ground floor of the County Buildings, home of Lanarkshire County Council. Not only were the motor tax people relieved of an irritating chore, they gained cheap, or more accurately free, labour.

You can imagine the enthusiasm that prospect generated when your turn came up. Just to make it all perfect you had to turn up in uniform for some inconceivable reason, thus standing out like a sore thumb in the tax office itself and when going for lunch in the council canteen at the top of the building.

It may well be that many an eighteen-year-old wanted nothing more out of life than to settle behind a desk in Hamilton Motor Taxation Department and carve out a career for himself shuffling paper and learning the mysteries and lore of the vehicle taxation system. Good luck to them, says I, but had I felt that way about it I wouldn't have been in Lanarkshire Constabulary at all, a position taken by most cadets who were sent to do penance in the place. If you liked that sort of thing, of course, it probably seemed an ideal location to embed yourself for a comfortable fifty-year Civil Service career but we regarded it as a sentence rather than a secondment and usually approached it in that spirit of keen anticipation.

If that sounds as if I had big ideas about myself and thought myself above working in an office, you're wrong. Horses for courses covers it, and as I had elected to pursue a career in an outdoor, active kind of environment, the sedentary life in an office wasn't for me. Conversely, more than one aspirant had joined the police with altruistic ambitions of public service only to be horrified at the realities of life like routinely engaging in violent clashes with various species of bad guys, dealing with decomposing bodies or calling at the door to tell people that their loved ones had perished in a fatal road accident. If you can't face doing things like that for a living it's perfectly understandable and there's certainly no disgrace in saying so, but if you've also joined the police you've made a bad career choice.

Policing, I'm afraid to say, is one of those jobs like being an undertaker or a hospice nurse where most people expect you to be there when required but are happier not to dwell too much on what you're doing on their behalf. Some come into these vocations with starry ideas about helping people but don't always last the pace when they find out what they've gotten themselves into. Put another way, the needy aren't necessarily the presentable good and deserving needy as portrayed by charity adverts when they're drumming up contributions. Of course it's equally true to say that someone has to work in local government offices and I for one, at that age at least, couldn't have stuck it at any price. Each to his own about covers it.

On arrival at my personal Devil's Island I was allocated a desk directly opposite the senior functionary of the office so that our furniture actually touched in the middle and we could eye each other all day long. It was obvious from the start that we weren't going to be best buddies. The tone of the visit was set on the first morning when my little tray of paperclips strayed over the boundary onto his side and was firmly pushed back with a prissy lecture about that side of the desk being his, the managerial, side and not an appropriate place for my clerical grade paperclips to be seen. I don't think he appreciated my priceless wit when I leapt to my feet with a gasp of horror, knocking my chair over in the process, and called on the god of civil servants to be my witness that I'd never to do such a thing again, which was a blatant lie as I did it constantly after that to annoy him.

In actual fact he wasn't the boss, being in reality the number two deputizing on an unpaid basis for the real boss who was "absent". The real boss, when he was there, occupied a desk which lay concealed behind a huge wall of filing cabinets and was completely hidden from the sight of mortals, rather like the Wizard of Oz. He was seldom seen and on his rare appearances didn't seem to do much except be the boss and pop out of the office a lot on mysterious errands. The reason for his almost permanent absence wasn't divulged to me, but it didn't take much working out from his florid features, slightly unkempt appearance and the unmistakeable aroma of strong mints which followed him about. My man, his number two, who was obviously embarrassed by the whole scenario, ran the place without complaint and had apparently been doing so for some time, though his sense of devoted loyalty and a naturally subservient civil service mentality had prevented his raising the matter and back-stabbing his way into a promotion.

I'd met the missing Great Oz once when he had allowed the light of his countenance to shine upon us and couldn't understand the almost religious awe in which he was held by virtue of his modest civil service rank, or the song and dance made when he deigned to turn up at work for a day or two. His status was more like the high priest of some mystic cult than a mid-ranking local government officer and rumours of his promised return circulated like reports of the Second

Coming. Personally, if I'd been his depute I'd have suggested that he get back to work or sling his hook permanently but then I don't have a civil servant's outlook on life. It wasn't a totally new situation, of course, as more than a few of my own bosses in Lanarkshire Constabulary gave themselves tremendous airs and graces, but the difference was that nobody else took their posturing seriously. In this place everyone did, or almost everyone.

The place was saved from terminal boredom by the presence of two retired polis supplementing their pensions by doing clerical work. Both were long retired from life's front line and perfectly happy to while away the days filling in forms, having done their bit for Queen and Country. For someone in their position it was a comfortable, congenial place to be with regular tea breaks and nothing to give them any grief.

My new leader clearly disapproved of them and their occasional vulgar remarks which were completely out of place in this twee little world of polite conversation and where a raised voice at the public counter was the talk of the office for days. Oh, we have our moments in here, the old dears would twitter proudly after a member of the public caused a shockwave to run through the building by questioning a decision made by a senior clerk, a person whose senior prefix bestowed a status verging on Papal Infallibility. To hear them you'd have thought they'd just survived a mortar attack. The two worthies, on the other hand, took nothing and nobody seriously but did take great pleasure in waiting their opportunity to pass well-timed comments guaranteed to horrify the old biddies who worked there, some being genuinely horrified and some who giggled and pretended to be.

The department head, or acting department head to be accurate, was in the invidious position of being responsible for them and extremely wary of them at the same time. Everything about them was alien to him. While no threatening behaviour had been used or was ever likely to be, he was astute enough to realise that these two were from a very different planet to his own and were better humoured, ideally from a safe distance.

The permanent staff in the department might cringe and grovel when reprimanded by some minor functionary one grade above them, but this pair wouldn't. On one occasion when he had cause to speak to one of them about some clerical misdemeanour or other, he had been reduced to a red-faced, stammering wreck without the object of his displeasure saying a word in return. The old boy had simply stared at him over his pipe until the boss dried up and retreated from the field of battle. This too became the subject of hushed whispers for days, the staff quivering with excitement as they re-lived the whole delightful episode over lunch to an awe-struck audience from other departments. One or two such incidents had raised the pair to the status of folk heroes among their ageing groupies in the department and the old devils played up to it at every chance.

That aside, it was boredom in the extreme and from my point of view a complete waste of time. You may well think I had a cheek complaining about the sort of tedious work some people have to do for their entire careers, but I don't. They applied for it and walked into it with their eyes open. I didn't, and took it personally although of course I shouldn't have. I wonder how one of these office-dwellers would have felt if they'd been thrown out on the street on a wintry night or told to search some urine-soaked pile of rags who'd just been arrested for drunken behaviour. Like me, I imagine they'd have taken the position that it was not what they'd signed up for and I would have been right behind them.

One day, however, just when I was losing the will to live, my temporary boss put his foot in it and gave me the opening to escape. My hours were exactly nine to five, just like everyone else, and at five on the button I downed tools and left. At that point the phone calls stopped so I was immediately superfluous. It wasn't the kind of job where you were expected to stay on to finish work or tidy up or feign dedication to duty. At five it stopped, period. On the fateful evening, however, the staff hung on for a couple of hours' paid overtime, a regular arrangement where backlogs were cleared, or files rearranged or knitting patterns swapped or something of the sort. Gripping stuff, I have no doubt, but I wasn't interested enough to look into it as it had absolutely nothing to do with me.

The boss, however, took umbrage at this and suggested that I might want to help out for the sake of the thing even although I wouldn't be getting paid, and that it would look good. I think he expected me to find the idea of unpaid overtime to clear their backlog an enticing offer.

I replied, civilly enough, that I didn't really work there, that the not getting paid part of the deal was the key issue, that I wasn't all that interested in looking good in my own time and that I would, with great regret, be heading off home without further delay so goodnight to all. For some reason which I never worked out he decided to make a stand and, metaphorically rearing up on his hind legs, turned his request into a formal order to go into the basement and carry umpteen boxes up, something he wasn't in the least entitled to do even during working hours.

Actually, had he only known it, I would have been perfectly happy to cart boxes up for him during my shift. I didn't much care how I passed the day and visits to the basement could – and frequently did – easily stretch into a long smoke break at the loading bay, but he had waited until home time to make the announcement. I politely declined to discuss it further and took myself off, leaving him to wave his finger at an empty space.

Next day, the atmosphere was tense and I was the subject of surreptitious glances from the old biddies who clearly saw the previous evening's events as the prelude to the revolt of the slaves. The old codgers chortled and suggested that I fetch their leader a crack round the ear if he said a word, but I wasn't so daft as to risk my own neck for their amusement and I doubt if they actually meant it anyway. The boss, when he arrived, made much of being cold and aloof then began a campaign of petty harassment which I ignored, to his annoyance, until after lunchtime when it started to get a bit tedious and a sudden idea popped into my head. That was my cue to leave early, saying truthfully that I had to visit the Training Department, something he couldn't object to, and lay my case before the Chief Inspector, a new model from the one who'd welcomed me to the job and who I understood to be an approachable type, not always the case among the mighty in Lanarkshire Constabulary.

I'd been told that claiming a conflict of personality was always a sure way of getting a move, provided you didn't try it on too often. The advice was obviously kosher and without commenting or going into it further he told me to go home for the day and report back to Motherwell the following morning. He would break the joyous news to the hierarchy at Motherwell and notify the motor tax office himself, he said, and I left with the impression that this wasn't the first time something of the sort had happened.

It must have put him in an awkward position, something I confess I didn't think about at the time, as he had been told by higher authority to send cadets to the motor tax office but also had a responsibility to look after their welfare. I heard later that a similar confrontation had occurred involving the cadet who replaced me, although in this case two visiting Traffic cops, in to check some files themselves, had overheard the exchange and intervened with a short, pointed word of advice in the great man's ear on the subject of how to address police cadets. I'm only sorry I missed it. I'm not normally vindictive by nature, I hasten to add, just sometimes.

Chapter 20

If I thought I was going to turn up at Motherwell next morning and take up where I'd left off, I was to be disappointed. I was told to go up to the Chief Inspector's room where I saluted smartly and waited to be welcomed back. I've no doubt he was overjoyed to see me back, but he managed to conceal it well, contenting himself by telling me that he didn't really need another cadet but as he'd been stuck with me anyhow I could find something to do in the uniform bar. He asked hopefully if I had any leave left so that I could disappear for a week or so and seemed to take it as a personal affront when I replied that I didn't. You'll note how the young lads were made to feel a part of things and boosted at every turn. I suspect that if I'd claimed to have a couple of weeks leave owing and taken it he'd have forgotten about me within ten minutes, but I confess I hadn't the nerve to try it.

He revealed that I was down for some course or other in the next few weeks which would have seen me out of the Motor Tax office anyway. When I asked the obvious question he shrugged and said that he didn't know anything about it, just what the Training Chief Inspector had told him on the phone. Something was coming up but as my arrival was at short notice, this accompanied by a suspicious glance suggesting that I had some dark secret to hide, he couldn't say more. It was fairly obvious that he couldn't have cared less either as I was just passing through and, as such, little or nothing to do with him.

I tentatively suggested that I might be of more use working with Bob which, given the relationship between them, wasn't the most tactful thing to say. It reminded him that I'd been hanging around during the car dealing fiasco, an episode so cloaked in secrecy as to have passed unnoticed by anyone else but still festering under the surface between the protagonists. It was with a satisfied smirk that he broke the news that Bob had a new apprentice and didn't need me back. I must admit I'd forgotten that, as with the motor tax secondment, I was only one of a string of cadets passing through Motherwell in rotation and attached to the great man. I took my leave and reported to the bar officer, close to spitting at the sight of Bob and his new cadet marching out of the office for a day's street trading.

The staff at Motherwell, most of whom I'd had little contact with having been out with Bob most of the time, were the same mixed bag as the ones to be found at Coatbridge and no doubt everywhere else, some being hard-working and sober, some not.

One of the bar officers, or office men as they were usually referred to, wore slippers on the nightshift, claiming that he had bad feet, and groused constantly. He was one of the school who was forty-five going on ninety and, although seldom seen to do much, couldn't so much as answer the phone without a theatrical sigh like an overworked camel about to have its back broken by the final straw. He shuffled around in a constant state of depression, giving the impression of a martyr who would rather end it all to save himself further suffering, but held on for the good of a public who didn't realise what he went through for them.

Another, of a similar age but of a much more lively disposition, had been done for the drink not long before, having been found by a senior officer while demonstrating Scottish country dancing on top of the office desk to the astonishment of several members of the public who had slipped in unnoticed and were waiting patiently to be attended to. He was one of the band of heroes who couldn't be allowed out of the office if he was to stay sober and vertical, although this was officially disguised as a chronic bad back, and had compensated for his enforced confinement by organising a network of hidden bottles so that he was never more than an arm's reach from refreshment.

A third had mastered the art of doing next to nothing while managing to convince the upper ranks that the office couldn't function without him in post. This one who was, or seemed to be, a bit older and whose snowy white moustache gave the grossly misleading impression that butter wouldn't melt in his mouth, had been getting away with conning the management for so long that he quite openly imbibed in the uniform bar, keeping a six-pack of beer chilled by storing it under the running tap in the medical room sink. Senior officers had no cause to step into the room which lay a mere few feet from the charge bar where they read the Daily Briefing Register and collected their mail every morning, while the bar officer wrung his hands unctuously and offered to have the cadet make tea for them. Not him, you'll notice – the cadet. They never guessed how close they were to finding the demon drink.

Strangely, none of the bosses ever commented on the constant sound of running water or made any attempt to locate its source, although there would be an unaccustomed flurry of activity to empty the sink when one of the police surgeons was called in to examine a drunk driver or treat an injured prisoner. On nightshifts and weekends, when management was absent, he too kept a bottle of the hard stuff in a drawer within easy reach and, like the other one, refreshed himself without moving from the chair.

By this time you will have noticed that I had met more than my share of colourful characters, mostly a law unto themselves and the bane of their bosses' lives, and mostly at or near the foot soldier level. I did, however, meet one who was a boss himself and a fairly senior one at that. This one, a Superintendent no less, seemed to regard himself as the chief of police in some minor dictatorship as he did, in a nutshell, exactly what he liked.

He was collected at home each morning by the van crew covering that end of town and taken home by the backshift lot, a perk someone of his rank was absolutely not entitled to and had probably been established because he was frequently unfit to drive his own car. The only time he was seen to drive was when he borrowed the unmarked supervisory car, a rather nice big Vauxhall Victor the street cops could have put to good use, and took his grandchildren off to the coast for the weekend in it, fuelled up and complete with police radio. He seldom wore uniform, in contravention of specific instructions to the contrary, and openly entertained friends in his office during the day.

Like his subordinates, he seldom found himself embarrassed by being asked to pay for drink which was delivered to him at work quite openly and in sizeable quantities. So much was delivered at the festive season that on one occasion a space was coned off at the front door of the office so that a builder's skip, supplied at no cost by a local firm of course, could lie there until it was filled with his empty whisky cases and removed in the early New Year.

As another aside, that was part of a larger issue which caused more than a few rumbles of Yuletide discontent among the rank and file. A great deal of Christmas cheer was handed in by well-meaning donors who thought it would be distributed to "the boys" who looked after them and their property all year round, day and night and in all weathers, which I thought very civil of them.

Sadly, between parasitic senior officers who thought they had a God-given right to it and thirsty bar officers who knew perfectly well that they didn't but latched onto it anyway, the "boys" on the street saw precious little of the stuff. Basically, if you heard that someone was handing presents in, and you felt you should be included in the share-out, you made a point of being about, dug yourself in and ignored any and all hints to take yourself elsewhere. You also ignored all kindly offers by the office men to take your share into safekeeping as it had a habit of evaporating in mysterious circumstances.

Naturally, the boys on the street had their own sources for festive cheer, but it wasn't the first time a beat man called in to wish Merry Christmas to one of his parishioners only to discover to his horror that the much-anticipated gift had been handed into the office in good faith. As you can imagine, diligent and often heated enquiries would be made without delay and the usual suspects questioned closely, but invariably the drink was gone, stolen by the fairies and never to be seen again.

Chapter 21

This stint at Motherwell proved to be, as promised, of short duration. Another summons to the Training Department revealed that the promised course was in fact the much sought-after one held at Aberdeen every year and that I had been nominated to go. I waited to hear the catch but there wasn't one. Aberdeen, unlike some venues, was a course widely regarded as the genuine goods which people in the know would have killed for. Basically, it was a four week stay in Aberdeen University, lodged in the student accommodation and using the facilities of the establishment while it was closed for the summer recess. During that month all manner of mind broadening activities would be provided which, given previous experience, would have caused me some concern if I hadn't already heard that it was mostly good stuff. We would have a private room each, be well fed, be granted lots of spare time to spend enjoying whatever the city of Aberdeen could offer in the way of low entertainment and generally have ourselves a whale of a month.

After some of the secondments already experienced, I felt that it was about time too. There was also the cheering aspect that as the cadets from all over Scotland selected to attend were, like me, in their final few months before being appointed Constable, we were all old enough to enter licensed premises without hiding in the toilets or bolting for the door should the Aberdeen law come in. Beyond the usual lecture exhorting us to fly the flag and be a credit to Lanarkshire, while refraining from base thoughts of fiddling expenses, there was nothing sinister tacked on and I headed home full of the joys of living, ready to expand my horizons and give my liver a workout in Aberdeen.

Aberdeen, at that time, was just about to discover North Sea oil and so was still a large, old fashioned city known mainly for its seaport, the ancient university and the bracing North Sea breezes which even in the summer could cut you in two if you didn't dress for it. It hadn't yet wakened up to being the thriving heart of the Scottish oil industry it would shortly become although there was, as I recall, a lot of optimistic talk in the air of great things to come.

The current university campus, which we expected to be ancient as advertised, was in fact a pleasant, modern place with lots of open space between buildings and situated within reasonable walking distance of the city centre. The rooms as promised were clean and reasonably comfortable and the canteen food came in good big platefuls. The staff in charge of us were, for the most part, a friendly and easy going collection being mainly youngish cops and sergeants from various forces with one or two senior ones running the show in the background. This couldn't be true, we thought, but it was. I gathered after a while that it was a good career move for the staff to be selected for this course, although most of them seemed happy to be doing it for its own sake and went out of their way to help us enjoy it. One wasn't, but we'll meet him shortly and guess who fell foul of him.

I have to say in all honesty that most of the month passed with very little to gripe about and nothing much in the way of scandalous stories. It was, in fact, a thoroughly good course and I enjoyed it tremendously. Some of the cadets got involved with the local riff-raff in a dance hall up town and came out second best, leading to some involvement with the local police, but I wasn't there so I didn't get too worked up about it or involved in the secret arrangements to have a return fixture the following week, a plan detected and stopped by our instructors who instead sorted it out quietly by themselves.

I did, however, fall for the old taxi driver trick of taking the obvious stranger the long way home. On the first evening out a few of us, having over-indulged to an extent which made walking home impractical, took a taxi. Our driver, of course, turned a trip of under a mile into a magical mystery tour of Aberdeen, a ruse which we didn't rumble until the next evening when we realised we could have crawled back in less time than he took to drive. Sadly, all efforts to find him again and raise the matter of a refund failed, which was probably just as well for all concerned.

We visited the Aviemore Ski Centre, where we didn't actually ski but put away a lot of beer in the hotels which suited almost everyone just fine, went hillwalking with a local mountain rescue unit largely staffed by cops from the hilly parts of Aberdeenshire and visited a disused lunatic asylum.

This cold, creepy place, with a strangely Hammer Horror-like atmosphere about it, lay within a larger hospital and was entered after much theatrical rattling of locks and creaking of doors. Boris Karloff or Christopher Lee would have blended in nicely. We were invited to make ourselves at home by trying on strait-jackets and throwing ourselves about padded cells like authentic Victorian lunatics, although it was emphasised that it wasn't obligatory, only if we felt so inclined. Why they thought anyone would feel so inclined I know not, but the character who showed us round had a strange glint in his eye when he described how the inmates were restrained and punished – presumably for being mad – in the good old days. He seemed disappointed when nobody took him up on the offer. He looked more like a patient than a member of staff and I still wonder about him. No doubt you know the little tell-tale signs I mean – the sly sideways looks and laughing at nothing in particular. Perhaps the real mental nurse was wandering about another part of the building looking for us, or locked up in a cupboard while we passed the time of day with an Aberdonian axe killer.

We also did a bit of community work, the announcement of the last generating a predictably lukewarm response. The community work lark involved spending a few days attached to some agency or department which could have been anything from a juvenile detention centre to a functioning mental institution but in my case turned out to be an obscure organisation which visited and supported the local elderly. I forget the name of it, and in fact probably didn't even take note of it at the time. I was told that I would be accompanying a lady known as Miss Something or Other and a certain amount of nudging and winking from the course staff suggested untold delights in store. From this I naturally assumed that Miss Something or Other would be an eighty-year-old spinster smelling of cats, but the staff assured me she was only about thirty or so which turned out to be true. Things, briefly, appeared to be looking up.

Unfortunately she also turned out to be about twenty-five stone, wore tweed skirts and disguised slightly dodgy personal hygiene habits by dousing herself with cheap talcum powder which you could smell downwind for miles. I walked several paces behind her everywhere we went, in silent horror, thankful that I didn't know anyone in Aberdeen who might have seen me. In the evening after the first day I reported back to the lads that she really was thirty, made a few suggestive leers and skipped over the rest, although our staff looked tremendously pleased with themselves and encouraged me to be more specific.

One event put a damper on the course and caused some embarrassment, for the Lanarkshire contingent at least. As most of the forces in Scotland were represented and it was regarded as a fairly prestigious event, no doubt because of the cost involved, all the Chief Constables turned up for an arranged visit and were suitably wined and dined and fussed over by the staff.

The cadets, scrubbed, sober and presentable, were split into force groups and given a private area to sit in where their own Chief could join them for coffee and a chat, a memorable occasion for the cadets if not necessarily for the Chiefs, and one which they would not quickly forget. The cadets gathered in their positions, chattering animatedly, and awaited the coming of the Chief Constables as they left their dining room and made their way individually into the lounge. I have to say that the Chiefs did it well, smiling and shaking hands all round as they sat down with their own group and encouraged an easy, informal flow of conversation. There was never any question of things getting too informal, of course, and the Chiefs were guaranteed gales of hysterical laughter at their every quip, feeble or otherwise, but the thing went well and was a credit to all concerned. Except for Lanarkshire, that is.

Our Chief arrived, partook freely of the hospitality, and left without giving us as much as a look in the passing. Instead, we were joined by the Superintendent in charge of the course, a senior officer at the Scottish Police College who it turned out was an old Lanarkshire man himself. He was clearly as embarrassed as we were and put himself out to make our evening a pleasant one. Much as we tried to make light of it, it was an appalling exhibition by the Chief and quite inexcusable. I heard later that the only reason he came up at all was to try out a new BMW demonstrator, the first to be seen in the force.

The staff laid on a sort of dance in the university hall which at first sight didn't seem too promising, there only being about seven or eight female cadets to almost a hundred males, until it was announced that student nurses from the local hospital would also be attending. I've no idea what rubbish our staff told them about us to encourage attendance, but it must have been good stuff for they arrived by the cartload.

That smartened things up and the Old Spice and Brut – remember them? – was well sloshed about in preparation. The evening even went well, drunken behaviour and foul language being kept in reasonable check, although we were reminded by the ever-present staff that, as gentlemen and hosts, we were required to see the young ladies home at close of play. Nobody told us that the nurses' home was on the other side of the city, of course.

Again we fell for the nods and nudges from the staff, replete with the unspoken promise of great things, which resulted in dozens of knights in shining armour eagerly walking the fair damsels home only to see them nip smartly through the door of the nurses' quarters, abandoning their dribbling admirers outside. The student nurses had also been well briefed by somebody, I reckon, and probably by the dragon – picture Hattie Jacques playing Matron in the Carry On films – who took up station at the door to ensure nobody else nipped in smartly behind them.

It was a long walk home on a cold night, everyone being convinced that he knew a better shortcut than anyone else, and the instructors were standing outside the halls of residence counting heads until well into the small hours as we staggered back in various states of sobriety and sore of foot, many of the gallant knights having spent hours lost and wandering all over Aberdeen. I heard that one of our number was found trying to board a trawler in the harbour while another fell asleep in a cemetery, both parties safely recovered and returned to base by helpful Aberdeen Police car crews, no doubt well briefed for the occasion, but there were no fatalities or casualties beyond some sore heads next morning. For that matter there were sore heads every morning. Naturally, everyone swore to having had the night of his life and the tales got better by the day until we went home.

My little run-in with the instructor, as touched on earlier, happened as follows. We were on an overnight stay in tents beside some nondescript loch with a strip of sandy beach. I won't bore you with a description of the picturesque Aberdeenshire hills which I'm sure you can manage without. One of the staff, a sergeant, was seized with the splendid idea of organising a wrestling tournament on the sand. As most teenagers love the idea of inflicting violence, although not necessarily getting their share back in return, everybody threw themselves into the fun with a will, female cadets excepted which caused widespread disappointment. One inventive lecher, showing initiative, offered to level the odds by wrestling them two or three at a time, an inspired idea which gained an immediate and vocal following, but was firmly vetoed by the female sergeant instructor. She was obviously there as official spoilsport and chaperone, whether anyone actually wanted to be chaperoned or not, and was probably in cahoots with the old bag at the nurses' home whose mission in life seemed remarkably similar.

The idea was that someone stood in the centre of a ring of bodies and accepted challenges, the winner staying in until defeated. You didn't maim your opponent or gouge his eyes out or anything like that, the idea being simply to make his shoulders touch the ground. Game over.

It was my turn in the middle, having seen off a challenger who was a hell of a lot heavier and stronger than me but handicapped by wanting to fight fairly. The loser, now wiser than before, stamped off complaining about cheating bastards from Lanarkshire and the instructor in question, from the same area as the fallen hero, decided to restore the pride of his force by stepping into the ring with the intention of putting me in my place.

Like his protégé before him he spent just too long posturing to the crowd and found himself the victim of a sneaky rear attack, landing face down in the sand which he didn't like at all as he turned nasty and threatened to cripple me when he regained his feet. Figuring that I had nothing to lose, I responded by taking advantage of my temporary upper hand by rubbing his face in the sand and asking him if he wanted to transfer to Lanarkshire where he could play with the big boys. He responded sportingly to my merry banter and the delighted hooting of the crowd by spitting sand and screaming threats, although at this point somewhat restricted by still being unable to get up.

Much as I would have liked to continue the conversation, I accepted the referee's right to call a halt and jumped clear as the enraged instructor came up swinging his fists and snarling. Things were turning nasty and I was considering the best route for a tactical retreat into the picturesque Aberdeenshire hills, as touched upon earlier, when the sergeant, acting as referee, jumped in and sent him off with a warning to accept defeat like a good loser.

The good loser left, muttering darkly, and you can bet I avoided him for the rest of the course. Just as an aside, he came back into my life many years later when he appeared at my division for a short spell as a Superintendent heading for greater things. He didn't seem to remember me and as you will no doubt guess I took good care to keep it that way.

The final event of note during the course was a happier one, in that it allowed an opportunity for some harmless fun at someone else's expense, always the most popular kind. Two cadets from somewhere up north had fallen in love, one male and one female I hasten to add, and had been so smitten by each other that they had become betrothed on the spot. The male half of the act, for reasons best known to himself, had followed the public announcement by playing a sad, haunting lament called The Dark Isle on his accordion. This instrument, which again for reasons best known to himself he had trailed behind him to Aberdeen and persisted in playing at all hours, was roundly detested by everyone else in the hall of residence and was charmingly referred to as Shut That Fucking Thing Up by the music lover in the next bedroom. Play it he did, however, until it was a wonder that he didn't land in the harbour with it wrapped around his neck.

One of our female number from Lanarkshire, a soft-hearted soul with a deeply romantic nature, hitherto unsuspected, was so moved by the fairy-tale engagement, complete with atmospheric Highland music, that she burst into floods of tears and cried happily, off and on, for the rest of the evening. Unfortunately for her it quickly became apparent, to the delight of her male colleagues who hadn't a romantic bone in their bodies, that whistling or humming a few bars of The Dark Isle was guaranteed to produce another bout of tearful howling. Predictably, for the remainder of the course and on the long journey home in the old minibus, the tune established itself as a firm favourite with all.

Chapter 22

That was more or less the swan song of my career as a Police Cadet. On returning, I was sent to Wishaw for a few weeks to make myself generally useful about the place, keep my nose clean and await my nineteenth birthday. The only memory of that short period is going out with a car crew and spending about an hour brandishing a long stick and knocking chestnuts out of a tree in a large estate near the town. No doubt I found other ways of making myself useful too, but I can't remember a thing about it. The training staff had communicated the startling fact that I had come up to scratch and that a decision had been taken to confirm my elevation to the office of Constable.

The training sergeant who conveyed the glad tidings made allusions to the Lord moving in mysterious ways His wonders to perform, and who was he to question the decisions of the Chief Constable etc. etc., an obviously contrived and threadbare comedy routine which had seen many an airing. It didn't bother me in the slightest, but I was wise enough to receive it with equally contrived appreciation and fell about laughing at the appropriate cues during the performance. Confirmed I was to be whether this prince of jesters liked it or not, but I was conscious of still having two perilous years of probation to survive before I could safely blow raspberries.

On the fateful day, therefore, Birthday Boy arrived at HQ, best and only uniform in parade ground order and neck washed. A thorough inspection followed where uniform, boots, haircut, cleanliness of fingernails, level of sobriety and so forth were given the once over. Personal possessions were examined in case I tried to enter the hallowed ground with a packet of Benson and Hedges bulging in my pocket. I had, but they were quickly transferred to my raincoat which I wouldn't be wearing during the event. A doom-laden voice, sounding like a sentence of death, told me I was to be presented to the Chief himself where by some as yet undisclosed process I would be transformed from cadet to cop. I was to stand to attention throughout, speak when spoken to and refrain from any word or deed which might cause offence. What did they expect me to do which would give offence, I wondered with some annoyance. Help myself to the Chief's fags? Fart during the oath of office? Present him with an expenses claim, even? No, apparently it was even easier than that to offend the Chief.

It seemed that even if the great man asked a question he didn't actually expect or want an answer and it was what my life was worth to engage him in conversation or ask questions of my own. So it was going to be a fun morning, then. On that subject, I sometimes wonder if the Chief was actually aware that he didn't expect to be answered or whether it was his minions who were afraid of what would come pouring forth if both parties had an informal chat. The Chief, for all I know, may have gone through life thinking that nobody loved him because his every attempt to talk to his troops was met with stony silence. Perhaps it was his one remaining ambition in life to chat to a humble cadet or probationary constable and he might have developed a complex about it, although thinking back to Aberdeen it was quite possible that the training staff had anticipated his wishes accurately. He hadn't seemed too keen to chat to the lower orders the last time he had the chance.

I was taken by one of the Training Department staff into the basement, given a chequered hatband to replace the blue one, handed a whistle, a set of handcuffs and a wooden baton and photographed for my warrant card. The camera used was a huge wooden-framed thing on an equally huge wooden tripod which looked like something men in bowler hats and moustaches carried around in the Wild West. I said so and got a lecture on how this was actually top quality equipment, being called a large-frame camera which left me as wise as before, though not why it was needed to take a small, passport-size black-and-white photo. It also wasn't explained why the process was so antiquated that the warrant card wouldn't be ready for about a week, which meant that I would be out and about for that time without the means to identify myself. The whistle went into a little pocket just inside the tunic and the chain had to be placed in view in a certain way, the one and only correct method. Unfortunately, everyone had his own idea of the one and only correct method depending on where they had originally been stationed, so no matter how you arranged the chain some boss with nothing better to occupy himself would pop out at you and make a noise about it. What would really have given them fits was the habit some of the old cops had of replacing the whistle itself with a Guinness can opener, freely available from pubs, in those unenlightened days when ring-pulls on beer cans had still to be invented. It was certainly more use than the whistle itself.

The cuffs were still of the old, heavyweight Victorian pattern which required the two-handed grip of Sandow the Strongman to close them and assumed that all criminals had wrists the same size. There was also nothing issued to carry them in so they went in the back trouser pocket and fell onto the pavement when you had to break into a run – mine later landed in my locker and stayed there until the new American ratchet style replaced them, at which point everyone went about looking for someone to arrest so that we could look like something out of *Hawaii Five-0* as the bracelets were snapped on with a flourish.

The baton slipped into a specially designed trouser pocket and the short leather strap was to be tucked completely out of sight, no doubt so that I could get my head punched in or stabbed while I was fumbling about for it. In fact, the reason given was that if the strap hung from the trouser pocket, members of the public were likely to succumb to fits of the vapours at this display of paramilitary might being carried about by the keepers of the Queen's Peace. It seemed we were still maintaining the fiction that we could quell the most violent outbreak of riot and tumult without resorting to anything more potent than a stern glance and a firm word. Utter rubbish of course, as most of the cops I had seen went around strap-out and some even practised quick draws, like gunfighters of old. There was also the aspect that the sticks being issued at that time were so lightweight and useless that we couldn't have successfully subdued a stroppy canary with one, which is why anyone with any initiative acquired one of the old models which were made of lignum vitae, or ironwood, and could split granite. If you think that's a bit belligerent, try finding yourself in the position where you need your baton to make sure you get home the same shape as you left and see what you think then.

Some of our bosses of that era obviously lived in a fantasy world of their own, or developed the amnesia senior managers everywhere seem to get when they're safely behind a desk and unlikely to re-emerge, and thought that their troops spent the day chasing naughty apple scrumpers round Camberwick Green. Some of them were so long away from the street they probably remembered Artful Dodgers nicking handkerchiefs from old gentlemen in top hats. Strangely enough, a few years ago when the current batch of Chief Constables saw the light and uniform cops began to dress like the SAS about to take out some terrorists there wasn't a trace of public outcry. None at all. If anyone gave it a thought – and I doubt if many did – it was assumed they carried all that kit because they needed it. The public panic and the end of civilization as we know it didn't happen.

I was, to my surprise, assured that a new, yes new, uniform issue would be with me in a few days. I was told that henceforth I would be Constable LC642 and had five minutes to attach metal shoulder numerals indicating same to my jacket and unpick the cloth cadet flashes. Luckily, my ancient tunic had already been pierced for the numeral screws by some previous owner and I had a small penknife in my pocket for the shoulder-flash stitches.

Accompanied by the training man, also in best bib and tucker, I double-timed upstairs to the office of the Chief Constable himself. I was told to fall in behind some ancient, white-haired Superintendent I'd never seen before, was shown in, introduced in a military bellow and found myself facing what appeared to be two Chiefs, neither in uniform. Even I knew that couldn't be right and sought guidance.

No, I was told in a sharp hiss when I seemed unsure which one to salute, there was only one Chief. The other one was a Justice of the Peace who at that exact moment jumped to his feet and without any preliminaries began to administer the oath of office, something I hadn't been warned about. He did so at the top of his voice, brandishing a raised Bible like some crusading evangelist from the American Deep South who has just spotted a sinner in the offing, while I repeated the oath line by line, or at least made a convincing show of appearing to.

In fact I was so taken aback by his leaping about and shouting that I missed the start and didn't really catch up, having expected him to introduce himself with some word of welcome or congratulations on being appointed. I caught the bit where he touched on the Almighty and there was, as I remember, some reference or other to Her Majesty the Queen but beyond that it went over my head a bit. I felt, somehow, that it would be a bad idea to interrupt the flow and ask him if he'd mind starting again, so instead I improvised. I threw my right hand in the air, clicked my heels together in a rather good impression of Erich Von Stronheim and mimed the oath like one of those politicians you've no doubt seen on TV trying to sing the party song at the end of conferences when they don't actually know the words. The evangelist JP, exhausted by his efforts, subsided into a chair and took no further part in the proceedings from which I took it that I was sworn in, and quite possibly Saved.

The other figure, who had yet to move or speak and who I deduced was The Man himself, had appeared asleep when I went in, or possibly just deep in thought. He still appeared asleep or deep in thought and as nobody looked like doing anything to rouse him it struck me that this could turn out to be a long day. Some minutes passed in silence apart from the odd muffled cough.

Suddenly, stirring at last, the great one looked up and peered at me for a moment as if unsure why I was standing on his carpet. Having satisfied himself that I wasn't up for sentencing over some disciplinary complaint or other, or trying to bankrupt him with a claim for bus fares, he launched into a short, mumbled speech I didn't catch a word of then seemed to fall asleep again – or return to his deep thoughts – rather like the Dormouse from Alice in Wonderland. It was all a bit like Alice in Wonderland.

After another longish silence, when it became apparent that nothing more in the way of dialogue was forthcoming, my attention began to wander as it does and I took in my surroundings, shuffling the feet a bit and surreptitiously scratching my arse which is invariably one of the bits which needs scratching when you're in polite company. Fortunately the other bit was fine. The Chief's office, while suitably large, was something of a disappointment being a bit moth-eaten and sorely in need of renovation. The carpet and furniture looked as if it they had come with the building and the wallpaper might have gone up to celebrate Victoria's Jubilee.

It was not unlike a studio set from the Forsyte Saga and you could imagine the Chief's predecessors – or possibly him – sitting in that same chair at the same desk and reading newspaper accounts of Suffragette Riots or the Relief of Mafeking. I doubt if anything had changed since then. To be honest I don't know what I expected, but a visit to another Chief's office, many years later, was a very different proposition being modern, bright and giving the impression of buzz and activity and professional management. This one was more like a mausoleum. The white-haired Super, who had obviously been here before, cleared his throat a few times then made a great show of coughing but raised no response apart from the JP who looked up with a slight frown of concern. The way things were going I wouldn't have been surprised to see him produce a bottle of cough mixture and a spoon and tell the invalid to open up.

Just as I was wondering if it would be all right to sit down, or at least nip out for a smoke, another hiss in my ear from the Ancient Super – whose function there I have yet to discover – indicated that the show was over and it was time to go. I saluted the motionless form at the desk, spun on my heel with a certain cavalier dash which drew a dirty look from the training man still hovering in the background, and left the room a newly appointed Constable, an ancient and honourable office I was exhorted to carry proudly.

And yes, I was told in yet another hiss when I asked the key question in earshot of the Chief, my wages would go up with immediate effect.